"A fundamental study on connections and contexts of two early modern trans-local, trans-regional and trans-continental business entrepreneurs in Europe, the Atlantic world and the Indian Ocean."

—*Holger Weiss, Åbo Akademi University, Finland*

Early Modern Overseas Trade and Entrepreneurship

Drawing on an impressive range of archival material, this monograph delves into the careers of two businessmen who worked for Nordic chartered monopoly trading companies to illuminate individual entrepreneurship in the context of seventeenth-century long-distance trade.

The study spans the Caribbean to the Indian Ocean, examining global entanglements through personal interactions and daily trading activities between Europeans, Asian merchants, and African brokers. It makes an important contribution to our understanding of the role of individuals and their networks within the great European trading companies of the early modern period.

This unique book will be of interest to advanced students and researchers of economic history, business history, early modern global history, and entrepreneurship.

Kaarle Wirta is a Postdoctoral Researcher at Tampere University, Finland.

Perspectives in Economic and Social History
Series Editors: Andrew August and Jari Eloranta

55 **Labor Before the Industrial Revolution**
Work, Technology and their Ecologies in an Age of Early Capitalism
Edited by Thomas Max Safley

56 **Workers, Unions and Payment in Kind**
The Fight for Real Wages in Britain, 1820–1986
Christopher Frank

57 **A History of States and Economic Policies in Early Modern Europe**
Silvia A. Conca Messina

58 **Fiscal Policy in Early Modern Europe**
Portugal in Comparative Context
Rodrigo da Costa Dominguez

59 **Workers, Unions and Truck Wages in British Society**
The Fight for Real Wages, 1820–1986
Christopher Frank

60 **Early Modern Overseas Trade and Entrepreneurship**
Nordic Trading Companies in the Seventeenth Century
Kaarle Wirta

61 **Credit and Debt in Eighteenth Century England**
An Economic History of Debtors' Prisons
Alexander Wakelam

For more information about this series, please visit www.routledge.com/series/PESH

Early Modern Overseas Trade and Entrepreneurship

Nordic Trading Companies in the Seventeenth Century

Kaarle Wirta

LONDON AND NEW YORK

First published 2021
by Routledge
2 Park Square, Milton Park, Abingdon, Oxon OX14 4RN

and by Routledge
52 Vanderbilt Avenue, New York, NY 10017

Routledge is an imprint of the Taylor & Francis Group, an informa business

© 2021 Kaarle Wirta

The right of Kaarle Wirta to be identified as author of this work has been asserted by him in accordance with sections 77 and 78 of the Copyright, Designs and Patents Act 1988.

All rights reserved. No part of this book may be reprinted or reproduced or utilised in any form or by any electronic, mechanical, or other means, now known or hereafter invented, including photocopying and recording, or in any information storage or retrieval system, without permission in writing from the publishers.

Trademark notice: Product or corporate names may be trademarks or registered trademarks, and are used only for identification and explanation without intent to infringe.

British Library Cataloguing-in-Publication Data
A catalogue record for this book is available from the British Library

Library of Congress Cataloging-in-Publication Data
Names: Wirta, Kaarle, author.
Title: Early modern overseas trade and entrepreneurship: Nordic trading companies in the seventeenth century / Kaarle Wirta.
Description: 1 Edition. | New York: Routledge, 2020. |
Series: Perspectives in economic and social history |
Includes bibliographical references and index.
Identifiers: LCCN 2020006222 (print) | LCCN 2020006223 (ebook)
Subjects: LCSH: Scandinavia—Commerce—History—17th century. | Entrepreneurship—Scandinavia—History—17th century.
Classification: LCC HF3640 .W57 2020 (print) |
LCC HF3640 (ebook) | DDC 382.0948—dc23
LC record available at https://lccn.loc.gov/2020006222
LC ebook record available at https://lccn.loc.gov/2020006223

ISBN: 978-0-367-33286-0 (hbk)
ISBN: 978-0-429-31906-8 (ebk)

Typeset in Times New Roman
by codeMantra

Contents

	List of illustrations	viii
	Foreword	ix
	Acknowledgements	x
	List of abbreviations	xi
1	Introduction	1
2	Formative years of overseas entrepreneurship and Nordic overseas trade	21
3	Entrepreneurship in the company	57
4	The vulnerability of being connected	89
5	Knowledge and overseas business	121
6	The sea was a violent place to work	146
7	Conclusions	170
	Sources and bibliography	179
	Index	199

Illustrations

Figures

1.1	Map of Swedish areas around the Baltic in the seventeenth century	9
2.1	Map of Nordic interests on the Elbe river	28
3.1	Map of Danish factories and support nodes in Asia	67
3.2	Map of the Gold Coast	76
5.1	Map of the region of Western Africa in which Carloff was active	131
6.1	Map of the attacks in the Caribbean Sea	160

Tables

1.1	Chronologies of the Northern European wars	7
1.2	Nordic monarchs during the first half of the seventeenth century	8
3.1	Table of the nine main investors during the second charter of the SAC	65
5.1	Slave trade voyages involving Carloff	135

Foreword

The study of early modern shipping and economies has blossomed in the last fifteen years or so internationally. This has a multitude of causes, ranging from new research projects, books, networks, and data. Many of these projects have been global by nature, and they have introduced new data and sources to the debate about the extent and importance of early modern trade. In many cases, the focus has been explicitly global, thus eschewing purely national analytical perspectives. This type of new research on trade and empires has been at the nexus of economic, business, and global history, all of which have experienced a resurgence in the same period as a whole. Moreover, many of these studies have focused on exposing and deepening the study of colonial and mother country relationships, as well as including new geographic dimensions in the debate, such as the trade routes connecting Asia, the Americas, and Africa. Kaarle Wirta's study of Nordic trading companies in the seventeenth century is a wonderful example of this new history of global trade. His approach is explicitly comparative, and he examines both the actors and the trade itself, in various geographic contexts. It also connects to an emerging literature, both theoretical and empirical, on the role trading companies played in the development of early modern fiscal states and institutions. Furthermore, Wirta's work combines both quantitative and qualitative evidence, and the analysis is nuanced and broad at the same time. This study is a fine example of the international scholarship in this field, and a welcome addition to this monograph series. In fact, one of the key themes in the series is to explore global trade, merchants, and networks. I am equally sure that this volume will find a keen audience globally, and Wirta's study will form a cornerstone in the study of early modern Nordic trade and merchant networks.

Jari Eloranta (University of Helsinki, editor of *PESH*)

Acknowledgements

This book is based on my PhD research conducted within the "Fighting monopolies, defying empires" project funded by the European Research Council between 2013 and 2017 (ERC-2012-StG-312657-FIGHT). I was lucky to be a part of an electrifying research team under the supervision of Professor Cátia Antunes. Our team. i.e. Cátia Antunes, Elisabeth Heijmans, Julie Mo Svalastog, Edgar Pereira, and Hasan Colak, has provided me with endless support and encouragement to finish this book. I am also thankful for my second supervisor, Professor Leos Müller, whose work and support have always been a true inspiration for me.

I would also like to thank my colleagues and friends in the Netherlands, Finland, and Sweden. They have all given me support and extensive feedback without ever wanting anything in return. Holger Weiss, Malin Johansson, Joris van den Tol, Erik Odegard, Kate Ekama, Marion Pluskota, Jeannette Kamp, Sanne Muurling, Bram Hoonhout, Matthias van Rossum, Lisa Hellman, Henrik Mattjus, Otso Kortekangas, Patrik Hettula, Katja Tikka, Henri Hannula, Kalle Kananoja, and Lauri Tähtinen: thank you for making this contribution to a much better book.

I would like to thank the series editor Professor Jari Eloranta for providing me with feedback and for having faith that the book will be finished. I would like to thank the editorial board and the anonymous peer reviewers for their comments as well. Especially, for his invaluable patience and language skills, I would like to thank Alex Jordan for language-editing the book. I also want to thank Panu Savolainen for making the great maps.

I would also like to thank the personnel of the multiple archives that I visited, and whose help was instrumental for finishing this research. I am grateful to my PhD committee members for their time and comments, especially Professor Henk den Heijer and Professor Margaret Hunt for all the additional feedback and inspiring discussions. I would also like to thank all the people I have met at various conferences, summer schools, workshops, and history departments. There are so many that have helped me with the research.

Finally, this book and everything connected to it is dedicated to the ones who have had all the patience with me, while I have been working on the book, especially my parents and my brother. Finally, without the support and love of my beloved ones, the book would never have been finished. Tuulia, Saga, and Hugo, this book is dedicated to you.

Abbreviations

ANOM	Archives nationales d'outre-mer
BN	Bibliothèque Nationale
DEIC	Danish East India Company
DK	Danske Kancelli
EIC	English East India Company
FBA	Finspångsbruk Arkiv
FC	Furley Collection
FWIC	French West India Company
H&S	Handel och Sjöfart
HCA	High Court of Admiralty
KKA	Kommerskollegium, Huvudarkivet
LA	Leufsta Arkiv
NA	Notarieel Archief
NL-HaNA	Nationaal Archief, Den Haag, Netherlands
OWIC	Oude Westindische Compagnie
RAC	Rigsarkivet Copenhagen, Denmark
RAS	Riksarkivet Stockholm, Sweden
RP	Riksrådets Protokoll
RR	Riksregistraturen
S.G.	States General
SAA	Staatsarchief Amsterdam
SAC	Swedish Africa Company
TKIA	Tyske Kancelli Indenrigske Afdelning
TKUA	Tyske Kancelli Udenrigske Afdelning
UUB	Uppsala Universitets Bibliotek
VLA	Vadstena Landsarkiv
VOC	Vereenigde Oostindische Compagnie
WIC	West-Indische Compagnie

1 Introduction

State of the art

In 1648, the commander of the Danish East India Company (DEIC), Willem Leyel (ca. 1593–1654), suffered a mutiny and was arrested by his subordinates, being accused of having traded for his own benefit. Leyel had been the commander of the DEIC in Asia for some years and was able to maintain an active and profitable business thanks to his knowledge of the Indian Ocean trade, which he had acquired during his service in the Dutch East India Company (VOC) in Batavia.[1] Also in 1648, while Leyel was facing a mutiny in Tranquebar, the prosecutor of the Dutch West India Company (WIC), Henrich Carloff, decided to leave the company and take employment in the soon-to-be established Swedish Africa Company (SAC).[2] Like that of Leyel, Carloff's career benefitted greatly from the knowledge and experience that he had accumulated in various trading companies, beginning with the WIC. After abandoning the WIC and later also the SAC, Carloff participated in the launching of both Danish and French Atlantic ventures, finally returning to Dutch employment in the 1670s.

From the perspective of business history, Leyel and Carloff serve to illustrate a hitherto overlooked category of early modern entrepreneurial behaviour, namely that of overseas entrepreneurship. This book's main aim is to study overseas entrepreneurship in action, tracing their social and economic affiliations to European companies, reconstructing their role in early modern European overseas business, and interpreting their use of violence as part of their entrepreneurial strategies. While Leyel and Carloff embody the core features of overseas entrepreneurship, neither of them was unique by the standards of the seventeenth century; there were many similarly business-minded Europeans willing to join royal monopolies or chartered trading companies, only to abandon them when new opportunities arose. Some examples include Francisco Vieira de Figueiredo, Samuel Blommaert, Peter Minuit, Arent de Groot, Augustine Hermann, John Smith, Thomas Dale, Jacob Leisler, and François Caron.[3] Indeed, such men effectively blurred the commercial borders imposed by European powers, particularly through their overseas entrepreneurial activities, their business

2   *Introduction*

connections, their social climbing, and their knowledge-accumulation. Although they have been studied by previous scholars, it is surprising how little is known about the role these entrepreneurs played in early modern European overseas business.

In this book, the focus is not on biographies but rather on the type of business behaviour that Leyel and Carloff represented. The book aims to analyse the role that individuals played in the development of overseas business during the seventeenth century, particularly in the Nordic kingdoms.[4] In what follows, *overseas business* refers to how individuals, trading companies, and states organised, planned, and maintained long-distance trade. Rather than merely studying how trade (the selling and buying of goods) was conducted, the business perspective adopted here concerns the overall structure of economic activities overseas. Business is understood as part of a long-distance economic system, in which goods and services were important, as were various forms of financial activities. Furthermore, within this context, personal privileges and prerogatives acquired a political dimension. In this sense, business-as-trade and business-as-organisation were two inextricably connected subjects.

The book revolves around the concept of *overseas entrepreneurship*. Each chapter focuses on a theme directly related to this concept. The concept of overseas entrepreneurship encapsulates the way in which individuals manoeuvred between competing networks in Europe and overseas, their unlimited access to asymmetric information, and how these elements were used to attain professional advancement and personal wealth. Through such processes, Leyel and Carloff accumulated experience, knowledge, connections, and reputation, ultimately attaining considerable upward social mobility. Finally, although entrepreneurship is often associated with attempts to reduce risk and avoid conflicts, in the overseas context, conflict and violence became instruments that enabled entrepreneurs to attain competitive advantages. A focus on the careers of Leyel, Carloff, and their entrepreneurial behaviour means posing questions such as: What were the backgrounds and the mechanisms of overseas entrepreneurship? How did these relate to the Nordic institutional context of the seventeenth century? By studying the entrepreneurial behaviour of individuals in relation to trading companies, this book will offer new insights into early modern European, and especially Nordic, overseas business.

The historiography of overseas expansion, trade, and business

Historians have been interested in European overseas expansion and trade for a long time. Since the nineteenth century, research has considered the motives, goals, and development of European overseas expansion. From the early twentieth century onwards, research on specific nations gained momentum. In Western Europe, research focused especially on the institutions that underpinned expansion, particularly the Dutch and English trading companies. Studies by James Tracy, George Scammel, Niels Steensgaard, Femme Gaastra and Leonard Blussé pioneered ideas about the role of European overseas trade in a broader context, comparing and contrasting various European trading empires.[5]

During the twentieth century, a regional approach to overseas trade also developed. In large part, this was a reaction against the somewhat one-sided focus on the role of European institutions such as the chartered companies. The rise of Indian and Atlantic Ocean historiography demonstrated that European expansion had repercussions on local populations, and, indeed, that the latter were far from passive, helpless, or inconsequential. Overall, this body of literature has clarified how local, non-European societies participated in European overseas business. The interactions between the local populations and the Europeans proved to be heavily intertwined. Furthermore, such studies of the Indian and Atlantic oceans have sparked interest in regional systems of trade. They have also addressed a wide range of other topics, including demography, economics, politics, religion, and ideas, as well as structures, trade, societies, and environments. Such oceanic perspectives have also yielded an understanding of the diversity of actors in the construction of trading systems, whether affiliated with the European chartered companies or not. In turn, this provided a more nuanced framework for the study of overseas trade, one which not only focuses on the perspective of states and companies but also considers the participation of European and non-European agents in the construction of early modern empires.[6]

Today, most scholars who work on European overseas expansion agree that the scope of analysis needs to be more inclusive in terms of European versus non-European agency. However, it is rather surprising that most studies are still conducted with a specific geographical region in mind. For example, in the Netherlands, the two main areas of expansion – the Asian (East) and the Atlantic (West) – have largely been treated separately. For a long time, the focus has been on the Dutch expansion into Asia, whereas the Atlantic expansion has begun to receive attention only during the last few decades.[7] From a Dutch perspective, trade in Asia was more successful, whereas Atlantic trade tended to falter. In general, the WIC has been perceived as an instrument for supporting warfare, whereas the East India Company (VOC) has been seen as a trading company, and, indeed, as the first modern joint-stock company.[8]

Conventionally, this distinction has also been explained with reference to how the two regions changed following the arrival of the Europeans. The Asian trade was an already established trading system prior to the entry of the Europeans, whereas the Atlantic trade was largely developed by the Europeans. Furthermore, the Atlantic trade has been considered more open and dynamic, due to shorter sailing distances and relative closeness to Europe. The Atlantic companies were weaker, and were thus more vulnerable to internal and external competition. In contrast, the Asian trade has been considered more closed. Trade in Asia required other types of

4 *Introduction*

organisation, since ships had to sail in convoys, due to longer distances and changing monsoon seasons. It has also been argued that the settlements established by Europeans were different. In the Atlantic, Europeans built plantation colonies (with the exception of Western Africa), whereas in Asia, they erected fortified trading stations and operated mainly through shipping services.[9]

Although the two ocean systems were not entirely the same, this does not mean that they ought not to be studied together. In fact, when greater emphasis is placed on the business patterns of the two regions, they turn out to be quite similar. In both ocean systems, companies applied violence and confronted individuals and merchant networks who challenged the companies from within. In neither system did the Europeans dominate trade. Instead, in both cases, they were dependent on the locally established powers, who exercised control over the European presence during the seventeenth century. Another problem is that the European maritime empires have mainly been studied from a "national" perspective. However, the rise of global and transnational history has shown that empires were constructed and connected through multiple contexts and relationships. As such, our understanding of empires has become more global. Consequently, recent research on the Dutch maritime empire has begun to consider both East and West alongside each other. For example, scholars such as Kate Ekama and Erik Odegard have demonstrated that the division between East and West does not do justice to the realities of empire. By studying the legal disputes of the VOC and WIC, Ekama has shown that it is more fruitful to focus on a single Dutch empire, rather than on two or more distinct empires existing within the Dutch Republic.[10] Similarly, in another context, Elisabeth Heijmans has demonstrated that French expansion can be studied from a comparative perspective in both the East and the West. In particular, Heijmans has revealed how the connections and strategies applied by the French company directors were identical in both the East and West. In both systems, the directors established cross-imperial connections in order to adapt to local contexts. Thus, Heijmans has shown how the French overseas empire developed through a decentralised process rather than through a top-down management.[11]

Following these recent currents in the historiography, this book will combine both oceanic spaces (the Indian and the Atlantic) with an actor-centred approach (focusing on Leyel and Carloff), and will thereby elucidate the role of individual entrepreneurial behaviour in the creation of overseas economic opportunities and the shaping of spaces of exchange. This means that although in both cases there were local specificities, behaviour was nonetheless shaped by common economic, social, and political backgrounds. By adopting this approach, it becomes possible to connect the actions of individuals to broader, and even global, processes.

Throughout the book, an attempt will be made to bear in mind larger historical contexts. At the core of the seventeenth century was European

Introduction 5

internal rivalry, which created constant political tension and often escalated into outright war. Central to this rivalry was a desire to attain a stronger international position. Thus, overseas expansion became an accelerator of European rivalry, which was thereby projected onto a global scale. In the seventeenth century, growing global connections would not have been possible without, on the one hand, the development of European overseas expansion, and, on the other, the growing willingness of European rulers to engage in expansion.

From a political perspective, the rivalry between European powers created many career opportunities in the maritime sector. A good basis for such a career was provided by the European trading companies. From an institutional perspective, the companies were still in the process of development. They were not yet modern trading organisations with sophisticated mechanisms of employee surveillance, although this would change during the eighteenth century. Thus, during the period under study in this book, there was still an institutional vacuum that afforded entrepreneurial opportunities.

This book will study the ways in which individuals, information, knowledge, trade, and social relationships cut across institutional, organisational, national, and imperial boundaries. By studying two regional systems, some of the entanglements that characterised the history of overseas business will be elucidated. Studying both connections and manifestations of difference will mean that individual cases will be understood both individually and collectively, and this will permit a more global approach to overseas entrepreneurship.

Business history from in-between

This book adopts an actor-centred approach, placing individuals at the centre of the development of Nordic overseas business. The contextual backdrop is provided by the development of the Nordic trading companies and, to a limited extent, the Dutch companies. Although these companies are constantly present, this book does not consider trading companies as agents themselves, but rather as instruments for individual initiative. The famous business historian Mark Casson argues that entrepreneurs establish firms and companies in order to exploit an opportunity they believe they have discovered. In short, in order to understand a business climate, it is crucial to study the careers of the individuals who established a firm. In this sense, the study of entrepreneurship is also partly a study of the firm (here: company).[12]

By adopting such an actor-centred approach to early modern overseas business, recent research has highlighted the role of merchant groups, diasporas, and networks.[13] Indeed, such agency-oriented studies have shed new light on how different groups and agents were involved in seventeenth-century overseas trade. For example, Cátia Antunes and Amélia Polónia

6 Introduction

have emphasised the importance of studying individuals operating both within and outside imperial monopolies, these two groups being linked through self-organised networks.[14] In particular, they argue that individuals in self-organised networks posed serious challenges to the state, the church, and the monopolistic institutions with which they were affiliated. Although early modern states were crucial to the construction of overseas empires, being based on large and complex logistical mechanisms, and commanding large-scale financing, they remained, nonetheless, implicitly or explicitly dependent on the cooperation of individuals. In the work of Antunes and Polónia, the dynamic of early modern trade is thus conceptualised as a series of individual relationships, which together amounted to a system of global interactions.[15]

Here, the aim will be to move away from an exclusive emphasis on networks, and to analyse instead the strategies of specific individuals within the nexus of these global interactions. Indeed, this implies an even smaller scale of analysis than that employed by Antunes and Polónia. In this regard, individuals acted on a smaller scale than the companies with which they were affiliated. However, this does not mean that they were unimportant. To the contrary, a number of studies of early modern overseas history have argued persuasively for the importance of focusing on individuals and small-scale case studies within larger oceanic and imperial spaces.[16] For instance, the historian Francesca Trivellato has explained how studying overseas expansion on a smaller scale can help to clarify those business practices that have often been overlooked or deprecated by histories written on a macro scale.[17] Indeed, it can also serve to nuance and refine concepts that are often taken for granted, such as trading companies, company officials, pirates, or merchants.[18]

Similarly, the historian Maria Fusaro has emphasised that in studies of oceanic spaces, micro-analysis can offer significantly new knowledge, and thus provide a means to revise grand narratives. Methodologically, micro-analysis eschews the nation-state paradigm, in the sense that it pursues research topics outside the bounds of the nation state. This does not mean that the state and its institutions were unimportant, but it does offer greater consideration to the actions of the individuals. According to Fusaro, "It is in the relationship between institutions and individuals that the results of research are proving to be most fruitful and challenging."[19]

The novelty of this book consists in the fact that it is not concerned solely with people "from below" or "from above" but rather "in-between." In the history of European overseas expansion, such intermediate individuals remain relatively unknown. However, if we study how they operated in an overseas business context, we can unravel various connections, overlaps, similarities, and differences, which stretched beyond specific states, regions, companies, and trades. This book will encompass concurrent events in several regions of the globe, such as the Indian Ocean, Western Africa, Central America, and Western, Southern, and Northern Europe.

Introduction 7

It thus spans from the Caribbean to the Indian Ocean, and studies global entanglements through human interactions and daily trading activities. As such, the book focuses on the individuals involved, rather than on any specific national or regional territory, and privileges the encounters between European and non-European merchants, whether these occurred in Europe, the Caribbean, Asia, or Africa.

Overseas expansion in a Nordic context

During the seventeenth century, the Nordic kingdoms became increasingly intertwined with the continental states commercially and politically, and this had both direct and indirect repercussions on prospects for Nordic overseas business. The origins of these intensified connections lay in the rivalry between the two Nordic kingdoms, which influenced their commercial and political aspirations. For both Denmark and Sweden, the question of *dominium maris baltici* was the main motive for participation in general European conflicts. They aimed to attain recognition amongst the continental European powers. For the Nordic kingdoms, expansion in the Baltic and overseas served to accelerate the process of empire building.[20]

Since the sixteenth century, as shown in Table 1.1, the two kingdoms had fought each other several times, and conflicts continued to break out during the seventeenth century (1611–1613, 1643–1645, 1657–1658, 1658–1600, 1675–1679). Because of its expansive ambitions, Sweden also waged wars against Russia and Poland. In particular, Sweden wanted to secure its political position and access to important Baltic ports, especially in relation to Russia. Sweden also had to deal with the Polish branch of the Vasa family, which laid claim to the Swedish crown. The Baltic rivalry culminated between the 1620s and 1648, when both Denmark and Sweden were drawn into the Thirty Years War. Once the war ended in 1648, Sweden emerged as an empire to be reckoned with, whereas Denmark experienced a considerable decline. In 1648, the treaty of Westphalia was signed, and Sweden acquired the region of Vorpommern along with Rügen, Stettin, and Wismar, as well as the Duchies of Bremen and Verden.[21] Denmark's ill-fated participation in

Table 1.1 Chronologies of the Northern European wars

	Sweden–Denmark			Thirty Years War		Anglo-Dutch
1611–1613	Kalmar War		1618	Beginning	1652–1654	First War
1643–1645	Torstenson's War		1625–1629	Denmark in War	1665–1667	Second War
1657–1658	Karl X Gustav's I War		1630–1648	Sweden in War	1672–1674	Third War
1658–1660	Karl X Gustav's II War		1648	Peace at Westphalia	1672–1678	Franco-Dutch War

8 Introduction

the Thirty Years War forced the kingdom to re-evaluate its expansive capacity, and waging war against Sweden became a part of its effort to reassert its power. The main motivation in annexing these German provinces was to gain a foothold inside the Holy Roman Empire and, to a certain degree, to gain control over tolls.

Indeed, the main question dividing the countries around the Baltic was control over waterways, and especially control over tolls. For his part, the Danish king claimed control over trade and customs through *Øresundtolden* (the Sound Toll). In this way, Denmark was able to maintain a leading position in the Baltic for a long time.[22] Throughout the century, the Dutch republic, as the main carrier of the European commodity trade, had a stake in the Baltic, and usually participated in the many Nordic conflicts there. The Dutch wished to maintain the status quo in Baltic power relations, and to make sure that neither of the Nordic kingdoms would grow too strong. Initially, Sweden and the Dutch Republic had a close relationship, especially during the first half of the seventeenth century. For example, the Dutch Republic supported Sweden in challenging the dominant position of Denmark, including through the conquest of Reval (Tallinn) in 1561, as well as the Nordic Seven Years War (1563–1570).[23] The Dutch Republic also assisted Sweden in developing its manufacturing industry. In exchange for Dutch capital, Sweden became the Republic's main supplier of goods such as bar iron, copper, and tar.[24] However, towards the middle of the seventeenth century, the Dutch grew concerned about the growing strength of Sweden. In particular, the Dutch were displeased by recent Swedish customs demands.

The situation worsened in 1655, when the Swedish king decided to attack Poland-Lithuania, which jeopardised the supply route for Baltic grain.[25] For the Danish king, this presented an opportunity to reclaim previously lost territories, and he once again declared war against Sweden in 1657. A list of the Nordic monarchs is seen in Table 1.2. In response, the Dutch switched sides and offered military assistance to Denmark. However, the terms of the peace treaty signed at Roskilde in 1658 were a disaster for Denmark: Sweden acquired Scania, Halland, Blekinge, and Bornholm, as well as Trøndelag in Norway. Although in another treaty, signed in 1660, after Karl X Gustav's death, Sweden gave up Bornholm and Trøndelag, war nonetheless broke out again in 1675, when Denmark, joined by the Dutch, attacked Sweden in hope of reclaiming the other lost territories.[26] As seen in Figure 1.1, the outcome of this 200-year rivalry was that Sweden experienced

Table 1.2 Nordic monarchs during the first half of the seventeenth century

Years	Denmark King	Years	Sweden King/Queen
1588–648	Christian IV	1604–1632	Gustav II Adolf
1648–1670	Fredrik III	1632 (1644)–1654	Queen Christina
		1654–1660	Karl X Gustav

Introduction 9

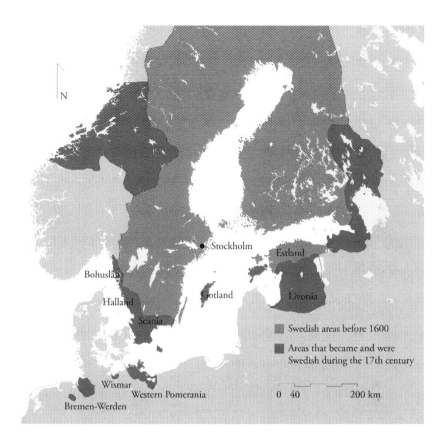

Figure 1.1 Map of Swedish areas around the Baltic in the seventeenth century.
Source: Map drawn by Panu Savolainen.

an age of grandeur, whereas Denmark, despite many attempts, experienced a period of decline. Ambitious overseas projects should thus be understood as an important part of this rivalry. As such, in the subsequent chapters, the general European situation and specifically the Nordic rivalry provide the political context for the book.[27]

Early modern entrepreneurship in overseas business

The concepts of *entrepreneurship* and *entrepreneurial behaviour* do not yet occupy an established status in the general historiography of the early modern period. Although there has been some research around the concept of entrepreneurship, it is by no means "mainstream" in economic and early modern business history.[28] Even in business history, the concept of *entrepreneurship* is still predominantly employed in relation to subsequent periods, especially the era of industrialisation in Great Britain. With regard to

10 Introduction

early modern overseas history, there is no shortage of works that designate individuals as "entrepreneurs." However, these lack analytic rigour, and entrepreneurship has not been dealt with in a systematic manner. The main problem is that there are no clear criteria as to what makes an entrepreneur. At times, individuals who have acted as entrepreneurs have instead been identified as explorers, prospectors, promoters, merchants, or even adventurers. This tends to romanticise their actions, and does nothing to bring about conceptual clarity.[29]

With regard to the early modern period and especially the European seventeenth century, the concept of entrepreneurship has been analytically applied mainly, although not exclusively, in the Dutch context.[30] Historians such as Clé Lesger, Violet Barbour, Peter Klein, Jan Willem Veluwenkamp, Karel Davids, Leo Noordegraaf, and Ferry de Goey have all studied the role of entrepreneurship in Dutch markets during the early modern period. Throughout, their aim was to understand the rapid advancement of the early modern Dutch economy, particularly during the period known as the Dutch Golden Age (1590–1660). During these years, Amsterdam witnessed the development of small- and large-scale businesses, as well as institutions such as a staple market, a bank, a stock exchange, notaries, and a booming shipping industry, all of which facilitated an array of entrepreneurial behaviours.[31] For the historian, they have also yielded a rich body of primary sources.

Studying entrepreneurship means studying agents of change. Entrepreneurship can change situations for better or for worse, and for private or for public benefit. In all cases, entrepreneurship always involves change, and the study of entrepreneurial behaviour is the study of why and how individuals act to change the status quo. In general, the term "entrepreneurship" refers to an individual's capacity and willingness to organise, manage, and develop business strategies, in order to make a profit, despite risks and uncertainties.[32] Casson, who specialises in business history, has defined an entrepreneur as "someone who specializes in taking judgmental decisions about the coordination of scarce resources."[33]

Ultimately, the function of entrepreneurship is always the same. What changes is the historical context. The key to the concept of entrepreneurship is the individual's motives in relation to the resources at hand, which are always bound to time and space. The context (or economic and social environment) is thus crucial to understanding the function of entrepreneurship.[34] As such, in order to understand entrepreneurship in the early modern period, it is not enough to focus merely on the personal capacities of individuals. In addition, it is equally crucial to focus on the social, economic, and political context with which the individual interacted. During the early modern period, entrepreneurship was not only about making profit but also about advancing one's social standing. In this sense, Clé Lesger, Luuc Kooijmans, and Leos Müller have stressed that early modern entrepreneurship was not only a matter of economics but also of sociability. They emphasise the

Introduction 11

importance of analysing entrepreneurship through a social lens, and particularly enquiring into the role played by friends, acquaintances, business partners, family members, and in-laws.[35] Lesger, Kooijmans, and Müller have all focused on how individuals used social networks, family relationships, and personal acquaintances as a means to improve their social status. They all emphasise the importance of social structures for entrepreneurial behaviour and stress that improvement of one's social standing provided sufficient reason to participate in business. Following in the footsteps of these historians, this book will demonstrate that early modern entrepreneurship was always socially embedded. However, in the overseas context, entrepreneurial behaviour did not always follow the same social structures as in Europe (as we shall see).

The context in which the individual acted always included the ways in which he or she dealt with risks and uncertainties. In order to change the status quo, individuals needed to confront risk and uncertainty. Casson has emphasised that individuals had not only to process information but also to deal with several overlapping social structures, using their imagination in order to reach their goals. These were the resources with which the individual operated, and it was his job to decide how. In short, we ought to ask: how did the individual deal with risk and uncertainty? Even if these concepts are often used interchangeably, they remain two different things. Risk refers to the probability of a future event, including the possible interference of internal and external factors. Risk can be minimised by preventive methods, such as risk analysis through market intelligence research, or various forms of insurance. In an economic sense, risk thus relates to the probability of returns on an investment. Uncertainty, on the other hand, arises from imperfect or unknown information. In short, risk is about the possibility of gaining or losing something of value, whereas uncertainty is the condition of not knowing. Risk can be minimised, whereas uncertainty remains uncontrollable.[36]

In early modern overseas business, such considerations were of paramount importance. Risks and uncertainties were multiplied due to the sheer scale of the threats to business. Gaps in information flows created considerable uncertainty, and it could be almost impossible to foresee specific outcomes. Unlike risk, in which potential undesirable outcomes can at least be measured and reduced, in the case of uncertainty, it is impossible to predict the outcome. Overseas business itself was considerably risky. Several potential threats were constantly present throughout the period, including long-distance voyages, shipwrecks, pirate attacks, war, and unsuccessful attempts to establish and maintain trade with local merchant networks. Irregular distribution of information and intermittent contact with headquarters and outposts created significant levels of uncertainty. Thus, from the perspective of maritime business, minimising risks and uncertainty was of crucial importance. From the perspective of the individual, these challenges proved to be an opportunity, as we shall see. Indeed, such long distances, uncertainty,

12   *Introduction*

and risks attracted a certain type of individual. Through studying entrepreneurial behaviour, it becomes possible to better situate the function of the individual and his entrepreneurship. However, the goal was always to change the status quo. Thus, in this book, overseas entrepreneurship refers to the activities of someone who specialised in making decisions in overseas business, in response to uncertainties and risks, on the basis of existing resources, in order to profit and to improve his or her social standing.

Literature and sources for the study

The Nordic historiography of overseas expansion, especially for the seventeenth century, has primarily been studied from a national point of view. The older studies by Georg Nørregård, Kay Larsen, and Victor Granlund employed an exclusively national framework, focusing on the Danish and Swedish presence in Asia and Africa.[37] Heinrich Sieveking has focused on Northern German overseas trade, including its close connection to Nordic trade.[38] In more recent research, Stephen Diller and Martin Krieger have studied the Danish presence in Asia in the *longue durée* but still from a Danish perspective.[39] A recent addition to the general overview of the Danish overseas expansion is a five-volume edited series on Danish colonialism.[40]

Particularly important for this book are the works of Ole Feldbæk and György Nováky on the role of the Nordic trading companies.[41] The former has studied the organisational aspects of the Danish East India and West India companies, and has demonstrated that their character was multifaceted. On paper, they strongly resembled the Dutch model. However, they also improvised novel solutions in response to local Danish political and economic contexts. Nováky's study of the Swedish Africa Company has shown that the SAC was not as unsuccessful as it might seem: at times, it managed to challenge the WIC, and even to turn a profit. Although in a different geographical context, Sune Dalgård's work on the competition between Dutch and Danish whalers in the Arctic has offered additional insights into the centrality of individuals to the development of Danish international trade.[42]

Currently, the predominant focus of Nordic overseas historiography is the eighteenth and nineteenth centuries.[43] Although giving more importance to the role of networks and agency, these studies are still primarily focused on particular companies and "national" empires. Although this book has benefitted considerably from these approaches, it focuses more strongly on the individuals who participated in the formation of the companies, and who subsequently managed them. In contrast to previous research, this book thus places individual employees or traders and their careers on centre stage, moving beyond a strictly Nordic overseas history, towards a more global scale of analysis.

The two case studies of this book, Leyel and Carloff, are not completely unknown. However, relative to the mass of sources available regarding their careers in the Indian and Atlantic Oceans, they have been understudied.[44]

Introduction 13

Leyel in particular has received only limited scholarly attention. His role in the DEIC features in several works of the older historiography, but always as a sub-narrative to the history of the company itself.[45] The two most important contributions regarding his career in Asia were by Kathryn Wellen and Asta Bredsdorff. Wellen provided a detailed and informative account of Leyel's involvement in attacks on local trading ships in the Bay of Bengal.[46] For his part, Bredsdorff provided a valuable biography of Leyel, which dealt with his life as well as his company employment in Asia.

In terms of primary sources, the most important are the Willem Leyel archives, which include material regarding his career between 1639 and 1648, and offer rich information regarding the relatively unexplored topic of Danish seventeenth-century trade in the Indian Ocean.[47] Moreover, they comprise documents written in Danish, Dutch, English, French, Spanish, Portuguese, Tamil, and Persian. Here, the focus is on the material in Danish, and the period between Leyel's arrival at Tranquebar in 1643 and the revolt he faced in 1648. All the reports that Leyel wrote to the directors of the DEIC in Europe have been rigorously consulted, as well as his correspondence with the other employees of the company. Additionally, the passports that Leyel issued and the instructions that he wrote during his period in command of the Danish company have been consulted. This material offers an unusual amount of qualitative information regarding the role that Leyel played within Danish business in Asia.

In addition to the Leyel archives, the correspondence of the Danish Chancellery, the personal letters of Christian IV, and the correspondence of the Leyel family have been analysed.[48] Moreover, the scarce and scattered sources relating to the first DEIC are also taken into account. Unfortunately, little material has survived in this regard. Although the surviving material mostly relates to the company's first voyage in 1620, rather than to the period when Leyel was in charge in Asia, the information regarding the finances of the company during the 1630s has nonetheless been beneficial.[49] In addition, useful contextual information concerning the Danish India trade between 1630 and 1648 has been gleaned from incoming letters from the VOC (the so-called *Generale Missiven*) as well as from the *Daghregister* (daily register).[50]

The career of Henrich Carloff is better known than that of Leyel. In most studies of Carloff's career, the dominant approach has been to observe Carloff from the standpoint of the trading companies. In line with the historiography outlined above, Carloff's activities in many different overseas business projects have been perceived through the "national lens" rather than from a business history perspective.[51] The most recent work on Carloff, by Henk den Heijer, is also the most accurate analysis of his role in the Atlantic trade. Den Heijer considered Carloff as a shrewd entrepreneur (*gewikste ondernemer*) and provided important information on his career in the Atlantic. In addition, György Noáky and Robert Porter have rigorously studied the activities of Carloff, especially in the West Africa trade.

14   *Introduction*

Although their focus was on the trading companies on the Gold Coast, they have also offered important insights as to how Carloff operated in West Africa.[52]

The primary sources relating to Carloff are scattered throughout multiple European archives. The Swedish Africa Company Archives in Stockholm include the correspondence between the company administrators, the de Geer family, and Carloff himself.[53] The material relates mainly to the administration of the company in Europe, and is less informative about events overseas. The Danish archives contain diffuse information regarding Carloff's role within Danish trade in Africa.[54] For their part, the French archives contain some clues as to how French West India Company officials saw Carloff.[55] In short, despite the extent of his role in early Swedish and Danish trade in Africa, Carloff has left remarkably little trace in the archives. The most fruitful archival material on his activities is located in the Netherlands. It includes material relating to the Dutch possessions on the Gold Coast,[56] the collection of the States General,[57] and the Notarial Archives of Amsterdam.[58] The early years of Carloff's life will unfortunately remain difficult to trace, due to a lack of material. By far the best documented period of Carloff's career are the years between 1649 and 1659, during which he served the Swedish and the Danish companies.

The details of Carloff's activities in Western Africa have become more accessible thanks to the Furley Collection (FC), which consists of various European archival sources collected, transcribed, and translated into English. However, this collection needs to be treated with some caution.[59] While it can offer initial directions towards relevant primary sources, it is sometimes difficult to know from precisely where the information originates. In other instances, the material has been re-arranged in the archives. Albert Van Dantzig has discussed the relevance and usability of the Furley Collection.[60] In this book, the N (Netherlands) section, which comprises Dutch sources, has been used. According to Van Dantzig, the Dutch material has limitations, since neither Furley nor his copyist was acquainted with early modern Dutch, something which led to occasional mistakes in translations. Here, the information from the Furley Collection has been checked against the primary sources held in the original archives, whenever it has been possible to do so. Through such cross-checking, any serious mistakes that would impact the argument of this book have been avoided.[61]

Outline of the study

The second chapter of this book will focus on cross-company behaviour and the migration patterns of northern European overseas veterans during the seventeenth century. It will discuss why the Nordic countries became such fertile ground for overseas entrepreneurship, particularly through a process referred to as *institutional sheltering*. The chapter will also pay attention to

Introduction 15

the background of the individuals concerned, and will ask why overseas business became an opportunity for so many people.

The third chapter will analyse entrepreneurship and specialisation in overseas business within the framework of the trading company. The focus will be on individuals, operating within the boundaries of the companies via entrepreneurial mechanisms. Here, it will be asked why early modern entrepreneurship was beneficial for both the trading organisations and the individuals concerned.

Chapter 4 will explore the importance of social relationships and business contacts for individuals, in both Europe and overseas. The main argument will be that overseas entrepreneurship was a difficult balancing act between various networks, revealing how vulnerable such overseas connections really were.

Chapter 5 will focus on the accumulation of knowledge necessary to building an entrepreneurial profile overseas. The chapter will study the ways in which individuals could influence how they were perceived by institutions, and the ways in which access to information and experience was crucial for overseas entrepreneurship.

Chapter 6 will focus on a seldom noticed aspect of overseas entrepreneurship, i.e. the use of violence. The chapter argues that violence played a crucial role in seventeenth-century overseas entrepreneurship. Even though individuals were not actively seeking out violent disputes, they at least had to be prepared to use violence in order to achieve their goals.

The last chapter of the book is a concluding discussion, elaborating on the results of the research. Here, the benefit contributed by the concept of overseas entrepreneurship will be discussed.

Notes

1 On Leyel and the Danish East India Company, see: Asta Bredsdorff, *The Trials and Travels of Willem Leyel: An Account of the Danish East India Company in Tranquebar, 1639–48* (Copenhagen: Museum Tusculanum Press, 2009); Ole Feldbæk, "No Ship for Tranquebar for Twenty-Nine Years. Or: The Art of Survival of a Mid-Seventeenth Century European Settlement in India," in *Emporia, Commodities and Entrepreneurs in Asian Maritime Trade, c. 1400–1750*, ed. Roderich Ptak and Dietmar Rothermund (Stuttgart: Franz Steiner Verlag, 1991), 29–36; Kay Larsen, *Dansk-Ostindiske koloniers historie* (Copenhagen: Centralførlaget, 1907). Rigsarkivet, Copenhagen (RAC), Danske Kancelli (DK) (Rentekammerafdelningen), B 246 A, B and C, Willum Leyel arkiv.
2 On Carloff and his Atlantic career, see: Henk den Heijer, "Een dienaar van vele heren – de Atlantische carrier van Hendrick Caerloff," in *Het verre gezicht – politieke en culturele relaties tussen Nederland en Azie, Afrika en Amerika*, ed. Thomas Lindblad and Alicia Schrikker (Franeker: Van Wijnen, 2011), 162–180; György Nováky, *Handelskompanier och kompanihandel – Svenska Afrikakompaniet 1649–1663 en studie i feodal handel* (Uppsala: Uppsala University Library, 1990), 82; Robert Porter, *European Activity on the Gold Coast, 1620–1667* (PhD dissertation, Pretoria: University of South Africa, 1975).

16 *Introduction*

3 Christian J. Koot, "The Merchant, the Map, and Empire: Augustine Herrman's Chesapeake and Interimperial Trade, 1644–73," *The William and Mary Quarterly* 67, no. 4 (2010): 603–644; Jaap Jacobs, *New Netherland: A Dutch Colony in Seventeenth-Century America* (Boston/Leiden: Brill, 2005); Jaap Jacobs, *The Colony of New Netherland: A Dutch Settlement in Seventeenth-Century America* (Ithaca: Cornell University Press, 2009); Alison Games, *The Web of Empire: English Cosmopolitans in an Age of Expansion, 1560–1660* (New York: Oxford University Press, 2008); Claudia Schnurmann, "Representative Atlantic Entrepreneur Jacob Leisler, 1640–1691," in *Riches from Atlantic Commerce: Dutch Transatlantic Trade and Shipping, 1585–1817*, ed. Victor Enthoven and Johannes Postma (Boston/Leiden: Brill, 2003), 259–283; C. R. Boxer, *Francisco Vieira de Figueiredo: A Portuguese Merchant-Adventurer in South East Asia, 1624–1667* (Gravenhage: Martinus Nijhoff, 1967).
4 In this book, "Nordic" refers to the present Nordic states: Denmark, Iceland, Norway, Sweden, and Finland.
5 Geoffrey Vaughn Scammell, *The First Imperial Age: European Overseas Expansion C. 1400–1715* (New York: Routledge, 1989); James D. Tracy, ed., *The Rise of Merchant Empires: Long Distance Trade in the Early Modern World 1350–1750* (Cambridge: Cambridge University Press, 1993); Niels Steensgaard, *The Asian Trade Revolution: The East India Companies and the Decline of the Caravan Trade* (Chicago: University of Chicago Press, 1973); Leonard Blussé and Femme Gaastra, ed., *Companies and Trade Essays on Overseas Trading Companies during the Ancien Régime* (Comparative Studies in Overseas History) (Leiden: Leiden University Press, 1981).
6 Ashin Das Gupta and Michael. N. Pearson, ed., *India and the Indian Ocean 1500–1800* (Calcutta; New York: Oxford University Press, 1987); Bernard Bailyn, *Atlantic History: Concept and Contours* (Cambridge, MA; London: Harvard University Press, 2005); John H. Elliott, *Empires of the Atlantic World: Britain and Spain in America 1492–1830* (New Haven: Yale University Press, 2007); John Thornton, *Africa and Africans in the Making of the Atlantic World, 1400–1800* (Cambridge/New York: Cambridge University Press, 1998); Mark Meuwese, "Indigenous Leaders and the Atlantic World: The Parallel Lives of Dom Antonio Filipe Camarao and Pieter Poty, 1600–1650," in *Atlantic Biographies: Individuals and Peoples in the Atlantic World*, ed. Jeffrey A. Fortin and Mark Meuwese (Boston/Leiden: Brill, 2014), 213–233; K.N. Chaudhuri, *Trade and Civilisation in the Indian Ocean: An Economic History from the Rise of Islam to 1750* (Cambridge: Cambridge University Press, 1985).
7 Victor Enthoven, "An assessment of Dutch Transatlantic commerce, 1585–1817", in *Riches of from Atlantic Commerce: Dutch Transatlantic trade and shipping, 1585–1817*, ed. Victor Enthoven and Johannes Postma (Boston/Leiden: Brill, 2003), 386–387.
8 For a useful overview of the differences between the WIC and the VOC, see Maarten Prak, *Dutch Republic in the Seventeenth Century* (New York: Cambridge University Press, 2005), 111–121 and Jonathan Israel, *Dutch Primacy in World Trade, 1585–1740* (Oxford: Clarendon Press, 1989), 156–187.
9 Ibid.
10 Kate Ekama, "Courting Conflict: Managing Dutch East and West India Company disputes in the Dutch Republic" (PhD dissertation, Leiden: Leiden University, 2018), 18; Erik Odegard, "Colonial Careers: Johan Maurits, Rijckloff Volckertsz, van Goens and Career-Making in the Seventeenth-Century Dutch Empire" (PhD dissertation, Leiden: Leiden University, 2018).
11 Elisabeth Heijmans, "The Agency of Empire: Personal Connections and Individual Strategies of the French Early Modern Expansion (1686–1746)" (PhD dissertation, Leiden: Leiden University, 2018).

Introduction 17

12 Mark Casson and Catherine Casson, *The Entrepreneur in History: From Medieval Merchant to Modern Business Leader* (Basingstoke: Palgrave MacMillan, 2013), 8.
13 Sebouh David Aslanian, *From the Indian Ocean to the Mediterranean: The Global Trade Networks of Armenian Merchants from New Julfa* (Berkeley/Los Angeles: University of California Press, 2011); Francesca Trivellato, The Familiarity of Strangers: The Sephardic Diaspora, Livorno, and Cross-Cultural Trade in the Early Modern Period (New Haven: Yale University Press, 2014); Francesca Trivellato, Leor Halevi, and Cátia Antunes, ed., Religion and Trade: Cross-Cultural Exchanges in World History, 1000–1900, 1 edition (Oxford/New York: Oxford University Press, 2014); Ina Baghdiantz McCabe, Gelina Harlaftis, and Ioanna Pepelasis Minoglou, Diaspora Entrepreneurial Networks: Four Centuries of History (Oxford /New York: Bloomsbury Academic, 2005).
14 Cátia Antunes and Amelia Pólonia, eds, *Beyond Empires: Global, Self-Organizing, Cross-Imperial Networks, 1500–1800*. Boston/Leiden: Brill, 2016a, see introduction, 2–11.
15 Ibid., 5.
16 Jeffrey Fortin and Mark Meuwese, ed., *Atlantic Biographies: Individuals and Peoples in the Atlantic World* (Boston/Leiden: Brill, 2013); Lisa Lindsay and John Wood Sweet, ed., *Biography and the Black Atlantic* (Philadelphia: University of Pennsylvania Press, 2013).
17 Trivellato, "The Familiarity of Strangers," 8.
18 Francesca Trivellato, "Is There a Future for Italian Microhistory in the Age of Global History?" *California Italian Studies* 2, no. 1 (2011), VII.
19 Maria Fusaro, "A Reassessment of Mediterranean History between the Northern Invasion and the Caravane Maritime," in *Trade and Cultural Exchange in the Early Modern Mediterranean: Braudel's Maritime Legacy*, ed. Mohamed-Salah Omri, Colin Heywood, and Maria Fusaro (London/New York: I.B. Tauris, 2010), 1–22, 10.
20 On the Nordic rivalry, see Michael Roberts, *The Swedish Imperial Experience 1560–1718* (Cambridge: Cambridge University Press 1979), Chapter 1.
21 Pommern 1648–1815, Wismar 1648–1903, Bremen-Verden 1648–1715; Rian, "Introduction," 23. Gustafsson, *Nordens Historia*, 103; Petri Karonen, *Pohjoinen suurvalta: Ruotsi ja Suomi 1521–1809* (Helsinki: WSOY, 1999), 225–227.
22 Mar Jonsson, "Denmark-Norway as a Potential World Power in the Early Modern Seventeenth Century," *Itinerario* XXXIII, no. 2 (2007): 17–27.
23 Reval was Swedish: 1561–1721.
24 Gustafsson, *Nordens Historia*, 116; J. Thomas Lindblad, *Sweden's Trade with the Dutch Republic 1738–1795: A Quantitative Analysis of the Relationship between Economic Growth and International Trade in the Eighteenth Century* (Assen: Van Gorcum, 1982), 12; Øystein Rian, "Introduction: Government and Society in Early Modern Scandinavia 1560–1721," in *A Revolution from Above? The Power State of 16th and 17th Century Scandinavia, ed. Leon Jespersen* (Odense: University Press of Southern Denmark, 2000), 13–30, 23.
25 Karonen, *Pohjoinen suurvalta*, 220.
26 Jörgen Weibull, *Sveriges historia* (Stockholm: Förlags AB Wiken Svenska Institutet, 1993), 29–49; Lindblad, *Sweden's Trade*, 14.
27 About the Nordic political context see, Paul Lockhart, "Denmark and the Empire A Reassessment of Danish Foreign Policy under King Christian IV," *Scandinavian Studies*, 63, no. 3 (1992) 390–416; Roberts, *The Swedish*; Jespersen (ed.), *A Revolution*.
28 Geoffery Jones and Daniel Wadhwani, 'Entrepreneurship,' in *The Oxford Handbook of Business History*, ed. Geoffery Jones and Jonathan Zeitlin (Oxford, Oxford University Press, 2008), 501–528.

18 *Introduction*

29 Casson and Casson, *The Entrepreneur*, chapter 1.
30 Leos Müller and Maj Britt Nergård have focused on seventeenth-century entrepreneurship in Sweden: Leos Müller, *The Merchant Houses of Stockholm, C. 1640–1800: A Comparative Study of Early-Modern Entrepreneurial Behaviour* (Uppsala: Uppsala University Library, 1998); Maj-Britt Nergård, *Mellan krona och markand: utlädnska och svenska entreprenörer inom svensk järnhantering från ca 1580 till 1700* (Uppsala: Acta Universitatis Upsaliensis, 2001).
31 Clé Lesger, *The Rise of the Amsterdam Market and Information Exchange: Merchants, Commercial Expansion and Change in the Spatial Economy of the Low Countries, c.1550–1630*, trans. J.C. Grayson (Aldershot; Burlington: Ashgate, 2006); Ferry de Goey and Jan Willem Veluwenkamp, ed., *Entrepreneurs and Institutions in Europe and Asia, 1500–2000* (Amsterdam: Aksant, 2002); Jan Willem Veluwenkamp, *Archangel: Nederlandse ondernemers in Rusland, 1550–1785*, 1st edition (Amsterdam: Balans, 2000); Clé Lesger and Leo Noordegraaf, ed., *Entrepreneurs and Entrepreneurship in Early Modern Times : Merchants and Industrialists Within the Orbit of the Dutch Staple Market* (Den Haag: Stiching Hollandse Historische Reeks, 1995); P. W. Klein and Jan Willem Veluwenkamp, "The Role of the Entrepreneur in the Economic Expansion of the Dutch Republic," in *Dutch Republic in the Golden Age, ed. Karel Davids and Leo Noordegraaf* (Amsterdam: Nederlandsch Economisch-Historisch Archief, 1993), 27–53; Karel Davids and Leo Noordegraaf, ed., *The Dutch Economy in the Golden Age* (Amsterdam: Nederlandsch Economisch-Historisch Archief, 1993); Violet Barbour, *Capitalism in Amsterdam in The Seventeenth Century* (Ann Arbor: University of Michigan Press, 1950).
32 Surprisingly, few economists have addressed the importance of entrepreneurship in economic development. Generally, economists consider individual agency to have had only a limited impact on economic development. See Mark Casson, ed., *Entrepreneurship: Theory, Networks, History* (Cheltenham, UK; Northhampton, MA: Edward Elgar, 2010), 3–4.
33 Mark Casson, *The Entrepreneur: An Economic Theory*, 2nd edition (Cheltenham, UK; Northhampton, MA: Edward Elgar Pub, 2003), 20.
34 Casson and Casson, "The History of Entrepreneurship," 1227.
35 Müller, *The Merchant Houses*; L. Kooijmans, *Vriendschap: en de kunst van het overleven in de zeventiende en achtiende eeuw* (Amsterdam: B. Bakker, 1997); L. Kooijmans, "Risk and Reputation: On the Mentality of Merchants in the early modern Period," in *Entrepreneurs and Entrepreneurship*, ed. Lesger and Noordegraaf, 25–35; Lesger and Noordegraaf, *Entrepreneurs and Entrepreneurship in Early Modern Times*.
36 For a general description of risk in a business context, see Casson, *Entrepreneurship*, 7.
37 Georg Nørregård, *Danish Settlements in West Africa, 1658–1850* (Boston: Boston University Press, 1966); Larsen, *Dansk-Ostindiske koloniers historie; Victor Granlund, En svensk koloni i Afrika: eller Svenska afrikanska kompaniets historia* (Stockholm: P. A. Norstedt, 1879).
38 Heinrich Sieveking, "Die Glückstädter Guineafahrt im 17. Jahrhundert. Ein Stück deutscher Kolonialgeschichte." *Vierteljahrschrift für Sozial- und Wirtschaftsgeschichte* 30, no. 1 (1937): 19–71.
39 Stephan Diller, *Die Dänen in Indien, Südostasien und China (1620–1845)* (Wiesbaden: Otto Harrassowitz Verlag, 1999); Martin Krieger, Kaufleute, Seeräuber und Diplomaten. *Der Dänische Handel auf dem Indischen Ozean (1620 - 1868)* (Köln: Böhlau Verlag, 1998). The study by Krieger has been crucial to a better understanding of the development of Danish trade in Asia. According to Krieger, Danish trade in Asia was based on a symbiosis between the interests of the companies and those of their employees.

Introduction 19

40 H.C. Gullov et al., ed., *Danmark og kolonierna,* five volume series (Copenhagen: Gads forlag, 2017).

41 Feldbæk, "The Danish Trading Companies"; Ole Feldbæk, "The Organization and Structure of the Danish East India, West India and Guinea Companies in the 17th and 18th Centuries," in *Companies and Trade,* ed. Leonard Blussé and Femme Gaastra (Leiden: Leiden University Press, 1981),131–158; Nováky, *Handelskompanier;* György Nováky, "Small Company Trade and the Gold Coast: The Swedish Africa Company 1650–1663," *Itinerario,* 16, no. 01 (1992): 57–76.

42 The whaling trade was lucrative. The oil produced from the whale fat was used to make soaps and lubricants, and was also sold for several other purposes. On the whaling trade in a Danish context, see Sune Dalgård, *Dansk-Norsk hvalfangst, 1615–1660 en studie over Danmarks-Norges stilling i Europæisk merkantil expansion* (Copenhagen: G.E.C. Gad, 1962), especially chapter 2.

43 Magdalena Naum and Jonas M. Nordin, ed., *Scandinavian Colonialism and the Rise of Modernity: Small Time Agents in a Global Arena* (New York: Springer, 2013); Holger Weiss, ed., *Ports of Globalisation, Places of Creolisation: Nordic Possessions in the Atlantic World during the Era of the Slave Trade* (Boston/Leiden: Brill, 2015).

44 Kaarle Wirta, "Rediscovering Agency in the Atlantic: A Biographical Approach Linking Entrepreneurial Spirit and Overseas Companies," in *The Biographical Turn Lives in History,* ed. Hans Renders, Binne de Haan, and Jonne Harmsma (New York: Routledge, 2016), 118–129.

45 RAC, håndskriftsamlingen VII E 1 a), De Ostindiske etablissementers historie, undated, but probably written in the late 18th century; Barthold G. Niebuhr, "Nogle efterretninger om Wilhelm Leyel Og Den Danske Ostindiske Handel under Hans Bestyrelse," *Det Skandinaviske litteratuselskabs skriften* 1 (1805): 142 69, 143; Gunnar Olsen, "Dansk Ostindien," in *Vore gamle tropenkolonier,* ed. Johannes Brøndsted, vol. 1 (Copenhagen: Westermann, 1952); Ole Feldbæk and Ole Justesen, ed., *Kolonierne i Asien og Afrika* (Copenhagen: Politiken, 1980); Larsen, *Dansk-Ostindiske koloniers historie.*

46 Kathryn Wellen, "The Danish East India Company's War against the Mughal Empire, 1642–1698," *Journal of Early Modern History* 19, no. 5 (September 2, 2015): 439–461.

47 RAC, DK, B 246, A, B and C, Willem Leyel arkiv.

48 There are several collected volumes of the letters, see for example, Erik Marquard, ed., *Kancelliets brevbøger vedrørende Danmarks indre forhold: 1635–36* (Copenhagen: C.A. Reitzel Nielsen & Lydische, 1940) (Henceforth: *Kancelliets brevbøger* with years); C.F Bricka and J.A. Fridericia, ed., *Kong Christian den fjerdes egenhændige breve 1636–1640* (Copenhagen: Selskabet for Udgivelse af Kilder til Dansk Historie, 1969). (Henceforth: *Kong Christian Den Fjerdes Egenhændige Breve 1636–1640*).

49 RAC, Tyske Kancelliet Indenrigske avdelnig (TKIA), Diverse akter vedr. det ostindiske kompagni og Guinea 1618 1659; RAC, DK, Diverse Breve Dokumenter og breve det ostindiska kompgani vedkommende 1616–1660.

50 W.P.H. Coolhas, ed., *Generale missiven van gouverneurs-generaal en raden aan heren XVII der Vereinigde Oostindische Compagnie, deel 1, 1610–1638* (Gravenhage: Martinus Nijhoff, 1960); H.T. Colenbrander, ed., *Dagh-register gehouden int casteel Batavia vant passerende daer ter plaetse als over geheel Nederlandts-India:1643–44* (Gravenhage: Martinus Nijhoff, 1902).

51 The Journal of Müller, as printed in Adam Jones, *German Sources for West African History, 1599–1669* (Wiesbaden: Franz Steiner Verlag, 1983); Nicholas De Roever, "Twee Concurrenten van de Eerste West-Indische Compagnie," *Oud-Holland; nieuw bijdragen voor de geschiedenis der Nederlandsche kunst, letterkunde, nijverheid, enz.* 7 (1889): 195–220; Granlund, *En svensk koloni i*

20   Introduction

Afrika; Cornelis De Jonge, *Geschiedenis van het Nederlandsche zeewezen*. Pt. 2. Vol. 3. (Gravenhage: Gebroedersvan Cleef, 1837); Cornelis Goslinga, Cornelis, *The Dutch in the Caribbean and on the Wild Coast 1580–1680* (Assen: Van Gorcum, 1971; Sievking, "Die Glückstädter Guineafahrt"; Nørregård, *Danish Settlements*; Feldbæk and Justesen, *Kolonierne i Asien og Afrika*; Kwame Yeboa Daaku, *Trade and Politics on the Gold Coast, 1600–1720: A Study of the African Reaction to European Trade* (Oxford: Clarendon Press, 1970); Angela Sutton, "The Seventeenth-Century Slave Trade in the Documents of the English, Dutch, Swedish, Danish and Prussian Royal Slave Trading Companies," *Slavery & Abolition* 36, no. 3 (3 July, 2015): 445–459.

52 Porter, *European Activity*; Nováky, "Small Company"; Nováky, *Handelskompanier.*

53 Riksarkivet, Stockholm, Sweden (henceforth: RAS), Especially in Handel och Sjöfart (henceforth: H&S), vol.42; Leufsta Arkiv (henceforth: LA), vol. 82.

54 RAC, TKIA, Diverse akter vedr. det ostindiske kompagni og Guinea 1618–1659.

55 I would like to thank Elisabeth Heijmans for assistance in the translation of the French documents.

56 Nationaal Archief, Den Haag (henceforth: NL-HaNA), Oude West-Indische Compagnie (henceforth: OWIC), 1.05.01.01, inventarisnummer *11* and *13A.*

57 Material related to Sweden and Denmark; NL-HaNA, Staten-Generaal (henceforth, S.G.), 1.01.02, inv.nr. *12571.38.1 and* NL-HaNA, Staten-Generaal, 1.01.02, inv.nr. *12572.41.*

58 Stadsarchief Amsterdam (henceforth: SAA), Notarieel Archief (henceforth: NA), several entries in this book.

59 John Talford Furley (1878–1956) was the secretary of Native Affairs of the Gold Coast Colony, 1917–1923. After his retirement, Furley collected both literature and primary sources for a history of Ghana. The collection is housed in the Balme Library at University of Ghana at Legon. I have accessed the Furley Collection through the digital collections of the University of Ghana, at http://ugspace.ug.edu.gh/handle/123456789/3 (accessed 16 September 2015). Recently applied also in the English context, see L.H. Roper, *Advancing Empire, English Interest and Overseas Expansion, 1613–1688* (New York: Cambridge University Press, 2017).

60 Albert Van Dantzig, *The Furley Collection: Its Value and Limitations for the Study of Ghana's History*, European Sources for Sub-Saharan Africa before 1900: Use and Abuse (Wiesbaden: Franz Steiner Verlag, 1987), 423–432.

61 Van Danzig stated that the seventeenth-century documents are much more elaborate than those for the later period, although less systematised. Ibid.

2 Formative years of overseas entrepreneurship and Nordic overseas trade

The Nordic kingdoms and entrepreneurial opportunity

In the seventeenth century, the Nordic kingdoms entered the overseas business scene. As had been the case with their western European counterparts, the Nordic expansion was carried out through commercial trading companies. The history of seventeenth-century Nordic business and entrepreneurship arose from a more general change in the development of the Nordic economies. The historian Mirkka Lappalainen has referred to the European seventeenth century as the "odd century," a period that was still characterised by a medieval political and economic system, but which also witnessed the development of premodern forms of business and capitalism.[1] Indeed, Nordic participation in long-distance trade served to accelerate this transition.

This chapter is divided into two parts. The first part will focus on the Nordic institutional context in which the trading companies were initiated. In particular, it will discuss the institutional business environment in the Nordic kingdoms, and what opportunities the kingdoms offered to individuals. The second part will focus on the individuals who were essential to the establishment of these companies. In particular, it focuses on the formative years of overseas entrepreneurship, and discusses how individuals accumulated the experience and knowledge required by the Nordic kingdoms.

As Nordic overseas ambitions grew, attention turned towards places where overseas trade had already been established. The trading networks and operations built by the Portuguese, the English, the French, and the Dutch also attracted the Nordic kingdoms, which lacked such already established practices, knowledge, capital, specialised labour, and connections. Above all, the Dutch republic was essential to early Nordic overseas endeavours. The Dutch had managed to develop a globally successful maritime trade and had become the most dynamic seventeenth-century economy on the continent. Of course, there were several reasons for Dutch success. However, the development of commercial specialisation and commercial culture was without doubt a key element. For example, Jan de Vries and Ad van der Woude suggest that seventeenth-century Dutch mercantile and

22 *Formative years of overseas entrepreneurship*

economic success was attributable to the fact that the domestic economy was able to respond to international specialisation.[2] According to Jonathan Israel, during the seventeenth century, a specific type of economic climate had developed in the Dutch Republic. One of the main reasons for this was the transition from "bulk trade" within the Baltic (grains, salt, and timber) to "rich trade" in Asia and the Caribbean (luxury products and goods).[3]

The lungs of the Republic's commercial success were in Amsterdam, which was at the time the world's central entrepôt for international trade. The city provided a platform for a set of new financial institutions, such as the merchant bank, the stock exchange, and a functioning insurance sector. Entrepreneurially minded people, both native and foreign, populated the elite quarters of the city. The elite of Amsterdam was not a traditional landed aristocracy but rather consisted of financially powerful merchants, who, through kinship and marital alliances, built a ruling elite that controlled both trade and politics.[4] The Republic also had an innovative maritime sector, not least in shipping, which grew to become one of the strongest shipbuilding industries of the era. For example, the introduction of the flute ship, which was specially designed for commercial purposes, became a symbol of the capacity of the Dutch merchant marine. It had several advantages, including its ability to carry a larger tonnage than its main competitors and its cheapness to build, maintain, and equip. The shipbuilding industry needed a lot of building material, and this pushed the merchant marine to broaden its import sector internationally, including with the Nordic kingdoms. The ropes and sails of the ship were produced using hemp and linen from the Baltic. Timber came mainly from Norway, and copper, iron, and tar from Sweden (incl. Finland).[5]

In connection to the expansion of maritime trade, Dutch skippers developed a special carrier service sector, which was responsible for shipping European goods from one side of the continent to the other. This carrier trade was especially strong in the Baltic. The Dutch republic was a maritime superpower, and its maritime institutions and agents, such as the trading companies, creditors, notaries, skippers, freighters, and entrepreneurs, were of central importance all over Europe, including in the Nordic kingdoms.[6]

Another important reason for Dutch success was the welcoming of different entrepreneurial networks, such as the Portuguese "Nation" or the German-Belgian manufacturers.[7] The Dutch also benefitted from immigration, especially from the Southern Low Countries following the fall of Antwerp in 1585. The immigrants brought with them capital, knowledge, and the ability to operate within international merchant networks.[8] During the early modern period, almost a million people travelled to the East Indies from the Republic. Of these, around 50 per cent were foreigners, and served in various positions within the VOC.[9] Approximately 40 per cent of the employees of the WIC were foreigners.[10] Also people from the Nordic kingdoms were employed in the Dutch trading companies. As Kristoff Glamann reminds us: "During the seventeenth-century the Dutch navy was

Formative years of overseas entrepreneurship 23

the main training camp for Northern-European naval officers and seamen, including those of the Nordic countries."[11] Indeed, there were also many Danes and Norwegians in the service of the VOC throughout its existence.[12] Many Norwegian sailors went into Dutch service in the seventeenth century.[13] Hiring Danish and Norwegian sailors on Dutch vessels was common, since they were often skilled and experienced. The attractiveness of the VOC came from its reputation for paying its personnel's wages punctually, and from offering a fair chance to climb the company ranks.[14] These exchanges and cooperative activities have been classified by the historian Erik Gøbel as a strong mutual influence between the Dutch and Danish.[15]

It has often been assumed that the companies were national enterprises tied closely to the state. However, they were not national enterprises in the modern sense. In reality, many of them, the VOC and EIC included, benefitted from foreign capital, foreign workers, and foreign knowledge, both European and non-European.[16] If we place too much emphasis on the supposedly national framework, we risk losing sight of such cross-imperial activities that can better explain how business was developed.[17] The companies were by definition multinational and were run by internationally organised business networks. The Dutch companies were also international. They provided an efficient platform to learn and to develop the skills required for maritime trade.

Dutch commercial and maritime success were not achieved overnight. To the contrary, they were the culmination of a process that had already begun in the fifteenth century. In the Nordic kingdoms, by contrast, this process occurred much later. In particular, the lack of skilled and well-capitalised local entrepreneurs forced the Nordic kingdoms to look for maritime knowledge and experience from abroad. Their preference for the Dutch was twofold. Firstly, from a purely practical standpoint, the Dutch were already experienced in overseas business. Secondly, a long-standing tradition of interaction in the Baltic trade made the connection with the Dutch seem natural.[18] For both these reasons, several large-scale investors and entrepreneurs moved from the Low Countries to the Nordic kingdoms, or at least built extensive trading networks there.[19] The Dutch worked on a larger scale in their international trade, and this suited Nordic merchants well: as will be discussed below, they could borrow capital, be hired as agents, and receive a basic training from their Dutch principals. Afterwards, some were even able to set up an independent enterprise.[20]

Migration in the early Nordic overseas ventures

From an early stage, the importance of internationally experienced entrepreneurs to the Nordic enterprises was obvious. In Sweden in the 1630s, growing interest in overseas expansion resulted in the establishment of the first overseas trading company, Söderkompaniet (South Company).[21] By 1637, two Dutchmen, Samuel Blommaert and Peter Minuit, had managed

24 *Formative years of overseas entrepreneurship*

to obtain a charter for the establishment of a Swedish settlement in the New World. The company settled at the Delaware River, in close proximity to the WIC, which had already had a settlement in the region since 1624.[22] Minuit and Blommaert had an extensive background Dutch trading ventures. In particular, both men had previously been employed by the WIC in New Netherland. Samuel Blommaert had begun his career in the 1610s in Dutch trade with Angola. For his part, Blommaert had also been involved in the New Netherland venture at an early stage in his career. In 1622, he became one of the directors of the newly founded WIC, but was simultaneously involved in the copper industry and arms trade. In 1635, he changed profession, starting a brass factory outside Stockholm, and in 1636, he became the Swedish consul in Amsterdam. Around the same time, Blommaert was engaged in equipping and fitting ships for a Swedish expedition to North America.[23]

Minuit, who had joined the WIC in the 1620s, was sent to New Netherland in 1625, in order to seek out new trading opportunities for the company, particularly by canvassing products other than fur.[24] Eventually, Minuit became the director of the WIC in New Netherland.[25] In 1631, he was suspended from his position, because the other directors doubted his loyalty, and was recalled to Amsterdam. There, he met with Willem Usselincx and Samuel Blommaert. The latter approached the Swedish chancellor, received privileges for a commercial company, and established the Swedish settlement in Delaware 1637.[26]

Willem Usselincx, Blommaert and Minuit's business partner, also had a career characterised by shifting affiliations.[27] After his travels in Spain and Portugal, Usselincx had learnt about the opportunities for colonial trade, and moved to the Northern Netherlands during the late 1590s. In 1621, he was among the founding members of the WIC, and was also part of the group that established New Netherland.[28] Much like Minuit, Usselincx eventually left the company and moved to Sweden. According to the royal charter that Usselincx received from the Swedish king Gustav II Adolf, his mission was to establish a permanent Swedish trading settlement in the Delaware region. As early as 1627, however, Usselincx had attempted to establish a colony in the Caribbean under the protection of the duke of Courland, but had ultimately failed to do so.[29]

Another Dutchman, Abraham Cabiljau, migrated to Sweden around 1604. The Amsterdam-based merchant participated in the founding of the city of Gothenburg, serving as mayor after 1609, and simultaneously became one of the king's financiers. After 1617, Cabiljau moved between Amsterdam and Sweden, before eventually settling in Stockholm. He introduced the Italian method of double-entry bookkeeping to Sweden, and became a director in the Swedish Shipping Company, which in 1631 merged with the South Company.[30]

This kind of cross-imperial migration also played an important role in the early Danish expansion to Asia. In 1615, Jan de Willem of Amsterdam and

Herman Rosenkrantz of Rotterdam approached the Danish king Christian IV, proposing to create a Danish trading company.[31] In March 1616, the king issued a charter, which gave the enterprise a twelve-year monopoly on trade between Asia and Denmark. Indeed, the early years of the Danish East India Company (DEIC) were strongly marked by foreign participation, especially by the Dutch.

According to Ole Feldbæk and Richard Willerslev, the strong connection to the VOC was also institutional as the company's charter, copied entire paragraphs from its Dutch counterpart.[32] A few differences can be found. One of the major differences was that VOC was divided into chambers for political reasons, whereas the DEIC retained a centralised administration. However, perhaps the most important difference was that the VOC had the right to sign contracts and treaties with local rulers and authorities. In the case of the DEIC, that right remained a royal prerogative. Curiously, the charter offered protection to navigators and merchants, including foreign navigators and merchants in Danish employment. It stated that:

> Everyone in the company, whether as skippers, pilots, sailors or other personnel, shall be treated in the same way as those who are born in the country of the king, and no additional burdens shall be laid upon them.[33]

This indicates that in the DEIC, international entrepreneurs were welcome, as both investors and employees. At this point in time, it was obvious that the company was designed to attract Dutchmen. The VOC responded quickly, and only nine months after its establishment, the VOC forbade Dutch seamen, skippers, and pilots from joining foreign enterprises.[34] Despite this prohibition, the first Danish expedition to India was mainly manned by a Dutch crew.[35]

In its initial phase, the company had problems sending out ships due to lack of financial support. However, the interest of potential investors increased after 1617, when a Dutchman, Marcelis Michielszoon de Boshouwer, arrived in Copenhagen with an enticing proposal. He had already worked for the VOC on the Coromandel Coast during the 1610s, and in 1612, he had served at the court of the King of Candy on the island of Ceylon. In 1615, he returned to Europe and requested Dutch assistance on behalf of the King of Candy in order to fight against the Portuguese. His request was rejected by the VOC, so he decided to approach the Danish king instead. Indeed, the king was drawn in by Boshouwer's claims regarding the riches that could be expected from Ceylon. Boshouwers's proposal was sufficient to convince the king, and most of the potential investors, to commit to an expedition to India. The idea was to enter Indian Ocean trade through Ceylon, where a friendly relationship with Candy appeared to be forthcoming.[36]

The company also managed to employ another former VOC employee, Roeland Crappe, as an advisor to the company. This was, in Crappe's own words, "After I had been employed by the Dutch East Indian Company for

26 *Formative years of overseas entrepreneurship*

many years."[37] In particular, Crappe accepted employment in the Danish company in order to secure a significant promotion, namely the post of Director-General of the DEIC.[38]

Roeland Crappe provides yet another example of internationally experienced individuals with a Dutch connection participating in the early Danish trade in Asia.[39] He was Dutch-born and a previous employee of the VOC, and became one of the key figures in early Danish entrepreneurship in Asia. Before joining the Danish Company, Crappe had also purchased property in Batavia.[40] His connections to the Republic should also be underlined, since his sister, Maria Crappe, was living in Amsterdam, and had a local merchant, Thijmon Jacobsen Hinlopen, as her guardian. In a letter dated 9 August 1636, the VOC was asked to pay 8000 *reals* to Maria. Indeed, Hinlopen himself was active in the Dutch Whaling Company, the Noordsche Compagnie, the fur trade through the New Netherland Company, and the slave trade on the Western Coast of Africa.[41]

After Crappe joined the company, a contract between the company and the King of Candy was drawn up.[42] After numerous drafts, the contract was signed on 30 March 1618, and by November 1618, the expedition was ready to set sail, with two company and two naval ships.[43] The naval ships were to provide protection during the voyage, and assistance to the King of Candy.[44] Admiral Ove Giedde was put in charge of the expedition, but lacked experience in Indian trade. The solution to this problem was to appoint Crappe and Boshouwer to take responsibility for trade in the east.[45]

When Crappe arrived in Ceylon, he tried to negotiate with the King of Candy, but in vain. He also opened up hostilities by attacking Portuguese vessels in Southern India, especially around Negapatnam. The Portuguese swiftly sank one of the Danish ships, and arrested Crappe. He was handed over to one of the local rulers on the Coromandel Coast, the Nayak of Tanjore, since Negapatnam, where the Portuguese had a trading post, was under the Nayak's jurisdiction.[46]

While the Portuguese detained Crappe, Giedde and his fleet arrived in Ceylon, and began negotiations to build a fort in Trincomalee. Boschouwer died before arriving in Ceylon, leaving Giedde without assistance in his negotiations with the King of Candy. Upon arrival in Ceylon, it became clear that Boschouwer had made up the tale of future trade with Candy. In this sense, the Boschouwer case illustrates the frequently unpredictable nature of European overseas expansion, whereby an experienced adventurer–projector would sell "dreams" to a king, hoping to gain favours, and possibly thereby to earn a fortune. Eventually, the Danish were unable to build a fort in Ceylon, and Giedde was forced to move elsewhere.[47] In October 1620, he decided to try his luck on the Coromandel Coast, and was permitted an audience at the court of the Nayak in Tanjore. In November the same year, a treaty between the Nayak and the king of Denmark was signed, allowing the Danish to build a fort in Tranquebar.[48] During these negotiations, Crappe was released from captivity. In 1622, Giedde set sail to Europe, and Crappe was placed in charge of Tranquebar.[49] Yet another Dutchman, Christoffer van der Molen, who had previously been employed by the VOC in Java, served as Crappe's assistant, and possibly his successor, in India.[50] When the first permanent Danish outpost had been built, and trade with the locals had been established, the day-to-day operations of the company in Asia were conducted by a number of previous VOC employees.

To conclude this section, many previous VOC and WIC employees participated in, or even initiated, the first Nordic overseas voyages. Whether in the Arctic, the Indian Ocean, or the Atlantic, experience in other European enterprises was vital for the establishment of the Nordic trading companies. Indeed, it was the previous experience of men like Blommaert, Crappe, Minuit, and Usselincx that provided them with tools, knowledge, access to information, and capital. Such experienced overseas veterans, with an entrepreneurial mindset, were the answer to the ambitions of the Nordic kingdoms. Indeed, within the early Nordic trading companies, the presence of such men was the rule rather than the exception. The following section will explain why so many previous VOC and WIC employees chose to transfer their allegiance to the Nordic Companies.

The institutional shelter

If, as is commonly accepted, Dutch business culture was the strongest in Europe during the seventeenth century, why did men like Minuit, Blommaert, and Crappe decide to seek out alternative opportunities in the Nordic kingdoms? Although Dutch markets and commercial companies were larger, they were not without their limitations. On the one hand, not everyone was able to participate in Dutch economic development, and, as such, some were forced to seek alternatives elsewhere, especially in the Nordic kingdoms.[51] On the other hand, due to the reasons described below, some experienced overseas veterans were also interested in diverting their business outside of the Republic.

Over time, a specific institutional environment evolved in the Nordic kingdoms. Nordic ambitions and desires for overseas trade created space for negotiations between rulers and internationally experienced individuals, who wanted to trade overseas, but who needed political protection. Here, this process is referred to as "institutional sheltering." This is best understood as the process whereby the individuals who had been recruited could negotiate with local institutions, organisations, or rulers regarding the prospect of joining a local enterprise, and thereby create the circumstances necessary for mutual benefit – whether social, political, or economic.[52]

A clear and illustrative example of this mutual process of institutional sheltering is provided by the Danish Empire under Christian IV and later Fredrik III. For his part, Christian IV founded a new city, Glückstadt, in order to pursue his overseas ambitions and to attract international expertise.[53] The Danish council of the realm had little say in matters concerning

28 *Formative years of overseas entrepreneurship*

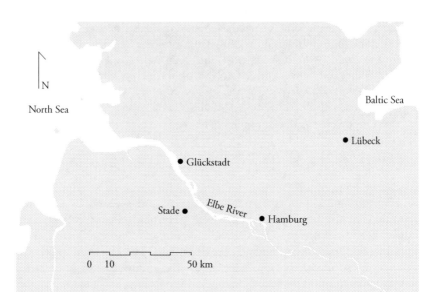

Figure 2.1 Map of Nordic interests on the Elbe river.
Source: Map drawn by Panu Savolainen.

the city, since the latter was situated in the duchy of Schleswig-Holstein, a private domain of the king. In Denmark proper, the king had to rule the kingdom on equal terms with the council, but in the duchy, the king could act as a feudal lord, and thus had almost complete freedom to pursue his ambitious overseas projects. In practice, as seen in Figure 2.1, Glückstadt was a protected environment within the Danish empire.[54]

Glückstadt was founded in 1619, in order to attract foreign merchants connected to international trading routes. In line with the overall development of the early modern Nordic kingdoms, cities were established as centres for trade, for accumulating capital and for garnering the monarch tax revenues.[55] By offering institutional shelter, including religious toleration, extensive privileges, and tax exemptions, the king was able to recruit Portuguese Sephardic Jews, as well as reformed Dutch merchants and skippers.[56] The Thirty Years War (1618–1648), Twelve Years Truce (1609–1621), and the Synod of Dordrecht (1618–1619) led some Dutchmen and Sephardic Jews to seek protection and/or business opportunities elsewhere.[57] For example, during the early seventeenth century, the aggravation of religious factionalism within the Republic drove certain groups of people away.

The Calvinist church of the Republic was divided into two factions: the Gomarians and the Arminians. Soon, the religious conflict escalated into a political one. In particular, the latter hinged upon the relationship between the church and the state, and developed into a controversy regarding the sovereignty of the seven provinces vis-à-vis the States General. The Arminians

Formative years of overseas entrepreneurship   29

supported the sovereignty of the seven provinces, whereas the Gomarians called for a division between the provinces and the States General. The conflict escalated further during 1618. By 1619, the Gomarians had seized power within the Republic and accused the Arminians of political treason. The Arminians were called to the Synod of Dordrecht, and were pressed to accept the outlawing of their religious practices. Those who disapproved of the Gomarians' plans were deported from the country, and this was one of the reasons behind some of the emigration to Glückstadt.[58]

Another reason for emigration to Glückstadt was the turbulence that occurred between the end of the Twelve Years Truce (1621) and the secession of Portugal from Spain (1640).[59] During these years, ships sailing with Dutch passports were barred from Iberian ports, which had clear repercussions on the Dutch carrier trade, and hit several merchants hard. Some of the latter thus moved to Hamburg and Glückstadt, seeking to take advantage of a treaty between the Spanish and Danish kings.[60] After the truce had ended in 1621, the Spanish monarchy had tried to put an end to the Dutch carrier trade between the Baltic and Iberian Peninsula. The Spanish king had approached the Danish King Christian IV, hoping for his cooperation in the struggle against Dutch dominance in trade; in particular, he wanted all ships sailing between the Iberian and Baltic ports to be inspected and certified by the authorities in Glückstadt. In short, the aim was to prevent Dutch skippers from continuing the Baltic–Iberian trade. Through the treaty signed between Spain and Denmark in 1630, Glückstadt became the staple market for Iberian products in the Baltic.[61] However, from the perspective of Christian IV, the treaty did not prevent international businessmen from trading with the Iberian world from Glückstadt. Therefore, the treaty prompted several Dutch skippers to request residency in Glückstadt, since they would thereby receive Danish passports and, thus, enjoy official Danish protection.[62] As such, residency in Glückstadt could open up new trading opportunities for individuals.[63] After the end of the Eighty Years War (1568–1648), Danish passports became less valuable. However, at least for a while, institutional sheltering worked to the benefit of Dutch merchants.[64]

The king granted businessmen residing in Glückstadt exclusive privileges for trade with Augsburg, Finnmark (today in Northern Norway), Iceland, and Northern Africa.[65] He also granted experienced producers and traders of Portuguese Jewish origin monopoly privileges over the import of sugar and the minting of coins.[66] The presence of foreign businessmen and their networks increased the availability of capital, as well as facilitating the introduction of new technologies and know-how. One notable example of the extensive privileges bestowed upon the Portuguese Jewish community was the Pallache family, who received exclusive privileges regarding trade with Morocco.[67] As early as 1647, the king issued passports to two Sephardic Jews – Simon and Henrique de Casseres – allowing them to sail to Guinea and the Caribbean.[68] By the 1680s, when the Danish West India Company

30 *Formative years of overseas entrepreneurship*

had established its headquarters in Copenhagen, the king appointed yet another Sephardic Jew, Moses Joshua Henriques, to be the factor of the company in Glückstadt, where he was largely responsible for sending company ships to the Atlantic, thus gaining the city a share of the products arriving from Africa and the Americas.[69]

However, the protection that foreigners received from the Danish monarchy was at the expense of their native Danish counterparts. Glückstadt, as a royal domain, insulated its residents from the competition of merchants in Copenhagen, as well as from the laws of the Danish kingdom. Understandably, this created tension within the kingdom, forcing the king to concede new privileges to Danish merchants in Copenhagen. The competition between the two cities regarding overseas commerce was severe, but the international business community in Glückstadt was more interested in profit than local politics.[70] For this reason, the king was able to outsource his own overseas designs to men whose political weight was low.

However, the structure and administration of the Dutch trading companies provided another reason for moving business to Glückstadt. These organisations, although large by seventeenth-century standards, did not offer equal opportunities to everyone. As will be discussed in Chapter 4, for those skippers and merchants who had been interloping or practicing illicit trade and smuggling while employed by the WIC, Glückstadt represented an opportunity to continue making profit under the official protection of the monarch.

For example, Willem Usselincx, already introduced above, recorded in his memoirs in 1644: "I was eager to see the new city of Glückstadt and Frederickstad in Holstein, as well as Gothenburg in Sweden."[71] Indeed, some entrepreneurially minded individuals were impatient and frustrated by the narrow conservatism and closed-mindedness of the Dutch companies.[72] The historian Violet Barbour states that this was the motive for Usselincx and others to join foreign companies. Furthermore, she indicates that there were several pamphlet attacks against the directors of the Dutch companies. According to Barbour, the shareholders had almost no control over the directors, and accused the board of incompetence, speculation, waste, and nepotism.[73] Thus, the individuals who looked for opportunities elsewhere were ready to use their entrepreneurial skills against the WIC and VOC if an opportunity arose, as the case of Usselincx and others demonstrate.

The reasons to accept Nordic employment, however, were not limited exclusively to Glückstadt. In the WIC and the VOC, employees worked on a contract basis, usually for four to six years, or at least in theory. After the contract expired, they had to choose what to do with their accumulated experience. Often, employees were forced to continue serving, due to a lack of manpower at the company's outposts. Others re-enrolled in the companies, because there was no better alternative. Thus, many employees continued to work for the company, whether out of free will or constraint. From the standpoint of the individual, dangerous working conditions were compensated

Formative years of overseas entrepreneurship   31

by the possibility of making a good career in the companies. This applied to foreigners, especially Nordic employees, but excluded German-speaking employees, who had fewer prospects.[74] Although good career opportunities existed, the highest positions were reserved for the Dutch, and, even among them, only for the elite classes. In this sense, exclusive networks of patronage rendered the highest positions inaccessible to outsiders, regardless of their origin.[75] For experienced but excluded individuals, the prospect of career progression within the Nordic companies could be an attractive option.

While working at the outposts, many officials had built up connections, developed private business initiatives, and were accustomed to the local trading cultures. This often meant that they had accumulated personal wealth (or knew how to do so) but were not allowed to bring it back to Europe on the company ships, since their contracts with the WIC and the VOC prohibited employees from engaging in private trade on an extensive scale. Therefore, after their contracts expired, such men were interested in the employment alternatives and transferability of wealth offered by the Nordic companies.[76]

The various push and pull factors described above attest to a process that was typical of the cross-imperial trading patterns that characterised the first Nordic overseas companies. At a time when trading companies claimed a monopoly over overseas trade, institutional sheltering enabled individuals to secure employment, and potentially also to raise their social standing. In the Nordic kingdoms, easy access to residency eliminated the issue of breaching the charter rights of the Dutch companies, which deprived all others than their own company investors from trading in the given charter areas. In exchange, the kingdoms received capable entrepreneurs, which they needed to compete – for example, business intelligence regarding local market prices and products, and other business-related information such as with whom to trade, or how to establish settlements. An experienced company employee knew how to operate locally, knowledge that was highly sought-after by the companies in Europe.

To employ someone with extensive connections, experience and knowledge overseas could confer a competitive advantage, just as much as having capable administrators in Europe. The aim was thus not only to protect assets and goods, but also to protect know-how and information within a highly competitive business sector. In other words, institutional sheltering was beneficial for both individual entrepreneurs and kingdoms. It was a type of business instrument, which was applied in order to reduce the risks involved in overseas trade. There were, however, complicating factors in the sheltering process. Since the city and its privileges were entirely dependent upon the king as feudal lord, the situation could change rapidly if the king or his successor so wished. The connection of the privileged trading groups to the king was thus highly precarious. Although the sheltering process was not perfect, however, it nonetheless provided an instrument to reduce risk and to limit uncertainty in business.

32 *Formative years of overseas entrepreneurship*

This chapter will now turn to two case studies. Together, these shed light on the years spent accumulating those skills that aspiring entrepreneurs could use to negotiate shelter. A particular focus will be the importance of experience accumulated within Dutch organisations. In short, how did overseas experience translate into entrepreneurial advantage when one sought employment in the Nordic trading companies?

The Leyel family

In 1593, Willem Leyel (Lejel, Leyll, Lyall) was born in Elsinore, Denmark, a city whose close proximity to the Sound made it important for Danish maritime trade.[77] In the sixteenth and seventeenth centuries, Elsinore was a transit port for itinerant voyagers – people with knowledge of, and stories about, distant lands, where great fortunes and prosperity could be attained.[78]

The city occupied a significant position in the Danish Kingdom, because it was also an entry point to the Baltic trading zone, and the place where the Sound toll was collected and administered. Indeed, this position lay at the foundation of the fortunes of several merchant families based there. The city, which peaked between 1590 and 1650, was also the place with the largest share of foreigners in the Danish Kingdom,[79] although this was still small in comparison with other European port cities, such as Hamburg, Lisbon, or Amsterdam.

The Leyel family, originally from Scotland, had migrated to the Nordic kingdoms during the first half of the sixteenth century.[80] Leyel's maternal great grandfather, Sander Leyel, had been an influential man in local Danish society, and especially close to the king. In 1548, he had been appointed collector of the Sound toll. From then onwards, the Leyel family had become the hereditary keepers of the Sound toll, and possibly the largest tax farmers in the kingdom. The Sound toll was a tax collected of every ship passing the Sound between Elsinore and Helsingborg, and constituted a great source of income not only for the king but also for the Leyel family. Indeed, the position of Sound toll collector was one of the most powerful positions that a person could obtain in the king's administration. As toll collector, Sander Leyel was also able to report to the king the latest events in international trade, since he was able to gather intelligence from abroad. Moreover, he also acted as royal factor.[81]

Another important aspect is that although Sander held the highest office in the city, he was not legally Danish, but remained a Scottish immigrant, married to a Scottish woman, Elline Davidsdatter, the daughter of David Thomson, mayor of Elsinore in 1521.[82] Sander's legal status changed only in 1558, when he was naturalised as Danish.[83] Willem's mother, Ingeborg Fredriksdatter Leyel, was married to Johan Willumsen (Willem's father), who became mayor of Elsinore in 1618. When Willem was thirty years old, his father passed away, and, in 1623, his mother re-married, to Matthias Hansen, a mayor in Copenhagen.[84] Willem was thus born into a family with

Formative years of overseas entrepreneurship 33

a relatively high socio-economic standing and with connections to trade administration. In turn, this suggests that Willem most likely received an education in the skills required for merchants and trade administration.

From Elsinore to Asia

As collectors of the Sound toll, the Leyel family was in a position to receive the latest news regarding maritime trade. Indeed, it is fair to say that they might well have been better informed about international trade than the king. How and why Willem Leyel initially entered the orbit of the Dutch empire, becoming a part of Dutch operations in Asia, is unclear.

In a report dated 1644, he wrote to the directors of the DEIC that he had in the past served in Batavia, with a captain called Jürgen Boddin.[85] There, Leyel had married a Dutch widow, who had given birth to a daughter, Christina.[86] Erik Odegard's research on the governors of the VOC has shown that marrying a widow in the Dutch East Indies could significantly improve one's prospects of career advancement. In this way, one could marry into an already existing network of members of the company.[87] In addition to his daughter, Leyel also had two sons: Hans and Anders.[88] Thus, it seems that Leyel was from an early date rooted in the world of Asian trade.

As gleaned from the archives in Copenhagen, Willem Leyel read and wrote several languages. He was apparently fluent in Danish, German, and Portuguese, and also in English and Persian. Such language skills were possible only due to a certain educational background, which his family had been capable of providing. He had probably learnt English and Danish at home, and German was the second official language in Denmark at that time. He possibly learnt Dutch and Portuguese during his early years in Asia, but it is equally possible that Leyel acquired the Dutch language through his family's business connections in the Republic. Dutch was, after all, widely spoken in Denmark – especially within maritime communities. Leyel joined the VOC at a time before Denmark had its own overseas companies, so it is possible that he was sent by his family to join the company in order to gain experience and expertise, particularly on how to conduct long-distance trade and how to manage a business. Whether the family had plans to subsequently participate in an Asian company in Denmark is less clear.

One might wonder why Willem Leyel did not continue in his family's footsteps, that is, by becoming a Sound toll collector. There are three possible reasons. The first is institutional – it is possible that Willem simply did not have the opportunity to continue his family's profession, due to a change in the administration of the Sound toll. Søren Mentz's research on English merchants in Asia has shown that many of the latter belonged to the gentry or to merchant families, but were younger sons, thus having no prospect of inheriting the social position of their fathers. Therefore, they had no choice but to establish their own careers. Such men often worked in sectors of the

34   *Formative years of overseas entrepreneurship*

civil service, in the army or the church, while others served apprenticeships at well-known merchant houses. In England, employment in the East India Company was a highly respectable option. Those who had connections to influential people in the company had a good chance of gaining employment.[89] Indeed, a somewhat similar situation must have pertained in the Nordic context. Thus, serving overseas might have offered Willem a chance to prove his abilities after the death of his father.

The second possible reason is a change in the strategy of the family. During Leyel's adolescence, the Danish king had issued charters for ventures in Asia, and it is possible that stories of great wealth and fortune attracted the attention of the Leyel family. Since they had a long history of involvement in maritime trade, it is plausible that Willem was sent to receive training in the Republic, where the family had trading connections. Indeed, Willem was not the only member of the Leyel family to enter overseas service. According to Steve Murdoch, Robert Lyall, a member of the same clan, entered DEIC service directly from Scotland. Other members of the clan continued to enter VOC service, as did John Lyall in 1641.[90]

A third possible explanation is that, after Leyel's father passed away, his new stepfather had no desire to maintain and provide for his stepson. Thus, Leyel would have had no choice but to strike out on his own. Whatever the reason for Leyel's entry into the VOC, it is clear that he began his mercantile career with the Dutch. During these formative years, Leyel developed his business skills, amongst which languages, bookkeeping, and knowledge of local trading practices were preeminent.

The first recorded reference to an association between Willem Leyel and the DEIC occurred in 1626 at Pipley, on the coast of Bengal.[91] He and his close business associate, Claus Rytter, were noted as trading for the DEIC.[92] Crappe, the commander of the company in Asia, had plans to establish a trading post there, but these plans did not meet with success. Leyel and Rytter were thus called back to Tranquebar, and then departed for Europe towards the end of 1628.[93] In a letter dated 22 February 1635, Leyel wrote that he had previously traded in Surat and in Persia. He expressed his belief that a trade connection with Persia was important for the DEIC, especially in order to acquire products that could be exchanged in Bantam (Banten) and Makassar. Furthermore, Leyel wrote that he had already tried to access Persian trade in 1626, when Crappe had sent him and Rytter to Pipley. They had, however, failed in their efforts, since the local rulers had deemed their gifts to be unsatisfactory.[94]

Ten years later, in 1636, Crappe was ready to return home. When he left Tranquebar, Danish trade in India was in decline, and he had failed to present the Nayak with a promised tribute.[95] Furthermore, he had negotiated with the VOC regarding the possibility of selling Dansborg to the Dutch.[96] These negotiations had never been concluded, but Crappe had secured factors in Masulipatnam (the East Coast of India), at Balasore (the Ganges delta), in Achin (the northern tip of Sumatra), at Japara and Bantam (on Java), and in Makassar (Celebes).[97]

Formative years of overseas entrepreneurship 35

Crappe's successor was Barent Pessart, an experienced overseas merchant, who, like Crappe and Boschouwer, had previously lived in Batavia as a free burgher (*vrijburger*).[98] As it turned out, however, he was a poor choice for the Danish company. The paucity of his accounts, unpaid rents to local rulers, and the enormous debts that he incurred all combined to weaken his reputation within the company.[99] Indeed, the period of Pessart's tenure shows that Danish operations in Asia were not on a solid basis, and testifies to the influence that individuals could have upon a small trading company like the DEIC. But why did Crappe, a man who was heavily involved in the organisation of the company in Europe, choose Pessart? It has been claimed that Pessart was "intelligent but unreliable."[100] The historian Martin Krieger has shown that Pessart was interested only in private gain, and treated the DEIC as an instrument for conducting private trade in the Indian Ocean.[101] However, it needs to be underlined that being an employee in a company was quite different from being in charge of the company overseas. A merchant was responsible for daily trade, whereas the person in charge was supposed to guarantee that the entire business was conducted correctly. Indeed, I will return to this issue in the next two chapters. As head of operations, Pessart was responsible for keeping the books, and for the improvement of trading relationships with local merchants and rulers.[102]

To make a successful career in the first DEIC, one needed not only to be experienced but also to be capable of running the business, and governing the company in Asia. In other words, governance and management required different types of know-how and experience to regular trade. Although this was true of most trading ventures at the time, it was especially crucial for a company that operated on such a small scale.

Leyel and the king

In 1628, Willem Leyel returned to Copenhagen after his years spent in Asia, in the midst of the Thirty Years War. He was appointed captain in the Royal Danish Navy, with an annual salary of 200 riksdaler.[103] However, he did not have to participate in the war for long, since Christian IV withdrew from it in 1629, as a result of having made peace with the Emperor. Leyel's appointment should be seen in the light of an experienced individual with family connections to the king. Indeed, this might have been a combination of two factors; it was possible that the king wished to show appreciation for Leyel's service in Asia, but at the same time, it is highly likely that he simply needed experienced officers to operate his fleet.

While Leyel was captain in the royal navy, two ships were due to be sent to India. The directors of the company had decided that all shareholders should pay a sum of 20 per cent over and above their original contribution, in order to cover necessary expenses and to maintain business. If they did not pay, the directors kept the investors' previous investments. Indeed, this is indicative of the challenging state of the finances of the DEIC. Put simply, the investors were simply compelled to keep investing. Despite this added

36 *Formative years of overseas entrepreneurship*

pressure, the company continued to experience financial difficulties, which eventually resulted in a financial rescue operation by the king, who, it was noted, paid a "considerable" amount. As a result, he became the lord of the company and used this position to appoint company directors, amongst other things.[104]

Despite the king's rescue operation, the administration of the company was facing overwhelming challenges by the 1630s. On 9 January 1634, the king expressed his dissatisfaction with the company's situation in India. He had appointed Albert Skeel, one of the main shareholders of the company, to investigate how to improve trade. In the same letter, the king had ordered Willem Leyel to express what he thought should be done regarding trade in India. "The king commanded this Vilm Leyel, who had recently returned from East India, to visit him (Skeel), and to give him a report on the state of affairs."[105] The king evidently considered that Leyel, having returned from Asia in 1628, had the most up-to-date knowledge regarding trade in India. This indicates how difficult it was to get reliable and up-to-date information in Copenhagen, a situation that confirms the thesis that individuals with access to information were of crucial importance.

Soon after the meeting between Skeel and Leyel, the king requested a meeting with his council, in order to discuss how the DEIC trade should be improved. In the king's letters to his treasurer, he informed the latter that Leyel was to receive 200 riksdalers in August 1634, in order to undertake a voyage to the Dutch Republic on his Majesty's service.[106] It was not specified exactly what Leyel's mission was. Supposedly, he was sent to the Republic in order to gather intelligence regarding the latest developments in European trade, and particularly in the Indian Ocean.[107]

The king also gave Leyel the task of equipping the vessel *St Anna* for a voyage to India.[108] In December 1634, the king requested that his treasurer hand over the requisite funds to Leyel, who was to manage the goods and the capital in the best interest of the company.[109]

In 1635, the king decided to further tighten his grip on the company, and on Leyel. In a council letter dated 14 September 1635, he announced that Leyel, now a director in the company, was to receive an annual salary of 300 riksdalers. In return, he was required to do his utmost to serve the company, as embodied in an oath of loyalty, sworn on 11 March 1636. In this regard, the council's letter books recorded that:

> In the presence of chancellor Christian Friis, Vincent Bilde, and Ove Juel, Villumb Lejel has taken the oath as director of the Danish East India Company. He promises to be loyal to the king, to do his best for the king and the participants of the Danish East India Company and to do his best not to cause any harm to them. He shall always act for the benefit of the company. He shall not reveal anything about the state of trade to the detriment of the company.[110]

Moreover, an earlier draft preserved among the papers of the Council included the sentence: "He promises to be loyal to the king and the company."[111] This means that in the actual oath, the company was given more prominence. On the one hand, this demonstrates that Leyel had become significant for the king. He was personally appointed as director, and as the king's representative in the company. At this point, it becomes clear that Leyel had a patron–client relationship with Christian IV. However, the appointment was in contravention of the original charter of the company. The latter stated that only directors were to appoint new directors, and only in the case that one of the previous directors had died. This time, however, Leyel was appointed by the king, which suggests that he enjoyed a unique position. On the other hand, it also shows that the king, who needed to save the company financially, assumed that he should have an active say in the way the company was managed.

The letter to the council further emphasised that the other directors should treat Leyel as their equal.[112] Indeed, this suggests that the directorship Leyel held was different from that of the other directors. In contrast to the appointment of Leyel, the king had in an earlier letter stated that he did not care who was appointed director, so long as he knew what he was doing.[113]

Leyel was appointed by the king to serve his and the company's interest in Asia (in this order). This was an extraordinary position for someone who had not invested money in the company. For the king, it was important to have a trustworthy director and employee, who would work for the benefit of the Crown and the company simultaneously. In exchange for safeguarding the royal interests in the company, Leyel was given a prominent position. Leyel's position changed yet again in June 1639, when he was appointed bookkeeper.[114] His experience in the Indian Ocean was reason enough for the king to appreciate and to reward him. He was also the right person to collect information, and to guard the king's interests vis-á-vis the directors of the company.

However, Asta Bredsdorff has identified an unresolved issue. At the time when Leyel was appointed as the director of the company and swore an oath to the king, he was supposed to be in India as the chief merchant on board the *St Anna*, which set sail from Copenhagen to India on 19 November 1635. Furthermore, in a letter dated 4 November 1636, the king had written that a certain Joachim Pedersen had been appointed director in the same company, and was to work jointly with Leyel.[115] As Bredsdorff has pointed out, Leyel could not have been in two different places at the same time. As an answer to this problem, Bredsdorff has suggested that the other Willem Leyel was perhaps a relative of the Willem Leyel in question here.[116]

Towards the end of the decade, Leyel's career would take yet a new turn. Commander Pessart's behaviour had caused the administration of the company great concern.[117] He had failed to send reports, and the directors were

38   *Formative years of overseas entrepreneurship*

unaware of the state of the company. However, the situation in Tranquebar forced the directors to act, and Leyel was dispatched to deal with the situation. In October 1639, two ships – the *Christianshavn* and *Den Forgylte Sol* – set sail for Tranquebar. However, it ultimately took Willem Leyel four years to reach the Coromandel Coast.[118]

To summarise, Willem Leyel was Danish, but with Scottish ancestry. He was unable to replicate the careers of his ancestors as Sound toll collector and mayor, and was thus educated in overseas and long-distance trade via his employment in the VOC. Upon his return to Danish service, he quickly climbed the military and social ranks. In this regard, his years of experience in Asia with the VOC were decisive. The Danish King Christian IV, acting as the largest shareholder of the DEIC, appointed Leyel as director, notwithstanding his lack of capital investment in the venture. In short, he was needed for his expertise, and in order to safeguard the royal interest within the company and in Asia.

Leyel's background shows that family connections were important to starting a career in overseas business, or at least to a certain extent. These connections provided him with reading and writing skills that enabled him to serve in the naval and commercial sectors. Nevertheless, his background was less decisive than his previous experience and knowledge of Asian trade, and his capacity to translate that experience into an entrepreneurial advantage.

Henrich Carloff in the WIC

Contrary to the case of Leyel, little is known about Henrich Carloff's (Caerlof, Carolof and Carlove) background. Judging from the sources, he was a German speaker. He is said to have been born in Rostock (Germany), in either 1621 or 1622.[119] However, Albert van Dantzig and Johannes Postma have suggested that Carloff was actually born in Pillau (Poland), and would thus have been of Polish origin.[120] In an Amsterdam notarial act dated 1644, he is mentioned as coming from Suomen.[121] In another source, Carloff is said to have come from Groningen, and to have gone overseas in January 1639.[122] This statement probably relates to the initial period of his overseas career. Indeed, he is likely to have started his career in Groningen by enrolling as a soldier in the WIC chamber, *Stad en Lande*.

In the employment records of the WIC, Carloff is registered coming from Rostock.[123] During the seventeenth century, it was common for young men from the small German states to seek employment with the Dutch trading companies, as a means to escape the perils of war, religious persecution, and poverty.[124] Based on the sources that Carloff produced, it is clear that he did not command any Scandinavian language, but was fluent in German and Dutch.

In 1639, Carloff enrolled in the WIC and served as a soldier and scribe for a company of landed militia under commander Gerrit Entes in

Formative years of overseas entrepreneurship 39

Dutch Brazil.[125] In 1630, the Dutch had seized the North-eastern part of present-day Brazil, which they duly lost to the Portuguese in 1654.[126] Serving in Brazil opened up the world of the South Atlantic to Carloff. In Brazil, most of the Europeans spoke Dutch, German, English, or Portuguese.[127] He thus began his Atlantic career surrounded by these languages, which would later become important for his career.

During his twenties, Carloff's career changed. In 1641, the governor of Dutch Brazil, Johan Maurits van Nassau-Siegen, gave orders to dispatch an expedition to Western Africa, in order to attack the Portuguese territories there. In charge of this attack was Cornelis Jol, who managed to capture the town of Luanda, in Angola, as well as the island of São Tomé. For his part, Carloff also participated in this expedition. Subsequently, he worked as a clerk in Western Africa for the WIC, although between November 1641 and June 1642, he also worked as an officer on the Island of São Tomé, where he was sent to mediate between the Portuguese sugar planters and the WIC.[128]

Unsurprisingly, the Portuguese planters were not particularly keen on the presence of the company on the island. The fact that he was selected for this role suggests that Carloff was capable of functioning as a broker between conflicting parties. It is also a strong indicator that Carloff spoke Portuguese, which was commonly used in Western Africa at the time. In 1644, he returned to Amsterdam, where he worked in the administration of the WIC.[129] First, this trajectory demonstrates that from an early age, Carloff had experience of warfare on sea and on land. Second, he gained experience as a mediator, using his knowledge of languages and of the local context to his advantage. Third, he was sufficiently educated to hold a job in the administration of the company in Europe. Like Leyel, Carloff was thus also able to work with protocols and salaries, as well as with other administrative tasks. Moreover, the fact that he decided to return to Western Africa despite having secured employment in Europe implies choice rather than imposition.

Carloff's early career thus clearly demonstrates that he was able to continuously improve his position within the WIC. However, it is difficult to verify exactly which variables made his early career possible. Indeed, demographic factors and luck might have been partly behind Carloff's rapid advancement: although he was ill for a long period in 1641, he did not die of the disease, nor did he perish in one of the shipwrecks that was common at this time.[130] There is no mention of a patron having assisted him in his career, as was the case with Leyel.

Fortunately, Carloff's career can be charted in greater detail between the years 1645 and 1649. The reports written by the two WIC Director-Generals, Jan Ruychaver and Jacob van der Wel, alongside his own reports, permit an analysis of the role that he played as a young employee of the company.[131] It also makes it possible to understand what experience and entrepreneurial skills he accumulated whilst in the employment of the WIC.

The mid-1640s had been a rough period for the personnel of the company. In particular, changes were occurring in the structure of the company's

40 *Formative years of overseas entrepreneurship*

management in Western Africa. Between March and July 1645, seventy company employees had died, and there was a constant scarcity of experienced and seasoned officials.[132] For Carloff, this scarcity turned out to be an opportunity. Among Carloff's formative years in Africa, 1645 holds a special place, because it provides the first detailed glimpse into his career. During this year, he was promoted to the post of prosecutor (*fiscaal*) in the WIC in Western Africa.[133] As such, he held one of the highest positions in the region. A prosecutor was expected to investigate and prosecute possible interlopers, as well as company personnel engaged in illicit trade, interloping, and smuggling. Initially, Carloff hesitated to take the job, although such a promotion clearly represented upward mobility within the company structure.[134] As such, his reluctance might seem surprising, especially considering his modest background. According to a report by the newly appointed director, Jacob van der Wel, he had had to encourage Carloff to accept the position – Carloff himself would have preferred to become a chief factor at one of the main trading posts.[135] Nonetheless, Carloff had promised to take the appointment until the Heeren XIX decided otherwise.[136] Van der Wel had initially served as a merchant on the coast, before being appointed prosecutor of the company in 1643, by Ruychaver, who was at the time Director-General.[137] As prosecutors, Van der Wel and, later, Carloff were less mobile, and more bound to the company headquarters.

In terms of income, the Director-General's salary amounted to 300 guilders monthly, whereas the prosecutor made only 72 guilders, although he also had the right to one-third of all goods confiscated from interloping ships. In spite of the differences in income, the prosecutor was also able to learn the best methods of smuggling and illicit trade through direct experience.[138] The position also posed certain challenges. First, as prosecutor, one did not make many friends, since the prosecutor was responsible for ship investigations and halting illegal activities, in which other company officials were frequently engaged. Second, as a factor, the prospects of eventually becoming Director-General were higher, since factors developed regular trading contacts with local merchants and rulers, and moved around extensively on the coast.[139] Factors thus had the best connections at a local level, whereas a prosecutor had greater responsibilities. In this light, it is not surprising that Carloff was not keen on assuming the position. However, as will be shown, this did not stop him from subsequently taking advantage of his position as prosecutor.

The reason for Carloff's hesitance was thus related to the hierarchy and possibilities that existed on the coast. Carloff's powerful position taught him much about local conditions, and how trade (in his own interest).[140] However, being a prosecutor for the WIC was not necessarily a desirable position for the entrepreneurially driven Carloff, the salary was modest, and his position had the potential to make him many enemies. He was also more accountable to the company as prosecutor, working under the Director-General, than he would have been as a factor in one of the

Formative years of overseas entrepreneurship 41

outposts. He was still young, and it is possible that the council in Africa did not consider him sufficiently experienced and connected to become a factor. Nevertheless, Carloff's appointment as prosecutor progressed quickly. Only one day after his appointment, he was instructed to board the *Eendracht* from Enkhuizen. The director had asked him to investigate the ship, looking for possible smuggling activities.[141]

During the following years, Carloff was to be involved in a number of other investigations, of ships both Dutch and foreign. During his investigations, Carloff often encountered ships sailing under English, French, and Nordic flags. These ships were frequently operated by international merchants, skippers, and crews. Of the confiscated goods, Carloff took one-third for himself, while the other two-thirds went to the company and the other employees. Carloff was often sent to different areas on the coast. He reported directly to Director-General Van der Wel, and often travelled together with Isaac Coymans.

In his report to the directors, Carloff testified to the vexed situation of the company on the coast. He described how many men had become ill, and how several employees had recently died. He also complained that the company had failed to send experienced men to Africa. All the lodges and forts were maintained without any reinforcements, particularly by promoting junior employees to senior positions. The death of the factor at Fort Nassau, as well as those of two of his sub-factors, had worsened the situation. Carloff also pointed out that because the previous factors, Cock, Foullon and Director-General Ruychaver, had left the coast, there were currently only four capable senior factors left. The situation on the coast also necessitated double appointments. For example, one of the most respected employees, Isaac Coymans, was initially appointed factor but was simultaneously asked to do the bookkeeping for trade in general and for the garrison.[142]

On 1 June 1646 Director-General Van der Wel reported that the company was in desperate need of manpower from Europe. He needed at least three experienced factors and three bookkeepers, otherwise the organisation would perish. By this point, Van der Wel claimed, the lack of competent men was doing more damage to the company than were smugglers. He also explained that factor Joris Hogenhoeck and Coymans, who had already served six years in Africa, wished to return home, but, due to these unfortunate circumstances, they had had no choice but to prolong their employment. Indeed, Van der Wel feared that if Coymans left, there would be no one capable of succeeding him in the directorship. The only one who could be educated to the task was Jeremia Loten, who was still learning bookkeeping and lacked experience.[143] Van der Wel did not mention Carloff as a potential successor, which gives the impression that he was never a contender for the position. With reference to the VOC, Matthias van Rossum and Roelof van Gelder have shown that, at least during the eighteenth century, it was difficult, if not impossible, for employees of German origin to attain the highest positions in the company.[144] Indeed, it is plausible that a similar situation prevailed in the WIC.

42 *Formative years of overseas entrepreneurship*

Van der Wel continued and explained to the directors that the situation in Accra, where the company had established a lodge some years before, had become worrying. Van der Wel had been forced to move the factor, Hogenhoeck, from Accra to Fort Nassau, due to the importance of the latter for trade. The director's solution to the problem created by the vacancy was to appoint Carloff, who thus suddenly became factor in Accra. This additional appointment of course threatened to undermine Carloff's campaign against smuggling. Evidently, it was difficult for Carloff to be in two places at the same time. Therefore, Van der Wel also instructed another WIC official, Van Perr, to return from São Tomé, and to take up the position of second prosecutor. According to the Director-General, Carloff had confirmed that Van Perr was a good and reliable employee.[145]

Upon arrival in Accra, Carloff explained in a letter to the directors that the situation was still volatile. There was a conflict between two local leaders, who were fighting for power in Accra. As such, he counselled, the WIC should approach Accra with caution, and make sure not to pick sides, otherwise trade could be ruined. Carloff was then ordered by the company to negotiate peace, and to help to diffuse the tensions between the contending parties. Carloff explained that he was uneasy about this request, but that the Director-General had promised him full support and supervision in this task.[146] Whether there was a real tension is unclear, but Carloff at least wanted the directors in Europe to believe so. In any case, his position as a broker in relation to intra-African conflicts on the coast was established.

Two examples of Carloff's activities on the Gold Coast can be used to show how diverse his employment for the company was, and how it taught him about local trading circuits. The first example is related to the arrival of competitors on the coast. On 12 January 1647, Carloff sent a letter to the Heeren XIX, explaining that on 1 August 1646, a ship sailing under the Swedish flag had arrived on the coast. The ship, the *St Jacob*, had sailed to Western Africa to buy slaves, and its captain was Arent Gabbesen. Carloff investigated the ship and came to the conclusion that most of the men onboard were actually Dutch. As such, Carloff protested and ordered all Dutchmen on the ship to leave and go ashore. Gabbesen replied that he could not give up the men on board, since the ship would be unmanageable with only the remaining Swedish and Danish sailors, and this would force the ship to seek refuge on the coast. Carloff agreed that this would indeed be the case.[147] In the company journal, Director Van der Wel explained that as soon as he had heard about a Swedish ship sailing on the coast, he had called for Carloff to quickly return to Elmina, and, alongside Coymans and Loten, to prepare to board the ship and investigate.[148] Furthermore, in Van der Wel's report to the Heeren XIX of 14 August 1646, he explained that a ship sailing under the Swedish flag had arrived on the coast. The Director-General was baffled by the fact that he had not heard from the directors in Europe regarding how to proceed.[149]

Formative years of overseas entrepreneurship 43

This incident was the first encounter that the company had had with a ship under the Swedish flag in Western Africa. In the near future, there would be many more. Van der Wel's concern regarding the lack of instructions from Europe in relation to the Swedes was an example of the irregular communication between Europe and the coast. As was the case with the Danish East India Trade, disruptions in communication were a constant issue in Atlantic trade.[150]

The second example is a series of events in Accra, where Carloff served as factor. In Carloff's report to the Heeren XIX, he explained that he had been forced to delay his report to the directors, since he was trapped in a complicated situation. He had understood that the king of Accra had closed the trading roads, but he needed to leave for Accra as soon as possible in order to investigate the rumours. According to Carloff, he had had a meeting with the king of Accra immediately upon arrival, which had gone well, and the king had promised to re-open the trade routes.[151] Already, on 16 November, Van der Wel received a letter from Carloff, in which the latter explained that he had visited the King of Oquy, approximately five miles north of Accra. Apparently, there was tension between the Oquy and the Kingdom of Accra. According to Carloff, someone from Accra had killed the father of the King of Oquy. Carloff then explained that he had helped to settle the question by mediating, and by offering gifts to the King of Oquy. The king had responded by promising to re-open the trade routes yet again.[152] These events in Accra demonstrate, on the one hand, the importance of connections between Africans and Europeans, and, on the other hand, the value of local knowledge in acting as a mediator and broker. Indeed, this will be discussed further in Chapters 4 and 6.

It can be argued that Carloff was chosen as prosecutor in Elmina and then factor in Accra not due to patronage, but rather due to the wider context. The death of other senior officials and the problems of the organisation offered Carloff a chance, and it seems that he made the best of the opportunities presented to him. Nevertheless, the experience that he gained in Western African trade and local politics was an important factor in building up his reputation. He had served the WIC in many places along the coast, and had obtained a significant amount of information regarding the means of trade. His competence and reputation, combined with a degree of luck, made his early experience important to his future career progression.

From Western Africa to Stockholm

Judging by the sources regarding Carloff's early career, it seems that he was an obedient employee of the company. When events are contextualised, however, it is clear that working for the company did not necessarily imply pride and commitment to the organisation. Indeed, Carloff most likely needed the income, and had for that reason signed the contract. He needed

44 *Formative years of overseas entrepreneurship*

a company to make his career move forward, and the WIC provided him with an opportunity.

The decision to accept the position of prosecutor suggests that he might not have had other alternatives. If this was the case, it shows that this was the only way to improve his position within the company structure in Western Africa. However, he might also have accepted the position because it allowed him to build up a reputation as a good employee, and, in this way, maintain the possibility of becoming Director-General. In addition, it also allowed him to accumulate capital in the form of the goods that he confiscated. In this regard, it was important for Carloff to sell the goods as quickly as possible. After all, the demand from African merchants determined the value of the goods, and their taste could change quickly. This meant that for Carloff, it was crucial to act swiftly. In this way, he entered the scene of local trade.

Whether Carloff had a patron in Africa is less clear. The increasing frequency of the correspondence between Van der Wel and Carloff suggests that at least on a certain level, the Director-General was involved in advancing Carloff's career. On at least two occasions, Van der Wel told Carloff that he enjoyed his full support as prosecutor and factor. The previous director, Ruychaver, had also assured the Heeren XIX that he had no doubts about Carloff's loyalty.[153]

From an entrepreneurial point of view, Carloff was able to provide recent updates regarding trade in Africa. This was something that would have been interesting to the newly established Swedish Africa Company. Indeed, Van der Wel's letter from 18 March 1647 to the Heeren XIX indicated that other employees were ready to change company affiliation. An English merchant, Metcalf, had approached Van der Wel, offering to work for the WIC. Metcalf had complained that the other officials working for the English in Africa had treated him badly, and that he was ready to join the WIC instead. In the same letter, Van der Wel explained that a French ship had arrived on the coast with a previous WIC employee, Henrick van den Burch, as skipper. During the investigation of the ship, Carloff had asked Van den Burch why he had gone over to French service. Van den Burch replied that he had been disappointed by the WIC, which had hindered his progress with empty promises, and that he had now found more trustworthy employers.[154] In Carloff's report from 5 March 1647, he communicated that the skipper, Albert Smit, had also previously been employed by the WIC and had subsequently accepted a French commission.[155]

This tendency towards changing company affiliation also became apparent to Carloff through another incident that occurred on the coast. In 1647, a ship sailing under the Danish flag appeared, and Carloff was dispatched to investigate. On board the *Prince of Denmark*, the Dutch skipper, Thielman Wilkens, explained to Carloff that he was sailing with a genuine commission, issued by the Danish king. He showed Carloff his documents, stating that he had received a licence from the king, and that he personally had right of residence in Glückstadt. According to Van der Wel, other factors on the Gold Coast had complained about the fact that the Heeren XIX had not renewed the contract of Wilkens, who had sailed to Africa on several occasions. Indeed, these rumours had fostered mistrust towards the company among the factors.[156] In this context, it becomes evident that Carloff was constantly confronted with cross-imperial activity.

Carloff's role, the loyalty that he felt towards the WIC, and his entrepreneurial career all changed abruptly in 1648. The aforementioned skipper, Arent Gabbesen, who had sailed under a Swedish commission, soon returned to Africa, at a time when a group of investors in Sweden had begun to plan a permanent company.[157] On 17 April 1648, Gabbesen left Sweden with the ship *Christina*.[158] The voyage was rather short, and the ship returned during the summer of 1649. An immediate result of this second voyage, however, was that an active plan for establishing a Swedish Africa Company came to the fore. A clear indicator that such a company was being established came on 12 October 1649, when a contract was signed between one of the founders of the company, Laurens de Geer, and Henrich Carloff.[159]

Carloff was recruited by Gabbesen. As the records of Gabbesen's first trip to the coast demonstrate, Carloff and Gabbesen already knew each other. Indeed, Carloff had referred to Gabbesen as a "well-known member of the fatherland's maritime community."[160] In the daily register from 1646, Jacob van der Wel also stated that Gabbesen was well known on the coast.[161] Even though Carloff had protested against Gabbesen, this had resulted in no actual harm, and this may have been the moment when Gabbesen offered Carloff the prospect of advancement within a future Swedish company. For his part, Gabbesen was a broker between the investors in Sweden and the people on the coast. It is thus likely that Carloff shared his experiences on the coast and the challenges the WIC was facing in Western Africa with his new partners in Sweden.

The WIC was facing serious challenges in the 1640s despite its strong position on the Gold Coast. The company's financial situation was vulnerable due to the war in Brazil.[162] Many WIC company officials had decided to seek new opportunities in Hamburg, England, Stockholm, and Glückstadt. As reflected in his reports from the Guinea Coast, it is clear that Carloff was aware of the serious problems confronting the company. Its position had become particularly precarious during this period, when new European competitors began to appear on the African market, making promises of career advancement to WIC employees.[163]

Unfortunately, the archives do not contain Carloff's employment contract with the WIC, which would have stated for how long he was on the payroll. After all, in his report of 26 September 1647, he had complained that he had already served the WIC for almost ten years, and believed that he had done everything he could for the company. From another perspective, it is possible that due to the poor internal economy of the WIC, as well as a lack of work force and deficient communication with Europe,

46 *Formative years of overseas entrepreneurship*

the Director-General had decided to keep Carloff on the payroll. Still, he had not received a proper promotion. Carloff suggested that if his wishes were taken into account, he would be willing to work for the company for another four years.[164] He was already factor and prosecutor, which were senior positions. The only possible advancement for him was the post of Director-General, which could offer upward social mobility upon return to Europe. For example, the previous Director-General, Ruychaver, had been rewarded with admission into the *Vroedschap* of Haarlem after ten years of service in Western Africa.[165] In the end, Carloff was not appointed Director-General, which suggests that his origin and lack of patronage in Europe made his desired career goals impossible to achieve within the WIC.

From Carloff's perspective, an offer from Gabbesen would have been appealing. He had realised that the WIC would never make him a Director-General, a position he desired. For Carloff, the Swedish company was offering a more senior position, and the Swedish rules regarding conduct were more relaxed.

Conclusion

Although Willem Leyel and Henrich Carloff began their careers in overseas business at a similar age, they hailed from different backgrounds. Leyel was part of the local elite in Elsinore. His family, originally from Scotland, had consisted of a long line of merchants, who had achieved upward social mobility in Denmark, becoming closely connected to the Danish king. His background suggests that he would have received an education and training in the skills of a merchant. For unknown reasons, Leyel was unable to pursue his family's hereditary position as mayor of Elsinore and collector of the Sound toll. He thus chose, or was forced to choose, a different path, and began his overseas career in the employment of the VOC.

Subsequently, his appointment in the DEIC show that the knowledge and experience he accumulated in Asia had a beneficial effect on his career prospects. Henrich Carloff, on the other hand, was of unknown background. What he had in common with Leyel was the fact that he had begun his career in the employment of a Dutch company, namely the WIC. Under its aegis, he was able to learn several languages, bookkeeping, how to operate on local markets, how to establish contacts with non-European and European merchants, how to take advantage of the privileges of the trading companies, and how to navigate organisationally.

This chapter has shown that the Dutch commercial companies served as an important stepping-stone in the early careers of these men. In particular, both Leyel and Carloff learnt and practiced their entrepreneurship within these organisations. The formative years of Leyel and Carloff were not unique, since several others, such as Crappe, Wilkens, Minuit, Blommaert, and Usselincx, had similar backgrounds. The close connection between previous Dutch company employees and the Nordic trading companies is undisputable. As entrepreneurs, such individuals could offer the financial means to establish trading companies, as did Crappe and de Geer. However, from an overseas business point of view, accumulated experience was equally important. In exchange for such capacity and experience, the Nordic kingdoms offered to provide political protection.

The process of institutional sheltering featured in the establishment of Nordic companies intended to trade with both the East and the West. The aim of the process was to reduce risk and to limit uncertainty. Using the experience of individuals, trading organisations were able to penetrate previously unexplored markets. Newcomers such as the DEIC and the SAC could avoid high business risks if their key employees had already established business connections, and were also able to navigate and take advantage of local trading hierarchies and power balances. From the perspective of the entrepreneur, the sheltering process made it possible for the individual to attain career advancement in foreign companies, since his or her business became politically protected. Indeed, this was particularly attractive if their careers in the Dutch companies had stalled.

The Nordic expansion coincided with a growing general interest in overseas trade among the European powers. For men like Leyel and Carloff, there were now more employment opportunities than ever before, and this provided considerable potential for private gain. The Nordic companies appealed to entrepreneurs previously connected to the Dutch companies due to the room for private trading that they allowed. From an entrepreneurial point of view, the largest trading companies were not always the most attractive employers. Finally, and most crucially, when employees left their original companies, they took with them important skills and knowledge, which were difficult to replace.

Notes

1 Mirkka Lappalainen, *Maailman painavin raha* (Helsinki: WSOY, 2007), 7.
2 Jan de Vries and Ad van der Woude, *The First Modern Economy: Success, Failure, and Perseverance of the Dutch Economy, 1500–1815* (Cambridge/New York: Cambridge University Press, 1997), 402–408.
3 About the role of the Dutch bulk trade, for example in Jonathan Israel, *Dutch Primacy*, chapter 2; Jonathan Israel, *The Dutch Republic: Its Rise, Greatness and Fall, 1477 1806* (Oxford: Clarendon Press, 1998), 315–318.
4 Cle Lesger, *The Rise of the Amsterdam Market and Information Exchange: Merchants, Commercial Expansion and Change in the Spatial Economy of the Low Countries, c.1550–1630*, trans. J.C. Grayson (Aldershot; Burlington: Ashgate, 2006); Julia Adams, *The Familial State: Ruling Families and Merchant Capitalism in Early Modern Europe* (Ithaca: Cornell University Press, 2005); Jan De Vries and Ad van der Woude, *The First Modern Economy. Success, Failure, and Perseverance of the Dutch Economy, 1500–1815* (Cambridge: Cambridge University Press, 1997); *Prak*, 2009, 128.
5 Israel, *Dutch Primacy*, 20–22.
6 Ibid., 1–15; Milja Van Tielhof, *The 'Mother of All Trades': The Baltic Grain Trade in Amsterdam from the Late 16th to the Early 19th Century* (Boston/Leiden: Brill, 2002).

48   *Formative years of overseas entrepreneurship*

7 Cátia Antunes and Filipa Ribeiro da Silva, "Cross-Cultural Entrepreneurship in the Atlantic: Africans, Dutch and Sephardic Jews in Western Africa, 1580-1674," *Itinerario* 35, no. 1 (April 2011): 49–76; Miriam Bodian, *Hebrews of the Portuguese Nation: Conversos and Community in Early Modern Amsterdam* (Bloomington/Indianapolis: Indiana University Press, 1999); Lesger, *The Rise of the Amsterdam*; Klein, *De Trippen in de 17e Eeuw: een studie over het ondernemersgedrag op de Hollandse stapelmarkt* (Rotterdam: Van Gorcum, 1965).

8 Oscar Gelderblom, *Zuid-Nederlandse kooplieden en de opkomst van de Amsterdamse stapelmarkt (1578–1630)* (Hilversum: Uitgeverij Verloren, 2000); Erika Kuijpers, *Migrantenstad: immigratie en sociale verhoudingen in 17e-eeuws Amsterdam* (Hilversum: Uitgeverij Verloren, 2005).

9 Jan Lucassen and Leo Lucassen, "The Netherlands," in *The Encyclopedia of European Migration and Minorities, From the Seventeenth Century to the Present*, ed. K. Bade, P. Emmer, L. Lucassen, and J. Oltmer (New York: Cambridge University Press, 2011), 36; One of the reasons for foreigners to work in the Dutch companies was in fact the prospect of having their wages paid. See Jelle van Lottum, *Across the North Sea: The Impact of the Dutch Republic on International Labour Migration, c. 1550–1850* (Aksant: Academic Publishers, 1632), chapter 1; J. R. Bruijn, F. S. Gaastra, and I Schöffer, ed., *Dutch-Asiatic Shipping in the 17th and 18th Centuries*, vol. 1 (Gravenhage: Martinus Nijhoff, 1979), 152–157.

10 Filipa Ribeiro da Silva, *Dutch and Portuguese in Western Africa: Empires, Merchants and the Atlantic System, 1580–1674* (Boston/Leiden: Brill, 2011b), 131.

11 Glamann, "The Danish East India Company," 476.

12 Gøbel, "Danes in the Service," 90.

13 Knut Kjeldstadli, "Denmark, Norway, Sweden, Finland," in *The Encyclopedia of European Migration and Minorities: From the Seventeenth Century to the Present*, ed. Klaus J. Bade et al. (New York: Cambridge University Press, 2011), 5–15, 6.

14 The Lucassens have mentioned high wages as one of the reasons why Northern Europeans and Germans migrated to the Republic. See Lucassen and Lucassen, "The Netherlands," 36.

15 Gøbel, "Danes in the Service."

16 Chapter 3 will study this question in greater depth.

17 Wim Klooster has made a similar observation that many Dutch capitalists did not necessarily experience loyalty towards the Republic but rather to their home community, Wim Klooster, *The Dutch Moment, War, Trade, and Settlement in the Seventeenth-Century Atlantic World*, 1st edition (Ithaca: Cornell University Press, 2016), 187.

18 On Dutch and especially Amsterdam's trade in the Baltic, see Milja van Tielhof, *The Mother of All Trades*, especially chapter 1; Leos Müller, "The Dutch Entrepreneurial Networks and Sweden in the Age of Greatness," in *Trade, Diplomacy and Cultural Exchange: Continuity and Change in the North Sea Area and the Baltic c.1350–1750*, edited by Hanno Brand (Hilversum: Uitgeverij Verloren, 2005), 58–74; Leos Müller, "The Role of the Merchant Network – A Case History of Two Swedish Trading Houses 1650–1800," in *Entrepreneurship and Entrepreneurs in the Early Modern Times. Merchants and Industrialists within the Orbit of the Dutch Staple Market*, ed. Clé Lesger and Leo Noordegraaf, 147–163 (Den Haag: Hollandse Historische Reeks, 1995); Cátia. "Amsterdam Cross-Cultural Partnerships in the Baltic-Atlantic Link, 1580–1674," in *The Rise of the Atlantic Economy and the North Sea/Baltic Trade, 1500–1800*, ed. Leos Müller, Philipp Robinson Rössner, and Toshiaki Tamaki, 103–119 (Stuttgart: Franz Steiner Verlag, 2011).

19 Erik Wilhelm Dahlgren, *Louis de Geer, 1587–1652, Hans lif och verk*, vol. 1 (Uppsala: Almqvist och Wicksell, 1923a); Thomas Lindblad, "Louis de Geer

Formative years of overseas entrepreneurship 49

(1587–1652); Dutch Entrepreneur and the Father of Swedish Industry," in *Entrepreneurs and Entrepreneurship*, ed. Lesger and Noordegraaf (Den Haag: Hollandse Historische Reeks, 1995), 77–84.

20 Hermann Kellenbenz, *The Rise of the European Economy: An Economic History of Continental Europe from the Fifteenth to the Eighteenth Century* (New York: Holmes & Meier Publishers, 1976), 165.

21 On the Swedes and the Finns in North America, see Stellan Dahlgren and Han Norman, *The Rise and Fall of New Sweden: Gov. Johan Risingh's Journal* (Uppsala: Acta Universitatis Upsaliensis, 1988); Amandus Johnson, *The Swedish Settlements on the Delaware: Their History and Relation to the Indians, Dutch and English, 1638–1664: With an Account of the South, the New Sweden, and the American Companies, and the Efforts of Sweden to Regain the Colony* (Lancaster: The New Era Printing Company, 1911); John Munroe, *History of Delaware* (Newark: University of Delaware Press, 2006), 19–26; Bernard Bailyn, *The Barbarous Years: The Peopling of British North America: The Conflict of Civilizations, 1600–1675* (Knopf Doubleday Publishing Group, 2012), 276–321.

22 On the Dutch in North America, see Jaap Jacobs, *New Netherland: A Dutch Colony in Seventeenth-Century America* (Boston/Leiden: Brill, 2005); Jaap Jacobs, *The Colony of New Netherland: A Dutch Settlement in Seventeenth-Century America* (Ithaca/London: Cornell University Press, 2009); John Munroe, *History of Delaware*, chapter 1.

23 Oscar Gelderblom, Jaap Jacobs and Peter Klein have several notes about Blommaert. See Oscar Gelderblom, *Zuid-Nederlandse kooplieden;* Klein, *Die Trippen*, 279; Jacobs, *New Netherland.*

24 Minuit was not Dutch by birth. Minuit was born in Wesel, Rheinland, in Westfalen. He was a director of the WIC 1625–1632 and governor of New Netherland 1626–1632. On Minuit, see *Peter Minuit,* https://sok.riksarkivet.se/sbl/artikel/9361, Svenskt biografiskt lexikon (accessed 21 February 2018).

25 Barbour, *Capitalism in Amsterdam*, 136.

26 *Peter Minuit,* https://sok.riksarkivet.se/sbl/artikel/9361, Svenskt biografiskt lexikon (accessed 21 February 2018).

27 On Usselincx, see, for example, Benjamin Schmidt, *Innocence Abroad: The Dutch Imagination and the New World, 1570–1670* (Cambridge: Cambridge University Press, 2001).

28 For a recent study of the role of Usselincx in the WIC, see Joris Van den Tol, "Lobbying in Company Mechanisms of Political Decision-Making and Economic Interests in the History of Dutch Brazil, 1621–1656" (PhD dissertation, Leiden: Leiden University, 2018).

29 Barbour, *Capitalism in Amsterdam*, 136–138; Goslinga, *The Dutch in the Caribbean*, 437.

30 Abraham Cabiljau, https://sok.riksarkivet.se/sbl/artikel/16310, Svenskt biografiskt lexikon (accessed 21 February 2018); Lindblad, *Sweden's Trade*, 12.

31 The initial licence of Rosenkrantz is to be found in RAC, DK, Diverse breve dokumenter og breve det ostindiska kompgani vedkommende 1616–1660; Olsen, "Dansk Ostindien," 22.

32 Willerslev, "Danmarks første aktieselskab," 614–615.

33 "Att alle och huer sierdelis, saauell Companiett sielff som schiperne, Styrmendh, Bodzmen, eller Huad naffn de haffue Kunnde, som for thete Companies Schall fare eller bruigs, Vdj deris thienniste maa Ahntagis och methandlis, som Kong: Maytts: eigen indföd Vndersotter, och dennom ingenn Ivdere besuerinng att paaleggis…" Charter 16.03.1616, Feldbæk, *Danske handelskompagnier*, 26.

34 The same issue was experienced within competition in the Arctic trade. The Dutch Noordsche Compagnie, which enjoyed a monopoly over the Dutch

50 *Formative years of overseas entrepreneurship*

whaling trade, complained to the States General that the Danish operations under Braem were making use of Dutch capital and expertise. In 1633, the States General decreed that Dutchmen were not allowed to invest in foreign whaling enterprises, and were also forbidden from taking employment in foreign enterprises. See Dalgård, *Dansk-Norsk*, 176–192.

35 Feldbæk and Justesen, *Kolonierne i Asien og Afrika,* 48; Richard Willerslev, "Danmarks første aktieselskab," *Historisk Tidsskrift* 10, no. 6 (1944): 609–36, 620.

36 Olsen, "Dansk Ostindien," 22.

37 "Na ick lange jaeren in dienst van Nederlandtsche oost indisch compagnie geweest," in *RAC, TKIA, Diverse akter vedr. det ostindiske kompagni og Guinea 1618–1659*, Roland Crappe declaration – undated document.

38 "hebbende ik wel genegen sijn maystet van denemarcken ende denselve oostindische compagnie te dienen met op de cust als director generaal....," in *RAC, TKIA, Diverse akter vedr. det ostindiske kompagni og Guinea 1618–1659*, Roland Crappe declaration – undated document.

39 Kay Larsen, *Guvernører: residenter, kommandanter og chefer* (Copenhagen: Arthur Jensens Forlag, 1940), 60.

40 RAC, DK, Diverse breve dokumenter og breve det ostindiska kompgani vedkommende 1616–1659, two letters dealing with Crappe's house in Batavia, 10.12.1635 and 7.12.1634.

41 J.E Elias, *De Vroedschap van Amsterdam 1578–1795*, vol. 1 (Amsterdam: N. Israel, 1963), 310; RAC, DK, Diverse breve dokumenter og breve det ostindiska kompgani vedkommende 1618–1660, Letter from Hinlopen 9 August 1636.

42 Several versions of the contract and its different drafts is located in the RAC, TKIA, Diverse akter vedr. det ostindiske kompagni og Guinea 1618–1659.

43 I would like to thank Professor Steve Murdoch for accessing this information: Anders Svensson, *Svensk agent ved Sundet: Toldkommissær og agent i Helsingør Anders Svenssons depecher til Gustav II Adolf og Axel Oxenstierna 1621–1626*, ed. Leo Tandrup (Aarhus: Universitetsforlaget i Aarhus, 1971), 117–118.

44 Olsen, "Dansk Ostindien," 25; regarding the first expedition, see Esther Fihl, "Shipwrecked on the Coromandel: The First Indian-Danish Contact, 1620," in *Beyond Tranquebar Grappling Across Cultural Borders in South India*, ed. Esther Fihl and A.R. Vēṅkaṭācalapati (Delhi: Orient Blackswan, 2014), 229–256; Torben Abd-el Dayem, *Ove Geddes rejse til Ceylon og Indien 1618–1622*, No, 19 (Esbjerg: Fiseri-og Søfartsmuseets, 2006).

45 Olsen, "Dansk Ostindien," 23–25.

46 The Nayak will be discussed further in Chapters 3 and 4; Larsen, *Dansk-Ostindiske koloniers historie*, 17.

47 A report by Crappe revealed that De Boshouwer had sold the Danish Company lies. See RAC, TKIA, Diverse akter vedr. det ostindiske kompagni og Guinea 1618-59, Ausführliche relativ von der Reise die die Jacht gethan auch wie die genommen under endlich das conto und fort off Tranquebar gebaut Von Roland Crappe 1621.

48 Fihl has also discussed the development of the trade relationship between Crappe and the Nayak of Tanjore. Fihl, "Shipwrecked on the Coromandel."

49 Larsen, *Dansk-Ostindiske koloniers historie*, 20.

50 Ibid., 23.

51 Such behaviour was typical within the maritime communities from the Low Countries. Many individuals also found themselves working for the English and French overseas enterprises. One of the most famous examples is François Caron (1600–1673). See Glenn Ames, *Colbert Mercantilism & the French Quest for Asian Trade* (Dekalb: Northern Illinois University Press, 1996), 30; Barbour, *Capitalism in Amsterdam*, 132; Christine Petto, *Mapping and Charting in Early*

Formative years of overseas entrepreneurship 51

Modern England and France: Power, Patronage, and Production (Lanham/Boulder/New York/London: Lexington Books, 2015), 164.

52 A similar idea has been developed by P.W. Klein, albeit for a different purpose and in a different context. The idea behind institutional sheltering in Klein's argument is that in the early modern period, entrepreneurs were offered "shelter" to invest their capital through monopoly privileges. As Jan Willem Veluwenkamp has pointed out, such monopoly privileges rarely worked. See Klein and Veluwenkamp, "The Role of the Entrepreneur."

53 Glückstadt is situated north of Hamburg on the Elbe river.

54 Paul Lockhart, "Denmark and the Empire: A Reassessment of Danish Foreign Policy under King Christian IV," *Scandinavian Studies* 63, no. 3 (1992): 390–416, 393–395.

55 Karonen, *Pohjoinen suurvalta*, 177.

56 Der Portugysen in der Glückstadt Privilegium, vom 3. August 1619, printed in Gerhard Köhn, *Die Bevölkerung der Residenz, Festung und Exulantenstadt Glückstadt von der Gründung 1616 bis zum Endausbau 1652: Methoden und Möglichkeiten einer historisch-demographischen Untersuchung mit hilfe der elektronischen Datenverarbeitung* (Neumünster: Karl Wachholtz Verlag, 1974, 165, appendix 3; RAC, TKIA, A.10.1, Patenten 1655–1656, 196b; RAC, TKIA, 1626–1669 Patenten, A10.1, several entries with privileges (e.g. privileges to the Dutch and the Portuguese); RAC, TKIA 1627–1704, Memorialer vedr. Hertugdøm kgl. Undersåtters commercium, B153–B154, several entries of different privileges to Dutch and Portuguese merchants; Kellenbenz, *Sephardim an der Unteren Elbe...*, 64; Jacobs, Joachim.,"Der Jüdische Friedhof von Glückstadt," in *Erinnerungsorte – im auftrag des heimatverbandes für den kreis Steinburg*, ed. C. Boldt, S. Loebert, and K. Puymnaa (Steinburger Jahrbuch, Itzehoe 2014), 65–82, 67.

57 Glückstadt, Das Stadtarchiv, Bürgerbuch, several entries between 1620 and 1660 show an increase in Dutch skippers and merchants receiving residency permits. Köhn has shown that until 1652, approximately 25 per cent of the inhabitants came from the Low Countries (either Dutch or Sephardic Jews). Gerhard Köhn, *Die Niederland und der Europäische Nordosten ein Jahrtausend weitäumiger Beziehungen* (Neumünster: Karl Wachholtz Verlag, 1992, 300 and 310; Israel, *The Dutch Republic*, 460–465.

58 Israel, *The Dutch Republic*, 460–465; Köhn, *Die Niederland*, 300.

59 The truce was part of the Eighty Years War (1568–1648), also known as the Dutch war of Independence, in which the Dutch provinces revolted against the rule of Philip II of Spain. The cause of the revolt was a combination of religious tension and resentment towards Spanish rule and hegemony. During this time, the Low Countries (Belgium and the Netherlands) were divided between Catholic southern provinces (present-day Belgium) and Protestant/Calvinist northern provinces (the Netherlands). Between 1568 and 1609, the revolt escalated into several armed conflicts. The conflict also extended beyond Europe into the overseas world. Exhausted with fighting, and frustrated with the decline in trade, a twelve-year truce was concluded in 1609. Due to the beginning of the Thirty Years War, the hostilities between the Republic and Spain escalated again. The end of the Eighty Years War was signalled by the peace treaty of Münster in 1648 (a part of the peace treaty of Westphalia), in which the northern seven provinces were recognised as the Dutch Republic, whereas the remaining ten provinces remained a part of the Habsburg Empire.

60 Israel, *Empires and Entrepots. The Dutch, the Spanish monarchy and the Jews, 1585–1713* (London-Ronceverte: The Hambledon Press, 1990), 428.

52 *Formative years of overseas entrepreneurship*

61 A Sephardic Jew Alberto Dinis represented the Danish part of the negotiations with the Spanish king.

62 Köhn, *Die Bevölkerung der Residenz*, 53.

63 Israel, Jonathan, "The Politics of International Trade Rivalry during the Thirty Years War: Gabriel de Roy and Olivares's mercantilist Projects, 1621–1645," in *Empires and Entrepots*, 213–247; Charles Hill, *The Danish Sound Dues and the Command of the Baltic* (Durham: Duke University Press, 1926), 104; Köhn, *Die Bevölkerung der Residenz*, 52–53; on the treaty between Spain and Denmark, see L. Laursen, Danmark-Norges *Traktater, 1523–1750*, Vol. IV (1626–1649) (Copenhagen: Nielsen & Lydische, 1917), 87–88.

64 Köhn, *Die Bevölkerung der Residenz*, 55.d

65 RAC, Regeringskancelliet i Glückstadt, 1630–1703 Akter. Vedr. Glückstad by og fæstning, 146, file, 1 Nr 3 Conv. 4.

66 Der Zucker refinirer privilegium in der Glückstadt, vom 10. August 1620, printed in, Köhn, *Die Bevölkerung der Residenz*, 167 anlage 4.

67 RAC, Regeringskancelliet i Glückstadt, 1630–1703 Akter. Vedr. Glückstad by og fæstning, 146, file, 1 Nr 3 Conv. 4; Mercedes García-Arenal and Gerard Albert Wiegers, *A Man of Three Worlds: Samuel Pallache, a Moroccan Jew in Catholic and Protestant Europe* (Baltimore: John Hopkins University Press, 2003).

68 Nørregård, *Danish Settlements*, 12.

69 RAC, TKIA, Inländische registratur 1685–1686, B12.10, Appointment of Moses Joshua Henriques.

70 Nørregård, *Danish Settlements*, 13.

71 I would like to thank Joris Van den Tol for providing this source. NL-HaNA, Staten-Generaal 1.01.02, inv. nr. *5758* Liassen WIC, *3.10.1644 Memory by Willem Usselincx*, "ik begeerich was om de nieuwe stede van Gluckstadt en Frederickstadt in Holsteijn ende Gottenborch in Sweeden te sien."

72 Barbour, *Capitalism in Amsterdam*, 137.

73 Ibid., 138.

74 Germans had difficulties in advancing within the VOC, because they had a bad reputation in the Republic, they did not speak or write Dutch, and they were not allowed to openly confess their Lutheran religion. Roelof van Gelder, *Het Oost-Indisch avontuur: Duitsers in dienst van de VOC (1600–1800)* (Nijmegen: SUN, 1997), 284.

75 Gelder, *Het Oost-Indisch avontuur*, 186, 284; on the role of patronage networks in the VOC, see Matthias van Rossum, *Werkers van de Wereld: Globalisering, arbeid en interculturele ontmoetingen tussen Aziatische en Europese zeelieden in dienst van de VOC, 1600–1800* (Hilversum: Verloren, 2014), 272–278.

76 In the Swedish East India Company, the supercargoes could bring parts of the return cargo for their personal benefit, which made the position very lucrative and competitive. Leos Müller, Trading with Asia without a Colonial Empire in Asia: Swedish Merchant Networks and Chartered Company Trade, 1760–1790," in *Beyond Empires: Global, Self-Organizing, Cross-Imperial Networks*, ed. Cátia Antunes and Amelia Polónia (Boston/Leiden: Brill, 2016), 236–252, for example, 244.

77 The city has become famous for its geographical location and its economic function. It is located next to the narrow strait close to Sweden. In the fifteenth century, the Danish King Erik av Pommern established the Sound toll, which meant that every passing ship had to pay a toll. The revenues belonged to the king, not to the kingdom. For a long time, this was the single most important revenue stream for the king.

78 For thorough studies on the importance of the Sound toll, see Torben Hvidegaard, "Øresundstolden på Christian 4.'s tid – Sundtoldens betydning 1613–1645

Formative years of overseas entrepreneurship 53

for forholdet mellem Danmark, Sverige og Nederlandene," *Fortid og nutid* 1 (2000): 199–219; Hill, *The Danish Sound Dues.*

79 For an overview of the Dutch merchants residing in Elsinore, see Allan Tøn- nesen, *'Al het Hollandse volk dat hier nu woont': Nederlanders in Helsingør, circa 1550–1600* (Hilversum Verloren, 2003). Harald Holck, "Om Slægten Leyel," *Personalhistorisk tidsskrift* 6, no. 13 (1958); Thomas Riis, *Should Auld Acquaint- ance Be Forgot: Scottish-Danish Relations C. 1450–1707* (Odense: Odense Uni- versity Press, 1988), 155.

80 During this period, it was not unusual for Scottish families to migrate to El- sinore and the neighbouring areas. See Kathrin Zickermann, *Across the Ger- man Sea: Early Modern Scottish Connections with the Wider Elbe-Weser Region* (Boston/Leiden: Brill, 2013).

81 Riis, *Should Auld Acquaintance*, 163.

82 Going back even further in the history of the Leyel family, there were several other mayors in both Elsinore and Copenhagen, dating back to 1477. See, ibid., 188–189.

83 Ibid., 169.

84 Bredsdorff, *The Trials and Travels*, 18.

85 RAC, DK, B 246 A, Leyel to the directors, 22.09.1644.

86 Bredsdorff, *The Trials and Travels*, 20.

87 Erik Odegard, "Colonial Careers: Johan Maurits van Nassau Siegen, Rijckloff Volckertsz. van Goens and Career-Making in the Early Modern Dutch Em- pire" (PhD dissertation, Leiden: Leiden University, 2018).

88 Bredsdorff, *The Trials and Travel*, 20.

89 Søren Mentz. *The English Gentleman Merchant at Work: Madras and the City of London 1660–1740* (Copenhagen: Museum Tusculanum Press, 2005), 229.

90 Victor Enthoven et al., ed., *The Navigator: The Log of John Anderson, VOC Pilot-Major, 1640–1643* (Boston/Leiden: Brill, 2010), 92; Steve Murdoch, Net- work *North: Scottish Kin, Commercial and Covert Associations in Northern Europe 1603–1746* (Boston/Leiden: Brill, 2006), 210.

91 RAC, DK, Diverse breve dokumenter og breve det ostindiska kompgani ved- kommende 1616–1660, Leyel recounted the expedition to Pipley in a letter dated 22.02.1635.

92 Bredsdorff, *The Trials and Travels*, 20.

93 Ibid, 20; Olsen, "Dansk Ostindien," 58.

94 RAC, DK, Diverse breve dokumenter og breve det ostindiska kompgani ved- kommende, Willem Leyel 22.02.1635.

95 Olsen, "Dansk Ostindien," 60–61.

96 Coolhas, ed., *Generale missiven*, deel 1, 1610–1638 (Gravenhage: Martinus Nijhoff, 1960), 265.

97 Bredsdorff, *The Trials and Travels*, 13.

98 RAC, DK, Diverse Breve Dokumenter og breve det ostindiska kompgani ved- kommcndc 1616–1660, in a letter dated 9.09.1636, Crappe wrote that he had made Pessart the president of the DEIC in Asia; H.T. Colenbrander, ed., *Dagh- register gehouden int casteel Batavia: 1636* (Gravenhage: Martinus Nijhoff, 1899), 14.03.1636, 95 and 294.

99 Olsen, "Dansk Ostindien," 66–67.

100 "Pessart var en intelligent, men højst utilforladelig man," Larsen, *Dansk- Ostindiske koloniers historie*, 30.

101 Krieger, *Kaufleute*, 207–211.

102 RAC, DK, Diverse kongelige ekspeditioner det Ostindiske Kompagni vedkom- mende, The instructions from the directors to the president of the DEIC in Asia and to the merchants, 1623.

54 *Formative years of overseas entrepreneurship*

103 *Kancelliets brevbøger, 1627–1629*, 1.05.1628: 406; Bredsdorff, *The Trials and Travels*, 24.
104 Bredsdorff, *The Trials and Travels*, 22.
105 "har kongen befalet denne Vilm Leyel, som for kort Tid siden er kommet fra Ostindien, at begive sig til ham og give ham Beretning om same Tilstand," in *Kancelliets brevbøger, 1633–1634*, 9.01.1634, 403–404.
106 *Kong Christian den fjerdes egenhændige breve*, Christian IV till rentemestere, 20.12.1634: 314–316.
107 This is confirmed by Bredsdorff, *The Trials and Travels*, 25.
108 *Kancelliets brevbøger, 1633–1634*, 31.01.1634, 433–435.
109 *Kong Christian den fjerdes egenhændige breve*, 20 Decemeber 1634, 314–316, 818–819.
110 "Ed, som Villumb Lejel har aflagt i nærvaerlese af Kansleren Hr. Christian Friis, Vincent Bilde til Nes og Ove Juel til Meilgaard, i hans Egenskab af Bewinthebber og Forvalter for det danske ostindiske Kompagni. Han lover og forpligter sig til at vaere Kongen huld og tro, vide og ramme Kongens og det ostindiske Kopmagnies participanters Bedste og af yderste Evne afvende deres Skade. Han skal ikke aabenbar nogen noget om Handelens tilstand til Skade for kompagniet", i, *Kancelliets brevbøger, 1635–1636*, 11.03.1636, 450; *Kancelliets brevbøger, 1635–1636*, 14.09.1635, 255–256.
111 han lover og forpligter sig til at vaere Kongen og Kompani huld og tro, Ibid., 451.
112 Ibid., 451.
113 Kong Christian den Fjerdes egenhændige breve, Christian IV to Christian Friis, 23.02.1626, 3–6.
114 *Kancelliets brevbøger, 1637–1639*, 20 June 1639, 868.
115 *Kancelliets brevbøger, 1635–1636*, 4.09.1636, 715.
116 Bredsdorff states that Leyel had himself written that he had been onboard the ship; I have not been able to locate the source. Bredsdorff, *The Trials and Travels*, 34–35.
117 Olsen, "Dansk Ostindien," 70.
118 His ship *Christianshavn* was captured in the Canary Islands by the Spanish fleet, suspected for piracy, causing a long delay. See more about this episode, Bredsdorff, *The Trials and Travels*, 64–71.
119 P.C Emmer, *The Dutch Slave Trade, 1500–1850*, trans. Chris Emery (New York, Oxford: Berghahn Books, 2006), 30; György Nováky, *Handelskompanier*, 87.
120 Johannes Postma, *The Dutch in the Atlantic Slave Trade, 1600–1815*, 1st edition (Cambridge: Cambridge University Press, 2008), 75; Albert van Dantzig, *Forts and Castles of Ghana* (Accra: Sedco Publishing, 1980), 23.
121 Stadsarchief Amsterdam (SAA) Notarieel Archief (NA):1289, fol. 8v-19, 8.02.1644; It is unclear which place is referred to here. The closest to Suomen would be Suomi, which refers to Finland. During this period, Suomi often referred to southwest Finland, mainly around the town of Åbo/Turku. This, however, seems not to be the real place of origin of Carloff. If he were from Finland, he would have been reading and writing Swedish, but he was not.
122 NL-HaNA, OWIC, 1.05.01.01, inv. nr. *25*, 13.09.1643 (scan 262).
123 NL-HaNA, OWIC, 1.05.01.01, inv.nr. *11*. Monster Rolle WIC (1645) (scans 242–249), FC, N3, 203. In the references of this book, the word scans refer to the Dutch National Archives and to those archival collections which are available online through the National Archives. The specific page numbers of the scans relate to the sources.
124 Only a few studies have acknowledged the Germans who served in the Dutch trading companies. See Postma, *The Dutch in the Atlantic*; Tim Wachelder,

Formative years of overseas entrepreneurship 55

"Avonturen in Brazilië en op de Goudkust. Vier duitsers in dienst van de WIC (1623–1645)" (PhD dissertation, Nijmegen: Radboud Universiteit Nijmegen, 2004); Van Gelder, *Het Oost-Indisch avontuur.*

125 Schrijver and Voetknechten.

126 For more on the Dutch in Brazil, see Van den Tol, "Lobbying in Company"; Charles Ralph Boxer, *The Dutch in Brazil, 1624–1654* (Oxford: Clarendon Press, 1957); Charles Ralph Boxer, *Salvador de Sá and the Struggle for Brazil and Angola, 1602–1686* (London: University of London, 1952); Michiel van Groesen, *Amsterdam's Atlantic: Print Culture and the Making of Dutch Brazil* (Philadelphia: University of Pennsylvania Press, 2016).

127 Many of the soldiers were of German and Scottish origin.

128 SAA NA: 1289, fol. 28v-29v, 3.05.1644.

129 Ibid.

130 Ibid.

131 Jan Ruychaver was the Director-General 6.01.1641–18.12.1645 and Jacob van der Wel was the Director-General 18.12.1645–9.04.1650.

132 Ratelband, *Nederlanders in West-Afrika 1600–1650: Angola, Kongo en São Tomé*, 1st edition, XLIV (Zutphen: Walburg Pers, 2000); NL-HaNA OWIC, 1.05.01.01, inv.nr. *11*. Jacob Van der Wel, to Heeren XIX, 1.06.1646 (scans 731–742); FC (N4), 34.

133 Ratelband, *Vijf Dagregisters,* LVIII.

134 NL-HaNA OWIC, 1.05.01.01, inv.nr. *11*, Jacob Van der Wel to the Heeren XIX, 21.12.1645 (scans 211–223, 215, 218); FC, N3, 197.

135 NL-HaNA OWIC, 1.05.01.01, inv.nr. *11*, Jacob Van der Wel to the Heeren XIX, 21.12.1645 (scans 211–223, 218); FC, N3, 197.

136 NL-HaNA OWIC, 1.05.01.01, inv.nr. *11*, Journal kept by Jacob Van der Wel, 11.10.1645 (scans 266–290, 268); FC, N3, 242.

137 Ratelband, *Vijf Dagregisters,* XLIX.

138 Ibid., LVIII.

139 Ibid., LVIII–LX.

140 Heijer, "Een dienaar," 162–180, 165–167.

141 NL-HaNA OWIC, 1.05.01.01, inv.nr. *11*, Jacob Van der Wel to the Heeren XIX, 21.12.1645 (scans 211–223, 218); FC, "N3 Collection," 193–197.

142 NL-HaNA OWIC, 1.05.01.01, inv.nr. *11*, Henrich Carloff to the Heeren XIX WIC 21.05.1646 (scans 785–787); FC, N4, 29–30.

143 NL-HaNA OWIC, 1.05.01.01, inv.nr. *11*, Jacob Van der Wel to Heeren XIX, 1.06.1646 (scans 731–742, 735); FC, N4, 35.

144 Van Rossum, *Werkers van de Wereld*, 272–278; Van Gelder, *Het Oost-Indisch avontuur*, 186, 284.

145 NL-HaNA OWIC, 1.05.01.01, inv.nr. *11*, Jacob Van der Wel to Heeren XIX, 1.06.1646 (scans 731–742, 730); FC, N4, 35.

146 NL-HaNA OWIC, 1.05.01.01, inv.nr. *11*, Henrich Carloff to the Heeren XIX WIC 21.05.1646 (scans 785–787); FC, N4, 29.

147 NL-HaNA OWIC, 1.05.01.01, inv.nr. *11*. Henrich Carloff to the Heeren XIX 12.01.1647 (scans 1067–1069, 1068); FC, N4, 127–129.

148 NL-HaNA OWIC, 1.05.01.01, inv.nr. *11*, Daily Journal (Dagregisters) 1.01.1645–1631 March 1647, 01.08.1646 (scans 1079–1237, 1105); FC, N4, 81; Ratelband, *Vijf Dagregisters*, 208.

149 NL-HaNA OWIC, 1.05.01.01, inv.nr. *11*, Jacob Van der Wel to Heeren XIX, 14.08.1646 (scans 879–887, 880), FC, N4, 41–49.

150 For more on the importance of information and communication, see Chapter 5.

151 NL-HaNA OWIC, 1.05.01.01, inv.nr. *11*. Henrich Carloff to the Heeren XIX, 12.01.1647 (scans 1067–1069), FC, N4, 127–129.

56 *Formative years of overseas entrepreneurship*

152 NL-HaNA OWIC, 1.05.01.01, inv.nr. *11*, Daily Journal (Dagregisters) 1.01.1645–31.03.1647, 16.11.1646 (scans 1079–1237, 1161); FC, N4, 98; Ratelband, *Vijf Dagregisters*, 262.

153 NL-HaNA OWIC, 1.05.01.01, inv.nr. *11*, Jan Ruychaver to the Heeren XIX, 22.02.1646 (scans 371–393, 375), FC, N4, 50–59, especially 53.

154 NL-HaNA OWIC, 1.05.01.01, inv.nr. *11*, Jacob Van der Wel to the Heeren XIX, 18.03.1647 (scans 988–992); FC, N4, 129–157.

155 NL-HaNA OWIC, 1.05.01.01, inv.nr. *11*, Henrich Carloff to the Heeren XIX, 5.03.1647 (scans 1061–1065); FC, N4, 163–165.

156 NL-HaNA OWIC, 1.05.01.01, inv.nr. *11,* Jacob Van der Wel to the Heeren XIX, 18.03.1647 (scans 982–1022, 994); FC, N4, 129–157.

157 RAS, LA 82, 12.09.1647, Licence for Gabbesen.

158 Nováky, *Handelskompanier,* 82.

159 SAA NA: 875, fol. 315, Contract between Henrich Carloff and Laurens de Geer, 12.10.1649.

160 "Welbekent van de vaderlandiesen bootsvolck," see NL-HaNA OWIC, 1.05.01.01, inv.nr. *11*, Henrich Carloff to the Heeren XIX, 12.01.1647 (scans 1067–1069, 1067).

161 NL-HaNA OWIC, 1.05.01.01, inv.nr. *11*, Daily Journal (Dagregisters) 1.01.1645–31.03.1647, 3.08.1646 (scans 1079–1237, 1106); FC, N4, 81; Ratelband, *Vijf Dagregisters*, 209.

162 Heijer, "Een dienaar,", 167.

163 See previous chapter.

164 NL-HaNA OWIC, 1.05.01.01, inv.nr. *11*, Henrich Carloff to the Heeren XIX, 26.09.1647 (scans 688–695, 695) FC, N4, 179–185.

165 Ratelband, *Vijf Dagregisters*, XLIX.

3 Entrepreneurship in the company

Introduction

There is a common misunderstanding that entrepreneurship always refers to self-employment. However, in many early modern trading companies, salaried administrators and officials were more entrepreneurial than one might expect. This was especially true in the Nordic context, where the only way of conducting overseas business was through companies that had been chartered by rulers. Here, entrepreneurship was a matter of specialisation in running a business. After all, the trading companies were run by individuals, and it was as individuals that they took more or less informed decisions in managing the investments of others. To manage a business, many decisions regarding investment, capital distribution, employment, and various other matters had to be made. Thus, entrepreneurship did not necessarily require a business of one's own. Receiving a salary, with additional benefits for successfully executed operations, was just as entrepreneurial as self-employment.[1]

In relation to early modern trading organisations, entrepreneurship presents a twofold, reciprocal aspect. In particular, it involves the intersections of interests between individuals and larger economic entities (such as trading companies), these being connected and co-dependent. Hence, trading companies must be analysed from their employees' perspective, and the latter must be understood as active historical agents. As Casson reminds us, entrepreneurship occurs in an institutional context (firms, potential competitors, and partners), and this should not be overlooked. In an international business environment such as that of early modern overseas trade, business-related challenges were more complex than in purely domestic (intra-European) settings, due to the presence of many additional competitors, risks, and threats. This means that studying the relationship between individuals and trading companies is particularly important to understanding overseas business.[2]

The task of this chapter is complicated by the fact that seventeenth-century trading companies varied significantly from one another. As such, an all-encompassing definition of how they were structured is impossible.[3] However,

58 *Entrepreneurship in the company*

this chapter elaborates on an idea put forward by Sanjay Subrahmanyam, who has presented an alternative view of the DEIC during the seventeenth century, emphasising that the Danish companies operated almost exclusively within intra-Asian trade, and that Asian-European trade was considerably less important for them than it was for the EIC and VOC. Consequently, the DEIC is better understood not as an intercontinental chartered company but rather as a private firm operating in the Indian Ocean, not dissimilar to local firms such as those of Francisco Vieira (a Portuguese merchant, intermediary, diplomat, and factor of the sultan of Makassar) or Mir Kamal-al-din (an influential Persian merchant based in Masulipatnam).[4] As such, making comparisons with the bigger companies is not the best way to understand the role of the DEIC in Asia.[5] Given that the aim here is not to prove the importance or success of the DEIC, but rather to study the entrepreneurial opportunities that the company offered its employees, Subrahmanyam's argument offers a good interpretative framework. In this chapter, the approach will therefore correlate at least partly with Subrahmanyam's understanding of the role of the Nordic trading companies as private local firms.[6] Through a study of the entrepreneurship of Leyel and Carloff, the chapter asks whether Subrahmanyam's perspective on the DEIC also holds true in the Atlantic context. In doing so, it offers a new perspective on Nordic overseas business.

This chapter argues that overseas entrepreneurship did not necessarily have to take place outside the company structure, but could just as well occur inside it. In particular, the focus is on how Leyel and Carloff specialised in managing business within the Nordic trading companies. The chapter is divided into two parts. The first explains the structure of the company and thus explores its organisational setting in Europe. The second enquires into Leyel and Carloff's areas of specialisation overseas, and considers how their skills influenced their entrepreneurial opportunities, as well as those of the Nordic trading companies.

Leyel and the First Danish East India Company

In this section, the focus will be on the years between 1642 and 1648, the period of Leyel's rule in India. To situate Leyel within the wider context of the company, it will be necessary to understand the institutional environment of the first DEIC. According to Ole Feldbæk, "the First Danish East India Company was an economic fiasco."[7] Feldbæk argues that the only reason why the company survived until 1650 was that Christian IV refused to let the directors and shareholders liquidate it, hoping that it would eventually become profitable.[8] Martin Krieger, however, suggests a different interpretation. He underscores the fact that although the DEIC as a company was not able to compete with its larger rivals, it did, nonetheless, offer economic profit to those individuals who were engaged in private trade at the outposts.[9] The Danish East India Company thus offered a relatively strong institutional environment, in which entrepreneurially driven people could advance their careers. One of the best examples of such rapid advancement was the Dutchman Roeland Crappe, who was ennobled in 1635 for his services to the DEIC, receiving the name Crappé. He was allowed to trade privately alongside the company, and served as an inspiration to men like Leyel.[10]

Leyel became the director of the company at a time when it had already been active for nineteen years. From the beginning, the company had faced large challenges: the wars in which Denmark was involved hampered its development; the domestic market was insufficient for the goods imported from Asia; the merchants of Copenhagen were reluctant to invest; and, finally, there was heavy competition from larger enterprises, such as the English East India Company (EIC), but especially the Portuguese and the VOC.[11]

To begin with, the company's internal struggles help to explain the possibilities and limitations of Leyel's entrepreneurship. The company had considerable difficulties obtaining sufficient capital, and only did so by forcing the nobility and the richer merchants of Copenhagen to invest. By such desperate expedients, it managed to amass 180,000 riksdalers of start-up capital by 1620. The company had approximately three hundred shareholders. The individual shares varied greatly, from 50 to 16,000 riksdalers; the largest shareholder was the king, with an initial investment of 25,000 riksdalers.[12] This was partly achieved by making loans to potential investors who currently lacked the means to do so. The directors were supposed to invest at least 3,000 riksdalers, but, since it was difficult to find investors willing to invest such a large sum, during the early years, the directors' investments were pooled from multiple investors.[13]

The company had also taken loans from its directors in 1618 and 1622. Roland Crappe lent 7,000 riksdalers, and Jakob Mickelsen and Johan Braem 4,000 riksdalers each. The king continued to pour capital into the company: in 1618, 1619, and 1622, he invested an additional 42,000, 21,000, and 264,900 riksdalers, respectively. By 1624, the king had invested 307,395 riksdalers in total.[14] This means that in only four years, he had increased his investment from 25,000 to almost 308,000 riksdalers. Thus, from early on, the king played a central role in the company.

According to Richard Willerslev, at least on paper, the charter of the DEIC from March 1616 gave the nine initial directors a relatively strong position, similar to that of the directors of other contemporary Danish trading companies, such as the Danish Salt Company and the Icelandic Company.[15] In contrast to the SAC, the Danish trading companies thus initially had powerful directors, but this eventually changed. On 24 April 1621, the king decided to insert additional clauses into the charter. This increased the directors' responsibility for the administration: they were required to keep accounts, to produce reports, and to demonstrate their personal good conduct and loyalty to the company. The historian Jan Rindom takes a different view, claiming that the directors were not as powerful as Willerslev argued, merely because they had clear responsibilities.[16] In the first DEIC,

60 *Entrepreneurship in the company*

the investors had limited access to decision-making. The shareholders had no say in the purchase of cargoes for the ships, which remained a matter for the directors.[17]

With regard to the return on investments, Willerslev notes that it is impossible to calculate the value of the return cargos. Few ships made it back to Copenhagen, and the goods were sold to foreigners. Indeed, this did not please Christian IV, who had envisioned the goods being sold to Danish customers.[18] The challenges surrounding the import of goods, combined with modest interest from potential investors, had already exposed the company to financial problems by the 1620s. As such, the king decided to apply more aggressive methods in order to increase capital.

By 1628, twelve years had elapsed since the initial privileges were granted. The Thirty Years War had depleted the financial power of many of the investors, and inflation endangered the survival of the company. In 1629, the company required its participants to supply an additional 20 per cent outlay. If they failed to do so, their initial investment would be confiscated. This method was borrowed from the WIC, which, in 1624, had similarly demanded significantly increased investments.[19]

Similar requests for additional investment were successfully made in 1631, 1635, and 1636. To keep the company afloat, Christian IV also increased his own contribution. The company was thus becoming more of a royal-owned enterprise than a chartered company, with Christian IV as its "main protector and biggest participant."[20] This resulted in the directors becoming the king's servants, appointed with a fixed salary.[21] Rindom and Willerslev agree that by the mid-1630s, the king had effectively taken over the company, leaving little influence to its directors. According to Willerslev, this served to scare away foreign capital; by March 1636, the king owned more than half the company. In 1643, thanks to Roland Crappé's loan, the king's total capital had increased to 428,438 riksdalers.[22] He continued to invest in the company for reasons of symbolic power and prestige, since, as king, he had lost considerable political clout through his defeat in the Thirty Years War. Indeed, the East India trade became important for Christian IV as a means of regaining some of his prestige.[23]

The institutional environment in Denmark thus proved challenging for the DEIC. However, the contrary applied to Leyel; despite the many wars and lack of funding, the directorship of the company constituted a moment of entrepreneurial opportunity for him. Indeed, the king's constant support suggests that Leyel's East India skills had made him necessary. Thus, the king's frustration served to further augment this opportunity; the king needed someone who was experienced in Asian trade, and who could build up a regular relationship with Tranquebar. The king thus took control of the company, and initiated a patron–client relationship with Leyel (similar to the relationship that de Geer and Carloff would enjoy with the Swedish Africa Company, as will be discussed below). Although the fact that the king had personally appointed a director represented career advancement for Leyel, it also effectively split the administration of the company, which now included both royal and company-appointed employees. In other words, Leyel's appointment had a downside; being personally appointed by the king did not necessarily put him in a favourable position vis-à-vis the other directors. Another downside was that Leyel was left personally dependent upon the king's continuing favour. If the king should die, or change his mind, Leyel would most likely lose his job. Despite these disadvantages, however, the appointment should be seen first and foremost as a moment of career advancement for Leyel. Indeed, if Leyel were to be successful, he might be rewarded with ennoblement, as had been the case with Crappe.

Carloff with the Swedish Africa Company, 1649–1657

In this section, the focus will be on the period from 1649 to 1657 when Carloff was employed by the SAC. In the SAC, Carloff was a commander of the first expedition to West Africa. Moreover, Carloff was also the second largest investor in the company (the financing of his investments will be dealt with in the next chapter).[24] His participation in the company can be divided into two main periods. During the first, the *Louis de Geer* period (1645–1652), Carloff's patron de Geer ran the company with Carloff's assistance. Indeed, their partnership illustrates the blurring of lines that occurred between individual and company interests. This was the period for entrepreneurial opportunity, since it was when the SAC entered the African markets. The second period was that of *divided management* (1652–1657), during which other members of the company challenged Carloff's position, which resulted in the adoption of a second charter. This ultimately altered the institutional environment of the company, restricting concomitantly Carloff's entrepreneurial opportunities.

The institutional environment of the SAC is best understood through reference to the patron of the company, Louis de Geer, also known as the "father of Swedish industry." An iron-manufacturer, de Geer was one of the wealthiest men in the kingdom. Originally from the Low Countries, he had been naturalised Swedish.[25] Between 1645 and 1649, de Geer had expanded his business into the Atlantic trade. He had learnt of the potential of the growing Atlantic trade through his networks in continental Europe. When he embarked upon his Atlantic project, he lacked a complete trading company but benefitted from the protection of the Swedish Crown.[26]

The largest obstacle for the SAC was the limited funding that was available, due to the costly wars in which Sweden was currently embroiled. In this sense, the challenges faced by the Swedish were similar to those encountered by the Danish: the numerous wars on the continent and the internal Baltic rivalry had worsened the financial situation of both crowns, as well as that of potential investors. However, at the same time, warfare accelerated empire building: successful wars could make many aristocrats rich and encourage

62 *Entrepreneurship in the company*

them to signal their status by buying exotic and luxurious goods from overseas. This means that while imperial ambitions existed, the capacity of the Swedes to pursue them remained limited, due to the ever-growing demands of the war effort. In turn, this created an opportunity for foreigners with experience and capital to enter Swedish international trade. The protocol of the royal council stated that "our nation is not known in those lands" (referring to the Gold Coast).[27] In my view, this implies that the Swedish lacked know-how and recognition on the Coast, which internationally experienced Gold Coast veterans could supply. Finally, Queen Christina advocated de Geer's business plans, and, on 15 January 1648, yet another passport was issued. On the latter, the word "company" appeared for the first time.[28]

Like other trading companies, the SAC had directors. In the SAC, however, the latter did not play any significant role: for example, they did not receive a salary or commission. Indeed, they had little incentive to be involved in the management of the trade at all. Instead, their main function was to mediate between the traders and the administration of the central government. In his declaration of 1662, Carloff had referred to the company as a *simulatie* (a simulacrum or simulation).[29] The actual administration of the business in Europe was in the hands of a few key individuals in Hamburg and Amsterdam.[30] According to Carloff, the freighting of the ships took place in Amsterdam, and Hans Boor was the factor who bought and loaded the cargoes there. In 1649, Boor equipped the *Christina* and the *De Liefde* with Dutch crews.[31]

From the beginning, the SAC was primarily a private trading firm, the strings of which were pulled by de Geer and Carloff. Indeed, Carloff declared that after having unilaterally terminated his contract with the WIC and arriving in Amsterdam, he had met with Laurens de Geer (son of Louis de Geer). According to Carloff, de Geer had then offered him a contract, because he knew that he had the best knowledge and most up-to-date information regarding trade in Africa.[32] Carloff's contract made him the commander of the SAC for three years, and his monthly salary of 100 guilders was an improvement on that which he had received as prosecutor of the WIC. However, he no longer had a right to one-third of confiscated goods. On the plus side, he was now allowed to engage in private trade, up to the amount of 2,000 guilders, so long as it did not harm the interests of the SAC.[33] Beyond the provisions of the contract, it is also evident that Carloff was expected to invest in the SAC. Indeed, his investment of 10,000 riksdalers made him the second largest investor after Louis de Geer.[34]

Moreover, Carloff declared, the other large investors were Louis, Emmanuel, Steven and Johannes de Geer, and Jan Wouters. Thus, the business had two key aspects, namely the financial backing of the de Geer consortium, and the skillset and market access of Carloff.[35] The meeting between de Geer, representing the SAC, and Carloff, as an individual, suggests that both parties could benefit from a contract. In that contract, Carloff was given the highest operational position in the company, being made responsible for the overseas operations on the ground. Thus, even if the first charter has often been described as the "Louis de Geer Company," Carloff's role ought not to be underestimated. From his point of view, Carloff had achieved the position that he had desired but which he had been unable to attain in the WIC.

The contract between Carloff and de Geer was further strengthened through social mechanisms such as marriage. Indeed, it is tempting to argue that Carloff's choice of wife was at least partly related to the de Geer family. While employed in the SAC, Carloff married Sophia Felicitas Wolzogen.[36] The Wolzogens were an old Austrian noble family, who had migrated to the Low Countries in the sixteenth century. In Louis de Geer's personal correspondence, there are letters exchanged with Lodewijk Wolzogen, Sophia's brother.[37] One of de Geer's accounting books also reveals that when Carloff and Jan Wolzogen (likely another brother of Sophia, also known as Johann and Jean Andre) visited the de Geer mansion in Sweden, de Geer bore the costs.[38]

The planned structure of the company thus showed that the organisation would be tightly connected to de Geer. After all, he was without doubt the largest investor. The second in command of the company was Carloff, who was charged with managing the operation in Africa. This responsibility was a specialised task, which would rely upon his experience and skills. Finally, the importance of the specialised skills of Carloff for the SAC is reflected in the fact that the Queen fully supported giving Carloff and de Geer the freedom to plan and structure business in West Africa. Using power of attorney, Christina appointed Carloff the commander of the SAC and the head of operations in Western Africa. Moreover, the Queen stated that Carloff should contact his African business partners and aim to build up friendly commercial relations between the Swedish crown and local kings.[39]

While Carloff was in Western Africa, the SAC had undergone a period of considerable change. In particular, in 1651, the queen and her council had re-established and improved the old Board of Commerce, which was responsible for international trade, manufacturing, and shipping.[40] This restructuring indicates the growing desire of the state to participate more actively in company affairs.[41] The first councillor, Peter Julius Coyet, and the first president, Christer Bonde, were both investors in the SAC. Both men were attempting to bring the company closer to the state, leaving less space for individual entrepreneurial manoeuvres.[42] From an institutional perspective, the management of the company became more embedded in the state, particularly through the sharing of posts between directors in the company and councillors on the Board of Commerce.[43] The key figures on the board supported privilege-based trading companies, such as the Tar Companies, the Västervik Shipping Company, the Salt Company, the New Sweden Company, and the Swedish Africa Company.[44] Indeed, when Erik Oxenstierna was appointed president of the Board of Commerce, he also became director of the New Sweden Company.[45] The close connection between these enterprises and the board was also evident in the person of Erik Rosenholt, who was simultaneously director of the Tobacco Company, councillor of the Board

64 *Entrepreneurship in the company*

of Commerce, and mayor of Stockholm.[46] In 1652, de Geer died in Amsterdam. In 1654, Queen Christina abdicated, and Chancellor Axel Oxenstierna died. In 1652, when Carloff left Western Africa, he had fulfilled his contract, and was set to renegotiate his role in the company; however, these unexpected events would have serious implications on Carloff's position in the SAC.[47]

By 1654, the Board of Commerce had practically taken over the SAC. After Carloff had returned to Sweden, he was invited to Uppsala, where the board was temporarily seated due to the plague that was ravaging Stockholm. Here, he attended a meeting with the representatives of the Board of Commerce, to discuss the company's future, and, especially, its relationship to England. Indeed, this invitation shows that the Board of Commerce was interested in listening to Carloff. At the meeting, the reorganisation process was discussed, and plans began to take shape: in particular, the aim was to reduce the role of the de Geer family, and to tie the company more closely to Sweden, by preventing foreigners from investing in the company.[48]

Carloff approved the plans for reorganisation, but much remained unclear. Prior to the meeting, Queen Christina had spoken with Bulstrode Whitelocke, the English ambassador, regarding the possibility of withdrawing the privileges of the company and transferring them to a new English investor.[49] This might, however, have been an unwarranted inference on Whitelocke's part. In any case, at least in theory, there was an idea of bringing the English and the Swedish overseas interests closer together: for instance, the EIC and the SAC had plans for co-operation in the gold trade.[50] Indeed, this was at least partly the reason for Whitelocke's presence in Uppsala. At the time, the EIC held the charter for African trade and had direct access to the Western Coast of Africa.[51] If the relationship between England and Sweden had become closer, it would potentially have diminished Carloff's role, since new actors would have entered the scene.

However, the Swedish and English plans fell through, and the reorganisation of the charter proceeded. In 1654, the queen abdicated, and Karl X Gustav became the King of Sweden. The new king also issued new privileges to the company. A minimum investment of 500 riksdalers was explicitly specified, while a "principal shareholder" had to invest at least 3,000 riksdaler.[52] The new privileges excluded foreign investors, and stricter regulations regarding transparency and loyalty to the company were imposed.[53] However, in the second charter, the de Geer family estate remained the largest investor. Carloff was yet again the second largest, with an investment of 15,000 riksdaler. To judge from the list of new participants, it is clear that there were more Swedish noble families involved than had been the case in the first charter, among them Bonde, Brahe, de la Gardie, Sparre, and Oxenstierna.[54] Indeed, as seen in Table 3.1, these investors belonged to some of the most influential families in Sweden.[55]

Although the company allowed only Swedish investors, it tolerated the investment of foreign capital through Swedish principals, who would be recognised as shareholders. Nováky has illustrated this process in the case of

Table 3.1 Table of the nine main investors during the second charter of the SAC

Main participant	Riksdalers
Louis de Geer (estate)	90,500
Henrich Carloff	15,000
Erik Oxenstierna	6,000
Joachim Pötter Lillienhoff	6,000
Johan Beyer	3,000
Gustav Bonde	3,000
Christer Bonde	3,000
Ebba Brahe	3,000
Peter Julius Coyet	3,000

Source: Nováky, *Handelskompanier*, 175.

Joachim Pötter, who invested 6,000 riksdalers in the SAC, of which at least 4,000 originated from the Amsterdam merchants and brothers Guillaume, Matthias, and Volquin Momma.[56] Nováky suggests that this was probably an exception. However, I believe that this type of investment was in fact common. This phenomenon, which I call *ghost investing*, will be studied in detail in Chapter 4. Nevertheless, in order for Carloff to openly invest in the second charter, he had to be naturalised Swedish. Carloff was duly ennobled in 1654, and, as a Swedish nobleman, he could continue to invest.[57] However, it is possible that he was also representing other investors, as will be demonstrated in the next chapter.

The new company was led by a "Main Director," who was to be one of the main investors and "a renowned man." In practice, this referred to the president of the Board of Commerce. Directly under the main director were three directors responsible for the day-to-day running of the company, assisted by co-directors. The first main director was Erik Oxenstierna (son of Axel Oxenstierna), who had previously held the same position in the New Sweden Company. The three directors were Israel Lagerfeldt, Joachim Pötter, and Hendrick de Moucheron. Carloff worked as sub-director until 1656. Hans Kramer, who had also been responsible for the New Sweden Company books, was appointed bookkeeper.[58]

The contrast with the first charter is remarkable. While under the first charter, the company was administered by de Geer, under the second charter, it was officially governed by prominent Swedes. In practice, however, the de Geer family was still represented at the directors' meetings, through de Moucheron, even though the latter did not have his own shares, a fact that contradicted the company regulations. Consequently, the influence of the de Geer family remained strong. Notably, they owned their shares in the company not as individuals, but as a group.

Nováky has shown that Louis de Geer's death seriously diminished Carloff's room for manoeuvre. While this is true, it ought to be added that the

66 *Entrepreneurship in the company*

abdication of Queen Christina and the death of Axel Oxenstierna in 1654 also had negative consequences for Carloff. These deaths, along with the establishment of the Board of Commerce, represented setbacks in Christina's attempt to insert Sweden into a new international order. It can thus be concluded that Carloff's initial participation in the Swedish African trade relied on Sweden's inability to develop its own overseas business. With time, however, Carloff's advantage in this regard declined. Although Carloff was ennobled, his influence was diminishing, since bringing the company closer to the state was not in his interest. The development of the SAC demonstrates that a business that began almost as a private enterprise became more and more anchored in the state. In turn, this reveals that company trade was not only attractive to a few capitalists but also represented an issue of considerable contention within the institutions of the state. Having discussed the structure and administration of the companies in Europe, and the roles of Leyel and Carloff within them, I will now examine their activities on the Coromandel and Western African coasts.

Leyel as the commander in India

Leyel arrived at Tranquebar in 1643, where he found Danish operations in a precarious condition. Having arrived, Leyel informed the directors that Pessart had proved unsuitable as commander, and that the state of affairs was by now desperate. He reported that Pessart had stolen everything there was to steal, and, having inspected the accounts, he had realised that Pessart had not kept any records regarding trade. Trade with Ceylon, Masulipatnam, and Makassar was in shambles, and the factory at Masulipatnam had been lost, since the director had been unable to provide suitable gifts or to pay the expected tribute to the local ruler. Pessart's local creditors currently held his wife and family hostage in Masulipatnam.[59] Moreover, Pessart had also failed to pay the annual tribute to the Nayak, which had served to further worsen the overall situation in Tranquebar.[60] Finally, Pessart had also quarrelled with the Bengali rulers, and a broader conflict was looming.[61] According to Leyel, the other Europeans were laughing at the misery of the Danes.[62] Regarding the weakness of the company, and of the generally desperate state of affairs, Leyel wrote, "We must row with the oars that we have."[63]

In terms of solutions, Leyel intended to regain and improve the settlements that Crappe had established at Makassar (Celebes), Japara, Succadana, Mattam, Balasore, and, most importantly, Masulipatnam.[64] Balasore, Succadana, Mattam, and Masulipatnam had already been lost, and Leyel thus faced considerable challenges with regard to trade and politics in Bengal, Masulipatnam, and Tranquebar. By 1644, Pessart had left the employment of the DEIC, and Leyel had informed the company administration that the DEIC was now under his control.[65] In response, the VOC officials noted in their registers, "What will be the outcome of Leyel's rule, only time will tell."[66]

Entrepreneurship in the company 67

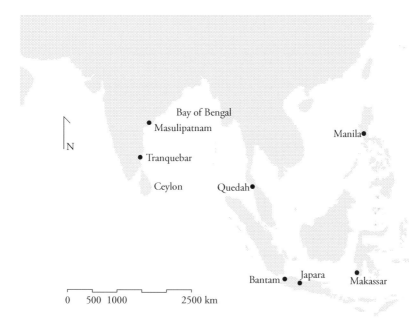

Figure 3.1 Map of Danish factories and support nodes in Asia.
Source: Map drawn by Panu Savolainen.

As illustrated in Figure 3.1, one of Leyel's most important tasks was, to manage the company's forts and trading factories. Indeed, he was worried about the company's weak infrastructure, and particularly its lack of functioning ships. In 1645, there had been the *Christianshavn*, the *St Michael*, and the *Wahlby*, of which the *Christianshavn* was the only large vessel. At the same time, Leyel noted that the Danish had only Fort Dansborg and a factor in Makassar at their disposal.[67] Leyel's reports to the directors reveal that he was gravely concerned regarding the status of Fort Dansborg. In 1645, he wrote that he had been repairing the fort between February and October, and that it was now in much better condition.[68] In the meantime, the town of Tranquebar had fallen prey to famine due to food shortages; people were starving, falling ill, or dying, and food prices had risen significantly, creating unrest among the inhabitants. To curb the crisis, Leyel ordered emergency food supplies from Ceylon.[69]

Leyel also faced problems with the company employees. He claimed that there were only seventeen European men in the fort, all married to local slaves. Of those seventeen, only six were Danes; most of the other had come to Tranquebar as runaways from Dutch Ceylon.[70] In 1623, by contrast, Dansborg had been garrisoned by no less than seventy European employees.[71] On

68 *Entrepreneurship in the company*

20 October 1645, Leyel wrote regarding the severe shortage of manpower at Tranquebar, and requested that the directors of the company hire more employees, and preferably trustworthy Northern Europeans.[72] At the end of his letter, Leyel listed the current employees stationed at the fort. The other inhabitants were locals, especially Portuguese-speakers and a Catholic priest.[73] Their number had decreased yet further from the previous year. Many of these men had already been in India for a long time, and there was a pressing need for new recruits from Denmark. He appointed Anders Nielsen, who had previously served as factor in Makassar, as acting governor of Dansborg, since he himself needed to travel in order to improve trade.[74]

Because navigation was dependent upon the monsoon season, the organisation of trading expeditions was subject to severe constraints. From Tranquebar, Leyel's ships crossed the Straits of Malacca to Bantam, from whence they continued via Japara (Jepara) and Charabon (Cirebon) to Makassar. They returned by the same route to Bantam, continued via Ceylon, and returned to Tranquebar at the time of the subsequent monsoon.

Coordinating negotiations

With regard to trade maintenance and development, his main priority was to resolve the conflict with the ruler of Tranquebar, the Nayak, which had arisen from Pessart's failure to pay the necessary tributes. At the time, there were several Nayaks ruling in the Tamil regions, which had functioned as commercial hubs for centuries, and which had also been central to interregional trade under the emperor of Vijayanagara. In the early seventeenth century, the Coromandel Coast was divided into two distinctive political regions: in the north, the Muslim Kingdom of Golconda; and in the south, the Nayak of Tanjore.[75] Tranquebar, on the Coromandel Coast, was part of the Kingdom of Tanjore. The Nayak of Tanjore was then an independent sovereign, with the formal title Nayakkan or Nayak. Often, the Nayak was considered a peace maker. If he could not bring peace via diplomacy, he could mobilise large armies to solve existing conflicts.[76] In 1645, Leyel sent the merchant Anders Nielsen to negotiate with the Nayak, particularly regarding the maintenance of the DEIC headquarters in Tranquebar (Nielsen's mission will be studied thoroughly in the next chapter).

In a letter to Nielsen, Leyel had explained that an official from the Nayak's court, Tiagapule, had visited Tranquebar the year before. He had perpetrated various outrages against the inhabitants, and burnt down several houses. Leyel's translator, Sima Marca, had been killed. Marca had been the company's best translator, and had worked for the DEIC during the reigns of both the current Nayak and his father. Tiagapule had also prevented the merchants of Tranquebar from accessing their ships and sailing to Ceylon. Indeed, Leyel claimed that it was due to these actions that the DEIC had been unable to pay its tribute to the Nayak. Thus, given the behaviour of Tiagapule, it was unreasonable for the Nayak to demand the

Entrepreneurship in the company   69

regular annual tribute, plus the support of the DEIC in times of war, plus courtly visits on demand.[77] Leyel claimed to have concluded peace with Tiagapule, and promised to pay him 500 *pardous* to end the hostilities. Although he lamented the fact that he had to pay this sum, he argued that it was the only way to restore good relations with the Nayak, who otherwise would transfer his allegiance to the VOC.[78] Indeed, Leyel was convinced that the VOC had been involved in the hostilities, supporting Tiagapule, bribing him and slandering the Danish. In 1645, an official visit to the Nayak's court resulted in an agreement regarding payment, and a promise of mutual aid at times of conflict.[79]

Thus, Leyel managed to re-establish the connection with the Nayak, which was the basis for the company's entire presence in the region. The episode with Tiagapule demonstrates that the VOC was intent on harming DEIC operations, and that the competition between the two companies had become intertwined with local politics. For Leyel, it was paramount to keep the Nayak friendly. Without paying the demanded tributes, the Danish company would have been ousted from Tranquebar, and without Tranquebar, the DEIC would have lost its headquarters and a large share of its income. Indeed, Leyel intended to redirect local ships travelling from Ceylon to Porto Novo into the port at Tranquebar, so that he could charge them import and customs duties. According to Leyel, this was a viable strategy, since many merchants from Porto Novo had already decided to settle and establish their operations in Tranquebar.[80]

During the period of Leyel's rule, the company participated in the Indian Ocean trade via three main networks. The first, and perhaps the most important, was that between Tranquebar and Ceylon. The second ran from Tranquebar to Makassar via Java, and the third from Masulipatnam to Emeldy in the north. Leyel's reports suggest that the main product for the DEIC at this time was Coromandel textiles, which were for the most part sold in the Sunda Islands.[81] On these islands, the Danish purchased in turn silk, tin, gold, and diamonds, which were then resold on the Coromandel Coast. Salt and saltpetre were traded through factories located in the Golconda towns. From the Indonesian archipelago, the DEIC obtained spices. The clove trade was especially profitable for the Europeans, since the purchases from Makassar were resold in Masulipatnam. According to Tapan Raychaudri, the Danes were primarily involved in the trade of cloves, sandal wood, radix china, tortoise shells, and silk from Makassar. From the Coromandel Coast, they exported textiles, and from the Bay of Bengal, sugar.[82]

The first regular trade network was with Ceylon, and consisted in arrack, cinnamon, and elephants, all of which were key products, providing access in the world of Indian Ocean trade. The key to entering the Ceylon trade was the ruler, the King of Candy. The Portuguese and the VOC had been fighting over dominance over the island, and the tensions between the two created an opportunity for the Danish to enter the Ceylon trade. In November 1644, Leyel wrote that the VOC and the Portuguese were at war over the

70 *Entrepreneurship in the company*

jurisdiction of Gale, a highly profitable region for the VOC, in which the Portuguese were not willing to give up their position. The VOC had already sent fourteen vessels with 2,500 soldiers to Ceylon, aiming to take over the Portuguese settlements, but had met with such fierce resistance that over half of the VOC soldiers had been killed, and the rest had had to retreat.[83] For Leyel, the ongoing tension between the Portuguese and the VOC represented an opportunity to penetrate a new and potentially lucrative market.

In 1644, Leyel appointed Adrian Jacobsen as his ambassador to Ceylon. His instructions were to sail to Cutiara, establish contact with the King of Candy, and attempt to procure an invitation to his court.[84] Jacobsen's task was to present the king with several lavish gifts, including a large Japanese chest, round mirrors, glasses, textiles, hunting dogs, and an instrument to distil water. If the king was dissatisfied with the gifts, Jacobsen was to assure him that his superiors would do their utmost to obtain whatever he desired instead. The aim was to establish a favourable relationship and, ideally, to access trade in Ceylon without having to pay customs duties. Jacobsen was to obtain a written agreement, if at all possible.[85] In October, Anders Nielsen reported to Leyel that one of their local contacts had returned from Ceylon with an elephant, given as a gift by the King of Candy. Jacobsen himself had not yet returned from his mission, since he was still visiting the king's court.[86]

The following year, Leyel reported that the King of Candy had granted the company trading rights and certain custom exemptions.[87] Leyel was apparently not entirely satisfied, given that a few years later, he sent yet another embassy to Ceylon, this time under the command of his son-in-law, Josias Stael.[88] Leyel equipped Stael with an array of gifts that were to be delivered to the king: four horses, three from Makassar and one from Java; a large Japanese scriptorium, a sombrero, globes, Javanese gold, and two cats. The aim of the mission was to boost trade, especially in wax, cinnamon, elephants, and rice. According to his instructions, Stael should ask for the king's permission to access the trade route between Cutiara and Jafnapatnam, and to be exempted from local taxation.[89] However, Stael's mission was in the end unsuccessful. Having received the news of the failed voyage, Leyel intended to send his own brokers, Chedam Benada and Antonio Gomes, with new supplies for yet another visit to the court, hoping that they would be more successful. Leyel suspected that one of the men in the former mission, Razia Pahsa Mudeliar, had not done his best, and stated that he should no longer be trusted.[90] There is no record of any further embassies to Ceylon. It appears that Leyel was successful in opening up a trade connection with Ceylon, but that a permanent route with completely free trade was never realised.

The second main trade network was with Makassar, one of the central trading ports of the Indonesian archipelago, and a hub for the collection and distribution of spices.[91] Leyel emphasised that the trade in cloves had been particularly profitable through Makassar, and that he had got a better

Entrepreneurship in the company 71

price for the cloves in Porto Novo than in Masulipatnam (on the Coromandel Coast). The intra-Asian clove trade was beneficial for the Danish, especially since the King of Golconda had been eager to acquire cloves from the company. The *Christianshavn* thus left Dansborg for Bantam, Charabon, and Japara on the coast of Java. From there, it sailed on to Makassar, where the DEIC traded in pepper with the Dutch.[92] Of particular significance was Leyel's participation in the journey that opened up the Makassar trade.

Following this journey, Leyel reported that he had conducted profitable trade in Charabon with the king, who was not favourable to the VOC, and who had appreciated Leyel's arrival. Indeed, he had granted Leyel exemption from customs duties, "for now and forever," and had promised to sell him as much pepper as his ships could carry annually. According to Leyel, this would provide sufficient pepper for both the European and the local markets. Leyel also received permission to build a factory in Charabon, and was welcomed in Japara, where a trading relationship was established with the local ruler. Upon arrival in Makassar, Pessart's outstanding debts were paid, and Leyel appointed Poul Hansen Korsør and Johan Polman as factor and assistant factor respectively.[93] The importance of the Makassar trade also stemmed from Leyel's desire to expand trade with Manila. Due to its central location, Makassar was vital for the trade in gold, silk, and cotton with Canton and Macao, silver with Manila, and textiles with the Coromandel Coast.[94] The Spanish sent silver from Mexico to Asian markets through Manila, and, in turn, textiles, satin and spices were sent from Manila to Mexico. As such, Leyel requested that the Danish king initiate negotiations with the Spanish empire, in order to establish a trade connection between the Spanish and the DEIC in Manila, which would facilitate the acquisition of valuable products. With these goods, the DEIC would have something to offer on the Asian markets. According to Leyel, the Danish king might try referring to the recent Danish–Spanish treaty of 1630, as a means to convince the Spanish king.[95] This request demonstrates that coordinating the company in Asia forced Leyel to attempt to influence decision-making in Europe, particularly by reporting his plans to improve trade in Asia. It also shows that Leyel had specialised knowledge regarding European diplomatic arrangements, which he used in an overseas context to advise the king. In this way, European and overseas diplomacy and trade became intertwined.

The third trade network began north of the Coromandel, and continued along the coast of Bengal. Masulipatnam was important, but since Pessart had failed to repay his debts, Leyel was unable to reopen trade there. In the Bengal delta, Leyel participated in the slave trade, which was then common in the Indian Ocean.[96] For Leyel, the slave trade was a means to obtain quick profits, which could then be used for gifts, tributes, and outstanding debts. In particular, the DEIC sold the crews of Bengali ships, which they had seized as prizes (Chapter 6 will study these seizures more closely). The slave trade was widespread in the Indian Ocean, and other powers also participated. Leyel, who was familiar with the region following previous visits to

72 *Entrepreneurship in the company*

Pipley during 1626, when the DEIC had attempted to build a trading station there, knew that due to developments within local politics, the Portuguese had lost their trading stations on the Bengal Coast, especially at Tamluk, Hughli, Balasore, and Pipley. These had traditionally been considered slave ports, and their loss coincided with the general decline of Portuguese dominance in the region.[97]

For Portuguese private traders, the Bengal slave trade had offered a solution to the declining strength of the *Estado da Índia*. Similarly, the DEIC also obtained slaves at the Bengali ports, whom they then transported to Ceylon for trade, and as gifts for the local rulers. For example, in his instructions to skipper Hans Ekman, Leyel stated that thirty-eight slaves (both Muslims and Hindus) could be offered as gifts to the king in Quedah (Kedah).[98] Indeed, Leyel was himself a slave owner. In a letter to Jørgen Hansen, the skipper of the *Christianshavn*, Leyel noted that if Ismael Nina, Leyel's business partner, brought slaves onboard, they should be considered his (i.e. Leyel's) property. In the same letter, he also discussed how to procure provisions for the slaves on board the ships.[99] This demonstrates that slave trading also took place among the DEIC and its officials. Indeed, such slave trading represented a gravitation towards the rhythms of intra-Asian trade, a gravitation that had been adapted by Leyel.

Under Leyel's administration, trade in the Indian Ocean was characterised by three strategies: first, the issuing of passports and instructions for company employees; second, the organisation of trading activities on the ground; and third, the use of a significant number of brokers and translators. By issuing passports on behalf of the Danish king, Leyel functioned as the king's representative. However, these passports were not the same as passports today. To the contrary, they were more like sea letters intended for a ship and its crew.[100] These passports and the instructions given to merchants were often issued simultaneously. An example of such instructions was a letter dated 19 September 1645, from Leyel to the skipper and pilot of the *St. Michael*, namely Simon Charstenson and Willem Mouridsen. According to Leyel, the ship was to sail to Quedah, on the Malaysian coast, where the crew would establish contact with the broker Seyed Nina, who had been hired by Leyel to handle trade for the DEIC. Together, they would undertake the purchase of elephants as their main goal. The ship was to be particularly wary of other Europeans, who might attempt to hinder its progress. If this happened, they were to show their passport and protest. Similar statements recurred in most of the instructions and passports issued by Leyel. However, issuing passports was not an activity specific to the DEIC; the VOC, and in particular the Portuguese, also issued passports.

Since the early sixteenth century, the Portuguese *cartazes* had been principally used to control Asian shipping and sea routes. The Portuguese, like the VOC after them, enjoyed naval superiority in Asia, which enabled them to stop other ships and demand the *cartazes*. If the ship failed to present such a licence, the ship itself would be confiscated, and the skipper and crew

Entrepreneurship in the company 73

accused of engaging in illegal trade.[101] The *cartazes* were thus primarily a means to extort money, and only secondarily a passport in the sense that the term would be understood today. The challenge with the *cartazes* was that it required the Portuguese to have sufficient force to control the seas. By contrast, the passports of Leyel were issued for a different purpose. The *cartazes* were sold to offer protection to local merchants and ships, whereas Leyel's passports were issued to offer protection for local merchants on-board Danish ships. After all, onboard the DEIC ships, a significant amount of both European and non-European private trade was conducted.

All in all, the DEIC passports demonstrate Leyel's capacity to adapt to the rhythms of local trade, a capacity that he had developed during his previous visits to the Indian Ocean. They also demonstrate his capacity to adapt to local business practices, in order to maximise the gains of the company and of himself.

The numerous passports contained in the Leyel archives show that Leyel was in a remarkable position overseas. He was acting similarly to the Portuguese viceroy in Goa, which again underlines the way he envisaged the activities of the company overseas.[102] The passports and instructions always stated the desired crew, the route they were to sail, the products they were expected to trade, and how to respond when facing threats. Leyel often wrote instructions to the skipper, the pilot, and the merchants of the ships. Here, he also clarified the hierarchy of the personnel, and even explained the hierarchy that would pertain in case of death.

A significant part of the instructions regarded how to act upon arrival at the different destinations, and how to undertake the various tasks assigned to the personnel. One of the issues that frequently recurred in the instructions was the abuse of alcohol. In this regard, Leyel stressed the need to avoid excessive drinking, which, he claimed, lay at the root of all the company's problems in India. Indeed, this suggests that during his years in the Asian trade, Leyel had seen many Europeans misbehave under the influence of alcohol, causing problems that then had to be resolved by authorities like himself. He also recommended purchasing as much arrack (a liquor or spirit) and as many elephants as possible.[103] These commodities were important, due to their widespread use in the Indian Ocean as gifts for rulers and merchants, helping to establish and improve business relationships.[104] Thus, while Leyel condemned heavy alcohol consumption, he nevertheless considered it as one of the most important commercial products.

Another common theme in the instructions was the role of brokers and translators in the company. Local brokers were instrumental for the development of business, since they were responsible for business transactions, and were often better connected and better informed than the company's own officials. For example, in relation to establishing trade in Porto Novo, Leyel described his local clerk, Canacapel Tayapa, as "a decent and trustworthy servant for our trade."[105] The use of brokers was also widespread in Bantam, Java, and Makassar. In Bantam, Leyel wanted the company

74 *Entrepreneurship in the company*

to trade through a Chinese merchant, Ziu Ziu. Even in Batavia, Leyel instructed Anders Nielsen to trade through Ambrosius van der Keer, to assist him in any way possible, and to diligently compensate him for his services. In Japara, Nielsen was to trade with Abdul Latif, with whom the prospects of the gold and timber trade were to be discussed.[106]

The brokers were also important for providing additional assistance in cross-imperial trade. The broker Simão D'Almeida, a merchant in Negapatnam, assisted the Danish with purchasing gunpowder, which could be used at Dansborg. D'Almeida exported some of this gunpowder to Ceylon, delivering it to the Portuguese general Don Filipe de Mascarenhas in return for cinnamon.[107] Even in Masulipatnam, where the DEIC had many problems, a broker called Virna acted as merchant and translator. Leyel wrote that Virna was to negotiate with the local governor, or with Thomas Penniston at the English factory. Furthermore, along the trade routes to Ceylon, Leyel had various other contacts, who were to assist the ships he had sent with purchasing elephants, cinnamon, and arrack.[108] The importance of brokers was also clear in Makassar. There, factor Poul Hansen Korsør was told to consult with broker Francisco Mendes in matters relating to the Manila trade.[109] Hansen, Leyel specified, should not act independently, but should rather consult one of Leyel's agents. Mendes most likely belonged to the "Portuguese tribe" that operated outside the control of the *Estado*.[110] Members of "the tribe'", or diaspora, as Halikowski-Smith has pointed out, were central facilitators of the international trade to-and-from Makassar.[111]

As these various reports, instructions, and passports indicate, the environment that Leyel faced in India was demanding: there was no support from Europe, there was a constant shortage of men, and there were serious trading issues with local rulers, often caused by unpaid debts and tributes. Leyel's lack of any direct connection with Europe further aggravated the situation – indeed, it is surprising that the company continued to trade at all. However, despite such challenging circumstances and limited resources, Leyel managed to keep the business afloat. This was possible largely due to his specialised knowledge of intra-Asian trade and management: he issued passports to his subordinates with detailed instructions, and traded in slaves to pay the company debts; he attempted to improve the infrastructure of the company, and allocated materials for repairs; and he personally travelled around the Indian Ocean, attempting to improve the company's business with the locals.

Carloff returns to the coast

Prior to Carloff's arrival on the Gold Coast as an employee of the SAC, an English merchant, Thomas Crispe, had received permission from the Fetu king to establish a trading station at Cape Coast (Cabo Corso).[112] The Fetu people were one of the older Kingdoms on the Cape Coast, being also referred to as Ogu.

Entrepreneurship in the company 75

The king of a larger town or state was called the *Onehe*, and the main officials were known as the *caboceers*.[113] In the Fetu Kingdom, power was divided between the king and his two closest men, the caboceers, the *Braffo* and the *Dey*. The king, who lived on the inland, was mainly responsible for politics and representation. The Braffo was a military commander, whereas the Dey managed finances and trade, and thus lived on the coast adjacent to the European forts, where most of the trade was conducted. In particular, the Cape Coast was one of the main markets for gold on the so-called Gold Coast. Indeed, gold was the main reason for Europeans to trade there. However, the Fetu were mainly fishermen, and offered transportation through their system of canoes.[114] Furthermore, much of the Fetu's trade was done via Elmina castle, which was situated at the border between the Fetu and the neighbouring Kommenda. Elmina had a semi-independent status as a result of Portuguese involvement on the coast, and was an import contact point for the Fetu and the Europeans alike. As such, the Fetu had the advantage of having two important marketplaces in relative proximity to their core region of dwelling. Although the Fetu played an important role as mediators in the gold trade, the Akani people, who lived in the interior, were the main exporters of gold, which they sold on the coast, and especially the Cape Coast. The importance of the gold trade was often noted by contemporaries, such as the Dutch Director-General, Valckenburgh.[115] Although the gold trade became the main reason for the European presence on the Gold Coast, it was not the only thing that Europeans traded; for instance, ivory, wax, and sugar from São Tomé were also in high demand. Although slave trading did occur, it was still of marginal importance during the 1640s.

Between the 1640s and the 1660s, the Fetu Kingdom was represented by the Onehe and two powerful caboceers: John Ahenakwa (Hennequa) and Jan Claessen (Acrosan). During the course of the 1650s, they became the most influential men on the Gold Coast, and when Hennequa died in 1656, Acrosan became *de facto* the most powerful man in the whole region.[116] As such, Acrosan's position is important to understanding Carloff's actions on the coast.

At one point, the relationship between the WIC and Acrosan deteriorated to such an extent that the company had plans to poison him.[117] After the death of the Fetu king, Bodema, the Fetu had tried to make Acrosan the Onehe, but he refused, and instead appointed one of his relatives as the acting king. As king, Acrosan would have lost the position of principal trader and thus significant amounts of money. Furthermore, on several occasions, he functioned as a mediator in European conflicts on the coast, successfully aiming to keep the African markets open to as many Europeans as possible.[118]

From the 1630s onwards, the English had increasingly begun to make their own voyages to the Gold Coast. The patron of the English trade, Nicholas Crispe, who played a role similar to that of Louis de Geer, was one of the earliest African trade capitalists of the 1630s and the 1640s.[119] In April 1650,

76 *Entrepreneurship in the company*

Hennequa gave the English permission to build a house on the coast. According to the English agent Thomas Crispe (a relative of Nicholas Crispe), Carloff, representing the SAC, arrived on the coast only a few days after the English, meeting with Hennequa and Acrosan. The outcome of this meeting was that Carloff was permitted to build another house next to that of the English, which, according to Crispe, violated the agreement that the English had made with the Fetu.[120] Crispe and the WIC Director-General, Henrik Doedens, protested against this decision but in vain. As Carloff himself explained, he had convinced the Fetu officials by offering them more lavish gifts and selling them goods at a lower price than the other Europeans. Furthermore, he also claimed to have purchased intelligence from Hennequa and Acrosan, particularly regarding the state of the WIC and the current market conditions.[121] Apparently, no WIC ships had been sent to the coast in 1648 and 1649; thus, it is possible that Carloff knew about the increasing weakness of the WIC and used this information to his advantage.[122] On 28 May 1650, Carloff signed a contract between the SAC and the King of Fetu – only a few days later than the contract that had been concluded between Crispe and the king.[123] Carloff soon managed to stabilise the SAC position on the coast, and acquired the right to build additional smaller lodges, at Anomabo, Takorari, Butri, Orsu, Jumoree, and Cape Apollonia, as shown in Figure 3.2.

To understand the events that took place around 1650, we must first analyse the period prior to the signing of the contract between Carloff and the Fetu king. During the 1640s, Carloff had worked for the WIC in Western Africa. His position as prosecutor had necessitated much travelling, and he

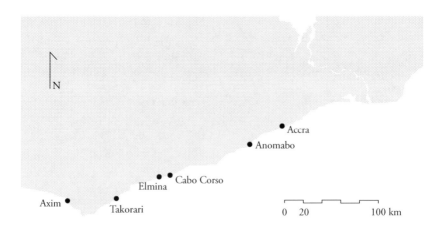

Figure 3.2 Map of the Gold Coast.
Source: Map drawn by Panu Savolainen.

Entrepreneurship in the company 77

had become familiar with the people of the region and their various trading customs. At that time, Carloff had also become aware of the ambitions of the English on the Gold Coast: he knew that Crispe planned to build a fort, but had so far failed to do so, due to competition from the WIC. Indeed, towards the end of the 1640s, the Dutch had once again regained control over the area. The WIC increased the price of the goods it sold to Africans, to such a point that the Fetu refused to pay, and, in 1649, trade came to a standstill.[124] Already in 1647, while still prosecutor for the WIC, Carloff had noted that English expansion on the coast had slowed. Moreover, Robert Porter shows that the Cape Coast had been devoid of Europeans for most of 1648 and the entirety of 1649.[125] As such, the shifting balance of power between the English and the WIC created a space for the SAC to enter the region in 1650.

For their part, the English were not at all pleased by the arrival of the SAC; one agent of the English company stated that the area already belonged to the English, and that the SAC should leave. Furthermore, the English also accused Carloff of being violent, and of having won the support of the Fetu by offering them goods at a lower price than the English.[126] At the same time, the disputes between Carloff and various WIC officials – namely, Henrik Doedens, Arent Cock, Jan Ruychaver, and Jan Valckenburgh – also offer insights into the specialised entrepreneurial strategies that Carloff applied on behalf of the SAC.

The Director-General of the WIC, Arent Cock, was not pleased with Carloff's arrival, and reported having sent the WIC prosecutor, Jan Valckenburgh, to Accra, in order to prevent Carloff from establishing trade there.[127] When the prosecutor returned, he informed Cock that Carloff had arrived in Accra before him, had already visited the local rulers, and had established an excellent relationship with them by providing lavish gifts.[128] Valckenburgh penned a missive of protest to Carloff in Accra on 26 July, in which he accused him of having used the same strategies on the Cape Coast. Valckenburgh claimed that Carloff was seeking to sabotage the WIC, and that he was motivated by his own personal hatred towards the company.[129] Indeed, Director-General Ruychaver confirmed in 1651 that Carloff had already begun to hate the WIC, even before the termination of his contract.[130] Furthermore, Valckenburgh indicated in 1650 that Carloff had also jeopardised the friendly relationship between the Swedish and the Dutch. He added that Carloff, more than anyone else, ought to be aware of the special relationship between the rulers of Accra and the WIC, and to respect the treaties that had been signed in 1643 and 1649 (that is, during the period of Carloff's employment with the WIC).[131] Cock subsequently reported to the directors of the WIC that Carloff had attempted to build a house in Accra, although the local officials of the WIC had succeeded in obstructing him. Seeking an alternative, Carloff had moved to nearby Orsu.[132] For his part, Carloff responded to Valckenburgh's protest in May 1650, arguing that he was sailing under the legal commission of the Swedish Queen, and

78 *Entrepreneurship in the company*

that documents proving this had already been presented to the previous Director-General. Carloff argued that the coastal waters were free to navigate for all, and that the WIC's jurisdiction did not extend beyond the area that it could defend by cannon.[133]

Carloff also knew the trade in Accra; for example, while he had been in the employment of the WIC, he had once travelled inland in order to resolve a dispute between local rulers.[134] Thus, Carloff's past diplomatic service on behalf of the King of Accra enabled him to open up a trading lodge there. The historian Van Dantzig has thus concluded that:

> Although Caerlof in fact did nothing more than establish a number of non-fortified lodges, he opened up new outlets for the African trade and thus laid the basis of a number of new forts, two of which were even to be raised to the status of castle.[135]

Carloff's protest exemplifies the strategies of argument and the experience that he had developed on the coast in his capacity as prosecutor of the WIC; in particular, he knew what to do in order to evade hostile accusations from his previous employers. Moreover, it also demonstrates just how little the WIC officials could do to prevent Carloff (and other competitors) from establishing a foothold in their area of interest.

Carloff was not satisfied with the SAC settling only at Cape Coast. To the contrary, he wanted to expand yet further, and he therefore also took possession of an abandoned WIC lodge at Anomabo, to the east of Cape Coast. After that, he turned towards the Western region of the coast, building small lodges at Takorari, Butri, and Jumoree. These districts had recently been subject to a degree of aggression from the WIC, in that the company had begun to levy a toll on local merchants. This practice had already been introduced by the Portuguese, and many African merchants had in fact welcomed the WIC, since its tolls were less onerous than those of the Portuguese. Now, however, they transferred their allegiance to Carloff, who promised to end the WIC tolls altogether.[136] Indeed, Carloff knew how to approach and establish connections with the coastal societies. Being aware of the weaknesses of the WIC, he turned them to his own advantage. On the African coast, as in Europe, the institutional environment was now propitious for Carloff's entrepreneurship.

In 1651, the newly appointed Director-General of the WIC, Jan Ruychaver (second-term as Director-General), decided to mount an even stronger stand against Carloff. He claimed that Carloff had overstepped his authority on the coast by attacking a WIC ship, harassing its crew, and ignoring the protests issued by the company. Ruychaver considered this disgraceful, stating that Carloff was devoid of all honour, and that he had ruined his own reputation.[137] However, two days later, Ruychaver sent another letter of protest to Carloff, this time in more moderate tones. Here, he claimed that he had nothing against Carloff and his subordinates personally but merely wished

Entrepreneurship in the company 79

to handle all matters on the coast according to the dictates of protocol and decency. Moreover, he also stated that he wanted to maintain his friendship with Carloff and the SAC, and even offered some slaves as a sign of friendship.[138] One cannot help wondering how this sudden change occurred. Ruychaver and Carloff were certainly known to each other. After all, it was Ruychaver who had appointed Carloff as the prosecutor of the WIC.

Regarding the confiscation of the ship, Carloff replied to have evidence showing that it did not fall under the jurisdiction of the WIC. Indeed, he continued, he could prove that both the ship and its cargo belonged to various Dutch, French, and Swedish proprietors. As such, the ship had departed from Texel without the appropriate documents.[139] Once again, it is clear that Carloff was here applying the methods that he had learnt at the WIC; particularly important were his references to the right to trade, the origin of the ships, the ownership of the cargo, and whether the official paperwork was in order. By these means, Carloff justified his actions and demonstrated his power.

From a broader coastal perspective, however, this intra-European quarrel had little significance. What really mattered were the connections between the Europeans and the African authorities, and the inner tensions within the company administration. Despite the existence of competitors, the SAC had managed to establish itself on the coast, and the other European powers had more or less accepted its presence. When Carloff left for Sweden in 1652, his position was precarious: he was the second largest investor in the company, and the commander of operations at its outpost. However, new appointments to the SAC administration in Europe would soon throw the internal politics of the company at Cape Coast into disarray.

In October 1653, the SAC appointed Jan Daniel Rosa as company prosecutor for a period of three years.[140] It seems that the intention was to then appoint Rosa as governor when his term as prosecutor ended. When Carloff left for Europe in 1652, he had been succeeded by Isaac Mivilla, but suddenly, in July 1654, Mivilla died, prompting a breakdown of organisation on the coast.[141] Rosa, who at the time of Mivilla's death was in Takorari, feared that he would miss out on the now vacant position of governor. When he attempted to re-enter Cape Coast, planning to seize the governorship, he was informed that the position had already been filled.[142] Indeed, another employee of the SAC, Joost Cramer (also a former WIC employee), had already been appointed. Furthermore, the WIC had already recognised the appointment: a WIC official, Loys Dammert, had acknowledged the death of Milvilla and congratulated Cramer on his selection.[143]

However, Cramer's governorship did not last for long. In August 1655, the SAC directors in Europe decided to send a new governor, Johann Philip von Krusenstierna.[144] Cramer remained vice-governor, but additional Swedish officials were now recruited, in the hope of bringing about a more organic connection between the company and its Swedish sponsors. Significantly, Nováky has stressed that none of these new officials had prior experience in

80 *Entrepreneurship in the company*

West African trade.[145] Thus, despite such new recruitment, many of the key positions on the coast remained in the hands of Dutchmen and Germans who did have such experience, Joost Cramer and Sigmund Jeunisch being the most prominent examples.[146]

This duality in the structure of the organisation on the coast created tension among those in the service of the company. While Cramer was governor (1654–1655), and later vice-governor, he and Carloff operated a smuggling network. A ship returning to Europe had been inspected by company officials, who had discovered gold worth 300 marks belonging to Carloff and his business associates. The gold was confiscated, by the same Rosa who had earlier missed out on the position of governor. Carloff's associates in this venture were a captain of the SAC, Alexander Loncq, his brother, the skipper Frans Gijsbertsen, and Cramer, at that time acting vice-governor. Following the confiscation, the company kept the gold, although Carloff was compensated for the goods that had been sent from Europe to Africa.[147] Notably, Nováky's research has elucidated these episodes. In 1656, Loncq had been accused of bringing cargo from Europe to Africa without the directors' knowledge, an activity in which Cramer had also been implicated.[148] Loys Dammert noted that when Cramer left Western Africa, he had obtained gold to the value of 27,000 guilders through private trading.[149] In a later investigation, this valuation was increased to 35,000 guilders, a truly remarkable sum, which clearly demonstrates the gains to be made through private trading in gold.[150] The trading activities in which Carloff participated thus had a considerable impact upon his relationship with the company. He argued in a letter to the president of the Board of Commerce, Christer Bonde, that he had been prevented from contacting Krustenstierna before his departure for the Gold Coast in 1655.[151] This was due to the fact that the other directors in Europe were already aware of the smuggling network that Carloff was operating. Nováky has thus suggested that there were two factions in the SAC. On the one side, there were Krusenstierna, Rosa, and their supporters, who remained loyal to the SAC directors in Europe. On the other side, there were the supporters of Carloff and Cramer, consisting largely of those officials most committed to continuing their own private trade alongside that of the company.[152]

The gold trade also helps to explain why Carloff wanted the SAC to establish itself at Cape Coast. After all, the latter was a major market for gold. In addition, the standing of the WIC there was in decline, and Carloff still had many valuable contacts from his time in the WIC. Therefore, despite his smuggling activities, the company still allowed Carloff to stay on. This can be explained by reference to the opportunities that his presence supplied: after all, he had the knowledge of the markets overseas, and knew how to navigate the complex competition between the different European powers. Moreover, he was also able to handle the competition and conflicts between the various African rulers and their representatives, as has been illustrated above. Furthermore, the directors also knew that if Carloff did not remain

Entrepreneurship in the company 81

in the company, he would probably offer his services to its competitors. Nevertheless, his controversial behaviour illustrates the challenges that the companies faced in attempting to access local markets. Although Carloff used his knowledge and skills to open up African markets for the company, his loyalty was conditional upon being allowed to privately accumulate capital. His partnership with de Geer provides an illustration of the entrepreneurial strategies pursued within this institutional environment. Thus, rapid shifts of institutional loyalty ought not to be considered exceptional but rather as an entirely normal strategy within seventeenth-century business.

Conclusion

The DEIC and the SAC were vehicles for the commercial expansion of the Nordic kingdoms. They hired individual entrepreneurs to direct their overseas endeavours, incorporating them into the company hierarchy. The DEIC and the SAC were obliged to pay tributes to local rulers, including lavish gifts, in order to access local markets, as were other companies. As such, it made sense to employ men who already knew how to operate in these regions. Leyel and Carloff attained a strong position within the companies in Europe and overseas, a fact that highlights the shortage of experienced and knowledgeable employees within the Nordic companies.

However, Leyel and Carloff also differed in the ways in which they participated in the Nordic companies. While they both had to deal with competitors, Carloff's main focus was to break the strong position of the WIC, whereas Leyel faced primarily internal problems within the DEIC itself. Carloff preferred to negotiate personally with his African counterparts, whereas Leyel used brokers. This difference was not inherent to the different trading mechanisms in the Atlantic and the Indian Ocean, but rather a personal choice, indicating different individual approaches.

In Chapter 2, it was shown that individuals needed the companies, at least in the Nordic context. In the current chapter, it is shown that the companies also need the individuals, and that this gave the latter considerable leeway in their activities. Mark and Catherine Casson point out that in early modern business history, the focus is still mainly on the firm as a managerial unit. Thus, they argue that "there needs to be more emphasis on identifying the individual entrepreneurs within the firms and analysing their influence in the decision making."[153]

Indeed, certain individuals were able to operate almost independently at the outposts. They took decisions on the ground regarding company business and, simultaneously, profited from the trade themselves. Most importantly, they coordinated the activities of the company overseas, using their knowledge of the local context to their own benefit. Thus, as Subrahmanyam has demonstrated, the best way to understand the DEIC is as a form of private trade in the Indian Ocean. This argument holds true in the case of Leyel as well as in the case of Carloff, given that the changing political

82 *Entrepreneurship in the company*

and trading patterns on the Gold Coast depended more on the decisions of individuals than on the ambitions of the directors in Europe.

The organisational environment could be both a blessing and a curse for entrepreneurship. Leyel was forced to make the Indian Ocean trade work without reinforcements from Europe. Ultimately, he succeeded in remaining active in Ceylon and Makassar, despite numerous institutional setbacks. Carloff, on the other hand, was mobile throughout his Swedish employment and enjoyed a rather unique position. He represented an asset that the company needed in order to access trade on the Western coast of Africa. However, his opportunities for professional advancement diminished as the company become more closely tied to the Swedish state and the domestic Swedish elite. As the organisational environment changed, Carloff encountered increasing hindrances to independent action. At the same time, the complaints that the WIC made against Carloff demonstrate that organisations were under constant pressure from individuals, who were able to manipulate the political and economic context to their own advantage. Indeed, this is why competing trading companies were willing to pay a premium for their services.

Notes

1 Mark Casson and Marina Della Giusta, "Entrepreneurship and Social Capital," 223.
2 Casson and Casson, "The History of Entrepreneurship," 1224; Casson, *Entrepreneurship*, 11.
3 Ole Feldbæk, "The Danish Trading Companies of the Seventeenth and Eighteenth Centuries," *Scandinavian Economic History Review* 34, no. 3 (1986): 204–218, 205.
4 Sanjay Subrahmanyam, "The Coromandel Trade of the Danish East India Company, 1618–1649," *Scandinavian Economic History Review* 37, no. 1 (1989): 41–56.
5 Ibid., 56.
6 Similarly in Kriger, *Kaufleute*, 230–231.
7 Ole Feldbæk, "The Danish Trading Companies," 206.
8 Ibid.
9 Krieger, *Kaufleute*, 231–232.
10 Larsen, *Guvernører*, 60.
11 See previous chapter for more detailed discussion.
12 In practice, the King invested even more. Some 5,000 riksdalers of his shares were actually invested by his son, Christian Ulrich Gyldenløve, and 1,500 riksdalers by his mistress, Kirsten Munk. The nobility invested 27,000 riksdalers, out of which Albert Skeel owned the largest share, worth 3,400 riksdalers. Erik Grubbe (2,500 riksdalers) and Holger Rosenkrantz (1,250 riksdalers) were also significant contributors. The rest of the participants consisted of professors and the Copenhagen political elite, such as the mayor. Citizens like Jakob Michelsen, Reinholdt Hansen, Jørgen Danielsen, Simon Surbeck, Mikkel Vibe, and Peter Andersen owned shares between 300 and 2,000 riksdalers. Jan and David de Willum invested 10,500 riksdalers together. These Dutch brothers had probably been naturalised Danish by this point. Willerslev, "Danmarks første aktieselskab," 622–625.

Entrepreneurship in the company 83

13 Ibid., 625.
14 Ibid., 623–628.
15 Ibid., 610; Feldbæk, *Danske Handelskompagnier 1616–1843,* 25–34 and 489–494.
16 Jan Rindom, "Ostindisk Kompagni 1616–50 – et Spørgsmål om organisatorisk udvikling og interne magtkampe," *Årbog | Handels- og søfartsmuseet på kronborg* 59 (2000): 99–125, 106.
17 Ibid., 107.
18 *Kancelliets brevbøger,* 1624–26, 570; *Kancelliets brevbøger* 1635–36, 138; Willerslev, "Danmarks første aktieselskab," 629.
19 Jan Rindom, "Ostindisk Kompagni," 110.
20 "hovedbeskærmer og største participant" Willerslev, "Danmarks første aktieselskab," 632.
21 *Kancelliets brevbøger,* 1635–1636, 255 and 714.
22 Ibid., 450; Willerslev, "Danmarks første aktieselskab," 633.
23 Rindom, "Ostindisk Kompagni," 108.
24 For additional information about the investments of Carloff in the SAC, see VLA (Vadstena Landsarkiv) FBA (Finspångsbruk Arkiv) inv.nr.62A. I would like to thank the Vadstena Landsarkiv for being helpful with accessing the sources.
25 About the business of de Geer, see Dahlgren, *Louis de Geer;* Lindblad, "Louis de Geer."
26 Nováky, *Handelskompanier,* 76. Also see previous chapter.
27 Severin Bergh, ed., *Svenska Riksrådets Protokoll* (RP), vol. XI: 1645–1646 (Stockholm: Norstedt & Söner, 1906), RP, 19.01.1946.
28 Nováky, *Handelskompanier,* 81; Dahlgren, *Louis de Geer,* 334.
29 Carloff declaration, 12.10.1662; NL-HaNA, Staten-Generaal, 1.01.02, inv.nr. *12572.41*; printed in De Roever, "Twee Concurrenten."
30 This is confirmed by an Account book of de Geer. VLA, FBA, inv.nr.62A.
31 Carloff declaration, 12.10.1662, Carloff declaration 12.10.1662, NL-HaNA, Staten-Generaal, 1.01.02, inv.nr. *12572.41*; De Roever, "Twee Concurrenten van de Eerste West-Indische Compagnie"; confirmed by the information in VLA FBA inv.nr.62A.
32 Carloff declaration 12.10.1662, NL-HaNA, Staten-Generaal, 1.01.02, inv.nr. *12572.41*; printed in: De Roever, "Twee Concurrenten."
33 SAA NA: 875, fol.315, 12.10.1649.
34 Dahlgren, *Louis de Geer,* 338.
35 Ibid.
36 The actual date of the marriage is unknown. On the marriage, see Heijer, "Een dienaar," 175.
37 RAS, LA 10, Correspondance with Jan Wolzogen, 1647, 55, 56; Correspondance between Wolzogen and de Geer, Louis de Geer, *Louis de Geers brev och affärshandlingar 1614–1652,* ed. Erik Wilhelm Dahlgren (Stockholm: P.A. Norstedt & Söner, 1934). October 1641, August 1648 and March 1651; Heijer, "Een dienaar," 175–177.
38 RAS, LA 111, Räkenskaper, C), Henrich Carloff and D) Jan Wolzogen accounts.
39 RAS LA 82, Power of Attorney, Christina to Carloff, undated. See also Nováky, *Handelskompanier,* 88; RAS, Riksregistraturen (RR) shows that there was a letter sent 20.11.1649, but I did not find the actual letter, only the register.
40 Swedish: Kommerskollegiet.
41 The Board was the central Swedish economic body during the seventeenth century. Its first presidents were Johan Bernds, Erik Oxenstierna, and Christer Bonde. In 1652, after the death of Johan Bernds, Erik Oxenstierna, who was also the governor of Reval, was appointed president. He was the son of Chancellor Axel Oxenstierna and Anna Bååt (another prominent Swedish noble

84 *Entrepreneurship in the company*

family). Erik Oxenstierna himself was married to Elsa Brahe, whose family also invested in the Swedish Africa Company. Nováky has shown that there was also another direct link to de Geer through Erik Oxenstierna. One of Erik Oxenstierna's advisors for war, trade, and politics was Lars Broman, who was also the brother-in-law of Arent Gabbesen. In 1645, he was in Amsterdam to meet various merchants. He was investigating whether there would be interest in a company based in Gothenburg. However, these plans were not realised. Erik eventually succeeded his father as chancellor in 1654, and was succeeded by Christer Bonde in the Board of Commerce. Nováky, *Handelskompanier*, 162–163 and 176–180; Gerentz, *Kommerskollegium*, 36–42.

42 The brother of Peter Coyet was Frederick Coyet, the commander of the VOC in Formosa.

43 Material about the investors and their role in the company in, RAS, H&S, vol. 45.

44 The secretary of the board, Johan Rising, had studied in the Dutch Republic. In 1653, he was sent as governor to New Sweden. He became the last governor of the Swedish settlement, Gerentz, *Kommerskollegium*, 36–37; on the investors in the companies, see Dahlgren, *Louis de Geer*, 337.

45 Nováky, *Handelskompanier*, 191.

46 Gerentz, *Kommerskollegium*, 43.

47 Carloff and three SAC ships were captured by the English navy at the entrance to the English Channel, being suspected of sailing with false papers. The English accused the Swedish ships of not really being Swedish but rather Dutch. The return voyage took place at the height of the First Anglo-Dutch War (1652–1654), and the English were keen to harm Dutch interests. Carloff and the SAC ships fell victim to this policy. After several petitions by Carloff and appeals by the Swedish queen, the ships and their cargo were released. Carloff Declaration 12.10.1662, Carloff declaration, 12.10.1662, NL-HaNA, Staten-Generaal, 1.01.02, inv.nr. *12572.41*; De Roever, "Twee Concurrenten"; Dahlgren, *Louis de Geer*, 342–343.

48 Kommerskollegium, Huvudarkivet (KKA), Protokoll, 1651–1654, A1 AA:1, protocol, 11.08.1654; Nováky, *Handelskompanier*, 163; Dahlgren, *Louis de Geer*, 346–348.

49 Nováky, *Handelskompanier*, 191; Bulstrode Whitelocke, *Journal of the Swedish Embassy in the Years 1653 and 1654*, ed. Henry Reeve (London: Longman, Brown, Green and Longmans, 1855), 6 May 1654, 200 (name: carloe), I have used the online the version; www.gutenberg.org/files/17407/17407-h/17407-h. htm (accessed 21 February 2018).

50 There are several documents related to the negotiations between the English and the Swedish about the Africa trade, Uppsala Universitets Bibliotek (UUB), N430. For a closer reading of the plans, see Nováky, *Handelskompanier*, 186–190.

51 For the most recent study of early English trade in Africa, see Julie Mo Svalastog, "Mastering the Worst of Trades: England's Early Africa Companies and Their Traders, 1618–1672" (PhD dissertation, Leiden: Leiden University, 2018); Porter, *European Activity*, 106–163, 219–278, 362–470; Roper, *Advancing Empire*.

52 In Swedish, *hufvudparticipant*.

53 Granlund, *En svensk koloni i Afrika*, appendix 3.

54 Nováky has compiled a useful list from the Swedish national archives: Nováky, *Handelskompanier*, 175.

55 Mirkka Lappalainen, *Suku, valta, suurvalta. Creutzit 1600-luvun Ruotsissa ja Suomessa* (Helsinki: WSOY, 2005), 45.

56 Nováky, *Handelskompanier*, 178.

Entrepreneurship in the company 85

57 Bernhard Schlegel and Carl Arvid Klingspor, *Den med sköldebref förlänade men ej å riddarhuset introducerade svenska adelns ättartaflor* (Stockholm, 1875).
58 Nováky, *Handelskompanier*, 164.
59 RAC, DK, B 246 A, Leyel to the directors, 22.11.1644; Bredsdorff, *The Trials and Travels*, 91.
60 RAC, DK, B 246 A, Leyel to the diretors, 22.11.1644.
61 Larsen, *Dansk-Ostindiske koloniers historie*, 32.
62 RAC, DK, B 246 A, Leyel to the diretors, 22.11.1644.
63 "wi maa roe med de aarer wy haffuer," RAC, DK, B 246 A, Leyel to the directors, 22.11.1644.
64 Ibid., 27.
65 There will be more about this transition in Chapter 4.
66 "Wat het uijteijnde van desen Leijel sijn bedrijf wesen sal leert den tijt," H.T. Colenbrander, ed., *Dagh-register gehouden int casteel Batavia vant passerende daer ter plaetse als over geheel Nederlandts-India: 1643–1644* (Gravenhage: Martinus Nijhoff, 1902), July 1644: 129.
67 RAC, DK, B 246 A, Leyel to the diretors, 12.12.1645.
68 Ibid.
69 RAC, DK, B 246 A, Leyel to P. Hansen, 17.09.1646.
70 RAC, DK, B 246 A, Leyel to the diretors, 22.11.1644.
71 Larsen, *Dansk-Ostindiske koloniers historie*, 24.
72 Leyel used the word "bequomme pershoner," which I translate to capable people.
73 RAC, DK, B 246 A, Leyel to P. Nielsen, 20.10.1645.
74 RAC, DK, B 246 A, Leyel to the directors, 22.11.1644.
75 Joseph J. Brennig, "Chief Merchants and the European Enclaves of Seventeenth-Century Coromandel," *Modern Asian Studies* 11, no. 3 (1977): 321–40, 322–323.
76 Daniel Jeyaraj, *Bartholomäus Ziegenbalg, the Father of Modern Protestant Mission: An Indian Assessment*, 20 (New Delhi: ISPCK, 2006); Radhika Seshan, *Trade and Politics on the Coromandel Coast: Seventeenth and Early Eighteenth Centuries* (Delhi: Primus Books, 2012), 30–32 and 42–43.
77 RAC, DK, B 246 A, Leyel to A. Nielsen, 3.03.1645.
78 RAC, DK, B 246 A, Leyel to P. Nielsen, 20.10.1645.
79 RAC, DK, B 246 A, A. Nielsen to Leyel, 23.03.1645; Bredsdorff, *The Trials and Travels*, 146.
80 RAC, DK, B 246 A, Leyel to the directors, 22.11.1644; Bredsdorff, *The Trials and Travels*, 130 and 136.
81 Seshan has written about the importance of the textile trade for the Europeans established on the Coromandel Coast. See Seshan *Trade and Politics*, 13–15.
82 Raychaudhuri, *Jan Company in Coromandel*, 113.
83 RAC, DK, B 246 A, Leyel to the directors, 22.11.1644.
84 Cutiara was also known as Koddiyaar and Cotiaar. It was located south of Trincomalee on Ceylon.
85 RAC, DK, B 246 A, Leyel to A. Jacobsen, 26.07.1644; Leyel also mentioned the sending of Adrian Jacobsen to the directors in a second report. RAC, DK, B 246 A, Leyel to the directors, 12.12.1645.
86 According to Bredsdorff, Jacobsen returned in October, having concluded the agreement with the King of Candy. I was not, however, able to date his arrival from the letters by Nielsen.
87 RAC, DK, B 246 A, Leyel to the directors, 12.12.1645.
88 There is only scattered information about Josias Stael in the archives.
89 RAC, DK, B 246 A, Leyel to J. Stael, 19.12.1647.

86   Entrepreneurship in the company

90 RAC, DK, B 246 A, Leyel to J. Hansen, 24 May 1647 and Leyel to N. Samson, 24 May 1647.
91 Stefan Halikowski Smith, *Creolization and Diaspora in the Portuguese Indies: The Social World of Ayutthaya, 1640–1720* (Boston/Leiden: Brill, 2011), 39.
92 RAC, DK, B 246 A, Leyel to the directors, 12.12.1645.
93 RAC, DK, B 246 A, Leyel to the directors, 15.11.1646.
94 Smith, *Creolization and Diaspora*, 39–40.
95 RAC, DK, B 246 A, Leyel to the king, 12.12.1645; Bredsdorff, *The Trials and Travels*, 158.
96 Martin Krieger has written about the Danish slave trade in the Indian Ocean. See Martin Krieger, "Der Dänische Sklavenhandel auf dem Indischen Ozean im 17. Und 18. Jahrhundert," in *Jahrbuch für Europäische Überseegeschichte*, vol. 12 (Wiesbaden: Harrassowitz Verlag, 2012), 9–30.
97 Rila Mukherjee, "Portuguese Slave Ports in Bengal 1500–1700," in *Seaports in the First Global Age Portuguese Agents, Networks and Interactions (1500–1800)*, ed. Cátia Antunes and Amelia Polónia (Porto: Uporto Edições, 2016), 221–41, 221–224.
98 RAC, DK, B 246 A, Leyel to H. Ekman, 21.09.1646.
99 RAC, DK, B 246 A, Leyer to J. Hansen, 19.02.1647.
100 A sea letter was a certificate issued by a maritime power to neutral merchant vessels during times of war, granting them permission to sail in the Indian Ocean. The document vouched for the neutrality of the vessel, guaranteeing that it would be allowed to continue its journey unharmed, especially if it encountered the naval forces of the issuing state.
101 Raychaudhuri, *Jan Company in Coromandel,* 96 and 119–123. About patrolling, Seshan, *Trade and Politics*, 23.
102 Jürgen Osterhammel has argued that *"a viceroy* [can be] *loosely defined as the head of the political hierarchy in a given territorial unit at the periphery."* According to Osterhammel, the viceroy represented the king at the local level, and was, in most cases, responsible for the specialised tasks of imperial crisis management. With regard to the VOC, use of the term "viceroy" might seem problematic, given that there was no king. Nevertheless, the function of the VOC *gouverneur-general* was broadly similar. While the VOC used the term *gouverneur-general*, the EIC used the term *proconsul*, and the Danish referred to the *commander.* See Jürgen Osterhammel, "The Imperial Viceroy: Reflections on an Historical Type," in *The Dynastic Centre and the Provinces: Agents and Interactions*, ed. Jeroen Duindam and Sabrine Dabringhaus (Boston/Leiden: Brill, 2014), 13–29, 20.
103 RAC, DK, B 247 B, Leyel Passport, 19.09.1645.
104 I will return to the topic of gifts in the next chapter.
105 RAC, DK, B 246 A, Leyel to P. Nielsen, 20.10.1645.
106 RAC, DK, B 246 A, Leyel to A. Nielsen, 1.02.1647.
107 RAC, DK, B 246 A, Leyel to A. Nielsen, 4.09.1644.
108 RAC, DK, B 246 A, Leyel to A. Jacobsen, 26.07.1644.
109 RAC, DK, B 246 A, Leyel to A. Nielsen, 1.02.1647.
110 Smith, *Creolization and Diaspora*; George Winius, "The 'Shadow Empire' of Goa in the Bay of Bengal," *Itinerario* 7, no. 2 (1983): 83–101; Sanjay Subrahmanyam, *The Political Economy of Commerce: Southern India 1500–1650* (Cambridge: Cambridge University Press, 2002).
111 Smith, *Creolization and Diaspora*, 39–40.
112 Van Dantzig, *Forts and Castles*, 24; Porter, *European Activity*, 296–297.
113 Porter, *European Activity*, 38.
114 Ibid., 42; Robin Law, "Between the Sea and the Lagoons: The Interaction of Maritime and Inland Navigation on the Precolonial Slave Coast (Entre Mer et Lagune: Les Interactions de la Navigation Maritime et Continentale sur la

Côte Des Esclaves avant la Colonisation)," *Cahiers d'Études Africaines* 29, no. 114 (1989): 209–237.

115 Valckenburgh mentioned the importance of gold several times in a report from 1659 (De Jonge gives the year as 1656, but this is mistaken), Cornelis De Jonge, *De Oorsprong van Nederland's Bezittingen op de Kust van Guinea* (Gravenhage: Martinus Nijhoff, 1871), 51–69.

116 Daaku, *Trade and Politics*, 107.

117 Brieven, confessie; mitsgaders, advisen van verscheyden rechtsgeleerden in de saeck van Isaac Coymans gegeven; als mede de sententie daer op gevolgt (Rotterdam 1662), 25.03.1660; W.B. Den Blanken, "Imperium in Imperio Sovereign Powers of the First Dutch West India Company" (M.A. Dissertation – Leiden University, 2014), 40.

118 Ibid.

119 On the English advancement in Western Africa, see Porter, *European Activity*, 118–140.

120 London, National Archives, HCA (High court of Admiralty) 24/111, no.182, declaration by Thomas Crispe; I would like to thank Julie Mo Svalastog for providing this source.

121 Carloff declaration, 12.10.1662, Carloff declaration 12.10.1662, NL-HaNA, Staten-Generaal, 1.01.02, inv.nr. *12572.41, printed in* De Roever, "Twee Concurrenten."

122 Dahlgren, *Louis de Geer*, 336.

123 NL-HaNa, OWIC, 1.05.01.01, inv.nr. *13A*, Contract, Carloff – King of Fetu, 28.05.1650, file: 512–514 (scans 514–516).

124 Nørregård, *Danish Settlements*, 10.

125 NL-HaNa, OWIC, 1.05.01.01, inv.nr *11*, Henrich Carloff to Heeren XIX, 26.09.1647 (scans 686–695); FC, N4, 179–185; Porter, *European Activity*, 294.

126 London, National Archives, HCA (High court of Admiralty) 24/111, no.182, declaration by Thomas Crispe (I would like to thank Julie Mo Svalastog for providing me this source); NL-HaNA, Staten-Generaal, 1.01.02, inv.nr. *12571.38.1,* Arent Cock to the Heeren XIX, 13.10.1650; FC, N5, 85.

127 The previous Director-General Henrik Doedens was succeeded by Arent Cock in summer 1650, Nováky, *Handelskompanier*, 101.

128 NL-HaNA, Staten-Generaal, 1.01.02, inv.nr. *12571.38.1,* Arent Cock to the Heeren XIX, 13.10.1650; FC, N5, 85.

129 NL-HaNA, Staten-Generaal, 1.01.02, inv.nr. *12571.38.1,* Jan Valckenburgh to Henrich Carloff, 26.07.1650; FC, N5, 86–88.

130 NL-HaNa, OWIC, 1.05.01.01, inv.nr. *13A*, Jan Ruychaver to Henrich Carloff, 10.07.1651, file.124–134 (scans 126–136,); FC, N5, 118–121.

131 NL-HaNa, OWIC, 1.05.01.01, inv.nr. *13A*, Jan Valckenburgh to Henrich Carloff, 28.07.1650, file.115–119 (scans 117–121); FC, N5, 96.

132 NL-HaNA, Staten-Generaal, 1.01.02, inv.nr. *12571.38.1*, Arent Cock to the Heeren XIX, 13.10.1650; FC, N5, 89.

133 NL-HaNa, OWIC, 1.05.01.01, inv.nr. *13A*, Henrich Carloff to the Heeren XIX, May 1650, file: 504–507 (scans 506–509); FC, N5, 90.

134 Klaas Ratelband, *Vijf Dagregisters*, 16.11.1646, 262; Heijer, "Een dienaar," 166.

135 Van Dantzig, *Forts and Castles*, 24.

136 Van Dantzig, *Forts and Castles*, 18; Nørregård, *Danish Settlements*, 10.

137 NL-HaNa, OWIC, 1.05.01.01, inv.nr. *13A*, Jan Ruychaver to Henrich Carloff, 10.07.1651, file, 124–134 (scans 126–136); FC, N5, 118–121.

138 NL-HaNa, OWIC, 1.05.01.01, inv.nr. *13A*, Jan Ruychaer to Henrich Carloff, 13.07.1651, file, 140–142 (scans 142–144); FC, N5, 123.

139 NL-HaNa, OWIC, 1.05.01.01, inv.nr. *13A*, Henrich Carloff to Jan Ruychaver, 14.07.1651, file, 142–149 (scans 144–151); FC, N5, 124.

88   *Entrepreneurship in the company*

140 Ibid., 167. A notary statement from around the same time indicates that Rosa was actually hired as head merchant of the company. SAA NA: 875, fol. 170, 09.10.1653. "opperkoopman." In the Amsterdam notarial archives, there are several entries between 1647 and 1661 regarding the business partnership between de Geer and Rosa.
141 Nováky, *Handelskompanier,* 166–167.
142 SAA NA: 870, fol.147, 29.08.1656; SAA NA: 878, fol. 170, 9.10.1653; SAA NA: 879, fol. 148, 29.08.1656; Nováky, *Handelskompanier*, 168.
143 NL-HaNa, OWIC, 1.05.01.01, inv. nr. *47*, Loy Dammerts Journal, 10.07.1654, 13.07.1654, 14.07.1654; Nováky, *Handelskompanier*, 168.
144 Although an experienced trader, Krusenstierna was not familiar with the Guinea coast. He was a close associate and advisor of Erik Oxenstierna, which suggests that the Board of Commerce in Sweden might have been trying to influence the trajectory of the company in Africa.
145 Ibid., 169.
146 Ibid.
147 Nováky, *Handelskompanier*, 172.
148 NL-HaNa, OWIC, 1.05.01.01, inv. nr. *47*, Loy Dammerts Journal, 29.05.1655; Nováky, *Handelskompanier*, 173. A notarial deed from 1657 reveals that Jean Neumann (probably Hans Neumann) had served under Laurens de Geer, and had thus been in Swedish employment. He had been on the coast in January 1657, as was Joost Cramer. According to Neumann, Governor Krusenstierna had asked Cramer whether he knew that skipper Alexander Loncq had been trading for his own benefit. SAA NA: 880, fol.88, 30.07.1657; UUB N 430 fol 309, Joachim Pötter, 22.12.1656.
149 NL-HaNa, OWIC, 1.05.01.01, inv. nr. *47*, Loy Dammerts Journal, 29.05.1655.
150 Nováky, *Handelskompanier*, 173.
151 RAS, H&S, 42, Henrich Carloff to Christer Bonde, 21.02.1657.
152 Nováky, *Handelskompanier*, 168.
153 Casson and Casson, "The History of Entrepreneurship," 1223.

4 The vulnerability of being connected

Introduction

Although the study of entrepreneurship is a study of individuals, this does not mean that the world surrounding individuals is unimportant. On the contrary, as has been argued by Leos Müller, Clé Lesger, and Luuc Kooijmans, also early modern entrepreneurship was always socially embedded.[1] In this sense, the connections and relationships that individuals maintained both in Europe and overseas can shed light on the social side of overseas business. The cases analysed in this chapter demonstrate that although Leyel and Carloff represented trading companies, the business that they did locally was always determined by the individual relationships and connections they maintained. This chapter argues that overseas entrepreneurship thus required individuals to balance simultaneously between different competing and cooperative networks.

When individuals engaged in the social hierarchies of business, they put themselves in a vulnerable position. Engagement via social relationships meant that individuals stood to both win and lose. As such, networks can be considered as relationships of exchange: collaborating with certain actors might result in exclusion from other networks; assuming a dominant role might empower a person, but might also expose the same person to tension with other members of the network.[2]

This chapter argues that overseas business involved far more than simply managing trade exchanges from the top down. In particular, it investigates the power relations in which individuals participated overseas. From the perspective of entrepreneurship, it did not matter whether one was employed in the Asian or the Atlantic trade; the challenges of balancing between various interest groups remained the same. There was an incessant pushing and tugging between different networks. Thus, when a social perspective on overseas entrepreneurship is applied, it becomes clear why individuals struggled to survive and why their entire careers revolved around uncertainty.

Leyel's relationships within the company

Leyel held the highest position within the DEIC, having sole responsibility for how the business was managed in Asia. Despite his high official position, however, he faced a different reality at the local level. Indeed, he arrived at Dansborg without knowing how the company's condition and relationships then stood. It was obvious that not everyone in the company was happy with the new commander, who arrived bearing new regulations and his own personal ambitions. For Leyel, this meant that he had to deal with already existing personal relationships between employees, as well as to establish his own relationships with his subordinates. The relationships that Leyel developed within the company in Asia were initially strongly linked to his predecessor Barent Pessart. The original reason for Leyel's departure for India was to investigate the state of the company, since Europe had heard nothing from Pessart for some time. Leyel demanded that Pessart send a report regarding the state of affairs in Asia, which he failed to do.[3] Leyel immediately went to great lengths to demonstrate Pessart's disobedience, and reported that he had been shocked upon arrival, particularly due to the decadent behaviour and heavy drinking of the company employees. Leyel doubted Pessart's administrative capacity and especially condemned his thirst for alcohol. Leyel outlined his concern that Pessart would seek to evade his duties and rob the company of its goods, leaving Leyel empty-handed. Since they were supposed to share the command of operations, Leyel had decided to keep a close eye on Pessart. While still sharing command, both men sailed to Masulipatnam in order to trade the goods that Leyel had brought from Europe.[4] During the trip to Masulipatnam, Leyel realised that a conflict was inevitable.[5]

Upon arrival at Masulipatnam, Leyel experienced problems with the locals, apparently, at least in part, due to the credit of the company having been exhausted by Pessart's outstanding debts. Pessart owed his creditors over 100,000 riksdalers, and although it was common for Europeans to borrow money there, Pessart had never repaid his debts. Unfortunately, Leyel did not specify whether Pessart's loans were personal or made in the name of the company. Pessart had apparently taken credit from several merchants and *moors* (i.e. Muslims) in Masulipatnam. This money had not been used to improve the trade of the DEIC, which suggests that it was rather intended for Pessart's private use. Due to these debts, no further credit could be obtained from the lenders concerned. Although loans were sometimes made to individual employees, companies still had to trade on the same markets, and were often called to stand as guarantors when the employees failed to pay their debts. In practice, companies were often forced to pay someone else's debts, either through repayment of loans or through gifts to local rulers and merchants.[6]

The hostile reception encountered at Masulipatnam forced Leyel and the DEIC ships to continue to Emeldy in the Kingdom of Golconda.[7] Leyel

The vulnerability of being connected 91

soon realised that Pessart, his skipper Michell Kroutsen, and several other crew members had planned to escape with the ship *Wahlby* and a large *shalup*. They eventually succeeded, despite Leyel's attempts to stop them.[8]

Leyel sent a messenger to the acting governor of Dansborg, Jakob von Stakenborrig, explaining the incident that had occurred at Masulipatnam and stating that he was on his way to Tranquebar. Moreover, Leyel demanded that Pessart be arrested if he appeared at Dansborg. However, Leyel's messenger was intercepted by Pessart, who had spent fourteen days at São Tomé of Meliapor.[9] Concerned with what Leyel might do to him, Pessart had been expecting a messenger, lay in wait for him, beat him up, and confiscated Leyel's letter.[10] Ultimately, Leyel was able to contact Stakenborrig by other means. In his second letter, Leyel declared that Pessart's command should be terminated, but that other employees should be forgiven. He insisted that he had the Nayak's support, and that therefore Stakenborrig had no choice but to arrest Pessart.[11] Promising the other employees that they would not be held responsible for Pessart's conduct was Leyel's way of gaining the support of the employees at Dansborg. However, the latter refused Leyel's command, stating that they had no obligation to assist in this matter, since they were already working in the interest of the Danish crown.[12] Moreover, it is unclear whether Leyel really had the Nayak's support, since he had not been in Tranquebar long enough to send a proper embassy to his court; in fact, at this point, Leyel hardly knew how bad his situation was.

When Leyel was in sight of Tranquebar, he requested that Governor Stakenborrig send supplies to the ship. However, he was denied not only supplies but also assistance and entry. Thus, Leyel decided to sail to Carical, south of Tranquebar, where he encountered Simão D'Almeida, who was a Portuguese merchant from Negapatnam. D'Almeida explained that several Coromandel merchants had been treated unfairly by Pessart.[13] Eventually, he decided to attack Dansborg with D'Almeida's assistance, a subject to which I will return in Chapter 6 in greater detail.[14] Before Leyel's takeover of Dansborg, however, Pessart had already escaped. He had bought a small ship from his Portuguese connections in Negapatnam, and had visited Dansborg and taken everything worth stealing. Leyel informed one of his subordinates, Hans Knutsen, that he could not tolerate Pessart and his associates' behaviour. Since Pessart had stolen or destroyed all of the accounts, Leyel did not know which employees had been paid their salaries, or which payments (if any) had been made to the Nayak. Leyel mentioned the bad reputation that Pessart had given the Danish, stating that "God shall forgive him who has so shamefully damaged our reputation in these lands."[15] In a sense, it does not matter if the money concerned was company money or not, because either way it hurt the reputation of the DEIC. This shows that the relationship between Leyel and Pessart also had repercussions on Leyel's relationships with others on the coast.

In June 1644, Leyel announced Pessart's official withdrawal as commander of the DEIC in Asia. All his rights were annulled, his salary was

92 *The vulnerability of being connected*

suspended, and his goods confiscated. The same applied to his companions, or fellow rebels, as Leyel called them. Leyel also summoned the council of the ship *Christianshavn* to open the instructions from Copenhagen, and he was placed in charge of the DEIC in Asia. Shortly thereafter, Leyel wrote out a statement, clarifying how Pessart had failed in Masulipatnam, the Bay of Bengal, and Makassar. He further claimed that his rival had stolen the accounts and records of the company. For all of these reasons, he argued, Pessart and his associates should have no right to represent the Danish Kingdom in the future. The statement was signed by Leyel, Jørgen Hansen, Carsten Loodewycksten, and Simon Janssen.[16] Leyel's relationship with Pessart demonstrates that in an overseas setting, being in charge meant having the power not only to determine the destiny of the company but also to use the company's resources to further one's own interests.

Leyel's relationships within the company also demonstrate that he did not really know how to relate to his subordinates; subtle signs of tension emerge throughout the sources. The reports and letters sent by Leyel reveal that he always had difficulties with the trust and behaviour of his subordinates. Thus, in order to manage the company on the local level, Leyel needed to deal with tensions and uncertainty within the company itself. Leyel was well aware of the potential problems within the company. For example, in a letter of instruction to merchant Poul Nielsen, he wrote that it was difficult to find trustworthy and capable employees.[17] For Leyel, it was important to deal with these problems not only when he was present at Dansborg, but also during his travels around the Indian Ocean. In 1645, Leyel appointed Poul Nielsen as governor of Dansborg during his own absence. Nielsen was to be in charge of all officers and soldiers, and also responsible for the town of Tranquebar. He could be released from his duties only by Leyel or the king (for example, if a royal ship arrived from Copenhagen during Leyel's absence). If Nielsen died, then his main assistants, Ekman and Sergeant Jakobsen, would take his place.[18] Once again, Leyel emphasised that the latter were among the very few people that he trusted.[19] To the letter was attached a copy of a document, containing oaths sworn by the officers and merchants of the DEIC, to the effect that they were committed to serving under acting governor Nielsen in Leyel's absence. They promised not to take any orders from Pessart or his associates, in the event that they appeared. The officers and merchants of Tranquebar also promised to defend the fort against all possible attacks.[20]

Anders Nielsen, who Leyel considered one of the most capable merchants in the DEIC in Asia, was also entrusted with diplomatic missions, as has been mentioned in the previous chapter. Nielsen was important because he understood local languages and customs, and was experienced in the Indian Ocean trade.[21] Leyel also sent Nielsen to Makassar to supervise trade with the surrounding areas, especially Java, and to utilise his Chinese business connections in the interests of the company.[22] The relationship with Anders Nielsen, however, was far from carefree. In fact, early in 1648, the

The vulnerability of being connected   93

relationship between Nielsen and Leyel took a new turn. Nielsen wrote to Leyel that he did not agree with the latter's plan to dispatch the *St Peter* and the *St Poul* to Makassar, due to the proximity of the monsoon season. Leyel, Nielsen added, ought to be aware that their mutual colleague, Claus Rytter, had tried to do the same thing in 1642, and had never reached Bantam. Nielsen hoped that Leyel would take his advice, especially since he had been a loyal servant for twelve years.[23] At this point, Nielsen demonstrated signs of discontent with Leyel. After all, Leyel's order to sail to Makassar put the lives of Nielsen and his crew at risk. Thus, the relationship between Leyel and Anders Nielsen highlights that Nielsen was specialised in the Indian Ocean trade, and Leyel was dependent on his skills and know-how. In particular, Nielsen's role was to streamline connections with merchant networks beyond the DEIC at Makassar. This gives the impression that Leyel was at the centre of the DEIC's web, striving to weave together connections with the outside world. However, as will be demonstrated below, the centre of the web could turn out to be a vulnerable position.

Leyel had problems with other company employees as well. In particular, the heavy drinking of his subordinates was a constant problem. According to Leyel's first report, chaplains Christer Sturm and Niels Udbyneder had been drinking every day and flouting all possible rules and regulations. A complaint from the people of Tranquebar had accused the priests of behaving badly towards Christians, Muslims, and pagans in the town; for example, they had ostensibly harassed and beaten some of the inhabitants.[24]

The behaviour within the company also occasionally escalated, and as a result, Leyel had to mediate between the company employees. On 30 January 1645, Jorgen Lauridsen, another company employee, wrote to Leyel that he had been involved in a fight with Christian Sturm aboard the *Fortuna* the previous year. According to Lauridsen, he had caught Sturm engaging in suspicious trading activities. As revealed by the correspondence between Lauridsen and Leyel, there was a dispute between Sturm and Lauridsen regarding for whose benefit the company's trade was to be managed. This suggests that the reason behind the quarrel was private trading, particularly by Sturm.[25] Finally, Leyel had had enough, and on 8 October 1645, Leyel sentenced Udbyneder and Sturm to exile.[26] This sentence increased the potential for unrest. Both priests were fairly popular among the other employees, and exile was a harsh punishment. Respect for Leyel, the man who held judicial power over the Danish community, subsequently withered.[27] Leyel's harsh sentencing arose from his need to improve his relationship with the locals, upon whom trade depended (this will be discussed further later).

Ultimately, Leyel's government had caused too many problems for his fellow employees. Late in 1648, Leyel's command of the DEIC abruptly ended, when his closest partners overthrew him in a mutiny, and he was replaced by Poul Hansen Korsør.[28] Korsør, Poul Nielsen, and Anders Nielsen collected information regarding Leyel's actions, and sent it to the directors in Copenhagen, using similar language to that which Leyel had used against Pessart.

94   *The vulnerability of being connected*

Indeed, Leyel's rivalry with Pessart had been one of the reasons for the mutiny in the first place. Korsør had written to Leyel in 1646 that Pessart had been a good employee, that he had done the best he could according to his knowledge, and that he ought not to be blamed for the severe problems of the DEIC.[29] One possible reason for the mutiny may have been that Leyel did not want to give any of the more experienced employees management positions, perhaps worried that his own status within the DEIC would thereby be challenged.

One of Leyel's last orders as commander had been addressed to Poul Hansen, appointing him acting governor of the fort during his absence. If something were to happen to Leyel, his son-in-law Josias Stael would be put in charge.[30] Thus, neither Poul Hansen nor Anders Nielsen would be promoted to commander, as they had probably been expecting. This is remarkable, especially given that Leyel had previously stated that Nikolai Samson and Anders Nielsen were his most trusted employees.[31] This demonstrates that trust was highly fluid, and that the constant presence of uncertainty undermined the company from within.

There is only scattered information regarding the mutiny. In a "memoria," it is claimed that Leyel had been trading for his own benefit.[32] According to this document, Leyel had traded at least 61 17/32 ounces of gold on his own account, and had also paid Tiagapule, the minister of the Nayak, the considerable sum of 500 *pardous*. The document also alleges that Leyel had traded arrack from Ceylon for his own profit. In addition, he was reported to have sold a large quantity of sulphur, tobacco, and pepper to local intermediaries.[33] The document states that these goods were booty that had been captured from Bengali ships, and that Leyel had sold them for his own profit. When Leyel was confronted with these accusations, he claimed to have traded only for the benefit of the king. However, the document contradicts this claim. If this is true, it demonstrates the possibility for accumulating personal wealth and power by conspiring with local authorities and merchants.

Another possible reason for the mutiny was Leyel's decision to prohibit DEIC officials and employees from privateering, one of the few ways in which they could make a significant profit. For example, the captured *St Michael*, a large Bengali ship, carried large amounts of cowrie shells from the Maldives, these being used as currency in local trade, in China and in Western Africa. The cargo of the *St Michael* was sold for 3,000 riksdalers, a considerable amount of money for a company that was continuously struggling to survive.[34] The temptation to pocket such gains was thus high. The fact that Leyel did not share the profits underlines the importance of balancing different loyalties.

It can be concluded that Leyel was unsuccessful in his attempt to maintain order within the company hierarchy. Although the men had sworn to serve both Leyel and the company, it is difficult to distinguish which took precedence. Leyel represented the interests of the king, but were these the

The vulnerability of being connected 95

same as the interests of the company and its employees? They now had a new chief of operations in Asia, who had not only overthrown the previous commander but had also implemented a far harsher regime. In the eyes of the employees, this could have negative consequences on their private trading activities. Such instructions and letters underline the fact that the various employees were not necessarily on good terms with each other. Indeed, this strengthens the argument that a shared nationality or employer did not necessary imply common goals and aims while overseas.

Relationships outside the company

This section focuses on Leyel's views regarding relationships outside of the DEIC. Of primary importance in this regard were the relationships with the local authorities, especially the Nayak of Tanjore and the King of Candy (Ceylon). To maintain good relations with the Nayak was of crucial importance, because only with the consent of the Nayak could Leyel and the DEIC remain at Tranquebar. From a business perspective, Leyel also wanted to access the lucrative markets of Ceylon, for which he needed the consent of the King of Candy. Leyel was especially interested in opening free access to the port of Batticaloa. In Tranquebar, due to the bad behaviour of Pessart and his men, relations with the Nayak had deteriorated, and Leyel thus needed to send an ambassador to court in order to re-negotiate terms.[35] Indeed, this was in accordance with local custom. Embassies were important, and companies such as the VOC appointed officials to undertake such visits to the courts of local rulers. Guido van Meersbergen refers to such emissaries as "merchant-diplomats," and emphasises their role as commercial agents with a political agenda.[36]

The Europeans understood that in order to improve their relationship with the Nayak, lavish gifts would be essential, particularly elephants. Indeed, the economy of gift-giving was a central part of early modern trade in the Indian Ocean. Throughout the region, elephants were prized for an array of economic, military, and cultural reasons.[37] Exotic gifts and gift-exchanging ceremonies demonstrated symbolic power, and thus served as an essential instrument for building trade connections, forging political alliances, legitimising authority, and making a statement about the power relations between Europeans and non-Europeans.[38] In Leyel's case, the elephants were mostly purchased from the Ceylon. Other gifts were also important, and Leyel referred to these various expenses as the *protection costs*, reflecting the importance of the security that the Nayak provided for the DEIC.[39]

Leyel's reports reveal that there were also issues of trust between the Nayak and the DEIC. Apparently, the Nayak had been disappointed with the behaviour of Pessart, who had not paid respect according to the rules. The Nayak expected personal visits by European officials, and Leyel thus dispatched Anders Nielsen to visit the Nayak's court in 1645. Apparently, the relationship with the Nayak was vexed, to the extent that the ambassador

96 *The vulnerability of being connected*

of the company would be risking his life. According to Leyel, it would thus be "better to lose an egg than a hen."[40] That Leyel attached little value to Nielsen's life is evident, and it is thus not surprising that Nielsen later turned against him. Although Nielsen provided the Nayak's court with gifts, especially elephants, the embassy proved to be difficult.[41] Nielsen sent several letters from the court of the Nayak in Tanjore, explaining that the Nayak constantly made new demands of the DEIC. According to Nielsen, the Nayak wanted to make sure that Leyel and the DEIC would respect the usual fees and pay their debts.[42] Thus, it seems that the Nayak wanted the DEIC officials to understand their position on the coast. Finally, when Leyel promised to pay an additional 1,000 riksdalers, the standing of the DEIC with the Nayak improved substantially.[43]

As with the Nayak of Tanjore, Leyel also tried to establish a friendly relationship with the King of Candy, similarly dispatching embassies with personally handpicked gifts.[44] According to Leyel, it was important to send trustworthy officials to visit the King of Candy, since trade with Ceylon was vital to the DEIC. From Ceylon, the DEIC imported wax, cinnamon, and arrack, all of which were important goods in the intra-Asian trade. It was thus imperative to have access to ports in Ceylon, despite the political conflicts then underway between Candy, the VOC, and the Portuguese.[45] In other words, free trade and friendly relations between the DEIC and Candy were crucial.[46] In his third report, Leyel reported that the King of Candy had rejected the VOC and, for that reason, was on good terms with Leyel's representatives.[47] As we have already seen, Leyel's grand design for a permanent free trade route between Tranquebar and Ceylon ultimately failed, but a profitable trade relationship was nonetheless established.

Leyel reported that he also wanted to improve relationships with Golconda, and especially with the governor of Masulipatnam.[48] For this reason, he had sent the *Ellefant* to Masulipatnam, carrying four elephants as gifts, in order to convince the governor of his good intentions. Masulipatnam was a central hub for the intra-Asian trade, especially for textiles.[49] The broker of the relationship was Virna, Leyel's veteran and capable translator.[50] In a report written in December 1645, Leyel wrote of his disappointment in participating in the trade at Masulipatnam. In the end, he had had as little success as Pessart and Crappe before him.[51]

Relationships with local rulers were volatile, and the DEIC had no choice but to adapt to already existing hierarchies. Despite the importance of these hierarchical relationships, Leyel relied almost entirely on his local contacts. For example, in the instructions that he provided to his fellow company employees, Leyel emphasised the need to listen to and to take advice from local merchants, due to their superior knowledge of trade. Leading by example, Leyel used the services of men like Anina Marca in Ceylon (who specialised in the trade of elephants), Ziu Ziu, a Chinese merchant in Bantam, Abdul Latif in Japara, and Francisco Mendes in Makassar.[52]

The goods carried on board the *St Michael* were co-owned by Seyed Nina and Leyel, within the framework of a partnership. Most of the goods were not recorded, but the ship certainly carried slaves.[55] Seyed Nina probably belonged to the Keling community, an originally Tamil-speaking people from India who had settled on the Malay Peninsula. Merchants from this community were the backbone of trade, and particularly trade with the Spice Islands.[56] Besides elephants, Seyed Nina was also able to provide timber for ship repairs, and was thus often entrusted with maintaining the DEIC's ships.[57] However, Seyed Nina was not the only broker upon whom Leyel relied. In addition, Ismael Nina was also involved in his network, and DEIC employees were advised to conduct any trade in Cutiara through him. For his part, Leyel transported slaves belonging to Nina, whilst the latter opened up the services of his agency to Leyel's colleagues.[58]

He instructed the Danish skipper, Simon Charstenson, and his pilot, Willem Mouridsen, to contact Seyed Nina, a local merchant, upon their arrival in Quedah. They were to maintain good relationships with him, since he was a crucial connection to the local markets, spoke the local language, knew the local customs, and, most importantly, specialised in the elephant trade.[53] Consequently, Leyel was dependent not only on employees such as Nielsen, but also, and perhaps more significantly, on local merchants. Indeed, Sanjay Subrahmanyam has argued that the 1640s were an important moment in the growing interconnectedness between European companies and local merchant networks on the Coromandel Coast.[54]

The goods carried on board the *St Michael* were co-owned by Seyed Nina and Leyel, within the framework of a partnership. Most of the goods were not recorded, but the ship certainly carried slaves.[55] Seyed Nina probably belonged to the Keling community, an originally Tamil-speaking people from India who had settled on the Malay Peninsula. Merchants from this community were the backbone of trade, and particularly trade with the Spice Islands.[56] Besides elephants, Seyed Nina was also able to provide timber for ship repairs, and was thus often entrusted with maintaining the DEIC's ships.[57] However, Seyed Nina was not the only broker upon whom Leyel relied. In addition, Ismael Nina was also involved in his network, and DEIC employees were advised to conduct any trade in Cutiara through him. For his part, Leyel transported slaves belonging to Nina, whilst the latter opened up the services of his agency to Leyel's colleagues.[58]

Leyel's relationships with local merchants offer important insights into how the latter were involved in company trade, but without being officially in the company's service. Making use of his royal commission, Leyel issued a passport to the *Trangabara*, a small ship belonging to Michael van Danzig and his partners, and under the responsibility of skipper Rama Pule. Danish protection enabled the ship to trade in the Indian Ocean, and the Danish passport made it possible to transport a cargo to Malacca.[59]

One of the most important relationships that Leyel maintained was with the Portuguese in India or, more precisely, with two different groups of Portuguese in India. First, Leyel had connections with the formal Portuguese empire, the *Estado da Índia*, which had its headquarters in Goa. Second, and far more importantly, he also had connections with the informal Portuguese empire, i.e. those Portuguese who operated outside of the *Estado*. In general terms, the dominion of the Portuguese crown in India lay mainly to the west of Cape Comorin, whereas the informal Portuguese networks lay to the east, extending all the way to the South China Sea and Timor.[60] During the seventeenth century, the *Estado* also had factories east of the Cape: Masulipatnam (1598–1610), Pulicat (1518–1610), São Tomé of Meliapor (1523–1749), and Negapatnam (1507–1657). In practice, by maintaining relations with both groups, Leyel was able to simultaneously participate in both European and Indian Ocean networks.

98   *The vulnerability of being connected*

Subrahmanyam has characterised the Portuguese-Asian society that existed east of the cape as footloose, freewheeling, mercenary, and renegade.[61] For his part, George Winius has referred to these elements of Portuguese society as a shadow empire, with its own logic and aims. Some of those involved were willing to work for other Europeans, and many were connected to Leyel.[62]

Leyel's relationship with the Portuguese in Tranquebar was particularly important. In his first report to the directors, Leyel wrote that he had allowed the local Portuguese community in Tranquebar to build their own Catholic church. In his explanation to the directors, he argued that it was important to let the locals express their faith, to worship their gods, and to have their own religious symbols, as this was beneficial for trade.[63] Leyel always wrote highly of the Portuguese agents and appreciated their knowledge and experience of intra-Asian trade.[64] Moreover, they were also involved in Leyel's personal trading activities. In a letter from Anders Nielsen to Leyel, Nielsen informed his commander of the arrival of Simão D'Almeida from Negapatnam, along with large quantities of tobacco and gold from Makassar. D'Almeida had announced that he wished to contribute to Danish trade, but Nielsen was suspicious, perhaps not without reason.[65] Although Nielsen did not specify the nature of his suspicion, it probably related to the partnership between Leyel and D'Almeida, which centred on trade in gunpowder with Viceroy Mascarenhas.[66]

Bearing in mind the importance of D'Almeida, Carvalho, and Pacheco, as well as that of the Portuguese merchants at Tranquebar, it is not surprising that local Portuguese merchants and their partners featured prominently in Leyel's correspondence. Leyel gladly invited Portuguese merchants to settle in Tranquebar. The DEIC headquarters became a safe haven for entire Portuguese merchant families from Negapatnam, São Tomé of Meliapor, Manar, and Ceylon, who had been driven out by the territorial advances of the VOC.[67] According to Tapan Raychaudri, Danish ships kept bringing Portuguese refugees from Masulipatnam to Tranquebar, and people thus continued to arrive in great numbers.[68] In his second report to Copenhagen, Leyel informed the directors that the Portuguese connections in Tranquebar were trading successfully with Ceylon, and were making a good profit for the DEIC.[69]

Leyel also used his Portuguese connections to improve trade with Ceylon, and sent Antonio Gomes and Razia Pahsa to visit the King of Candy, bearing gifts in the hope of opening up trade.[70] Furthermore, Leyel established strong relationships with the Portuguese merchants in Porto Novo. He sent one of his best brokers, Canacapel Tayapa, to establish a factory there,[71] since the trade in Porto Novo was particularly important to him.[72] The close connection with the Portuguese also included direct employment with the DEIC. In a list of the employees at Dansborg compiled in 1645, only six had Danish names, whereas the majority had either Indian or Portuguese names.[73] In fact, maintaining connections with the Portuguese on the

Coromandel was one of Leyel's priorities. Indeed, this was one of the reasons for his initial commercial success, since the local merchants were key to accessing local trading networks.

Leyel also developed a relationship with the formal Portuguese empire, the *Estado*. Indeed, he often stressed his good relationship with the viceroy, D. Filipe de Mascarenhas: "We correspond much with each other," he wrote. According to Leyel, Mascarenhas had received orders from the King of Portugal to remain friendly with Leyel. For this reason, the DEIC was allowed to trade in all Portuguese ports and factories in India. Moreover, the viceroy also offered support in the conflicts that the Danish were facing in Bengal.[74] According to Raychaudhuri, the Danish provided the Portuguese with secret intelligence regarding the VOC and carried their cargo on board Danish ships.[75] Leyel had also traded with a fleet of *barcos de remos* (canoes), which had been sent from Goa to the Coromandel.[76] Although it is unclear whether the fleet was sent specifically to trade with Leyel, it nonetheless reveals the trading connection between the headquarters of the *Estado* in Goa and Leyel.

The close collaboration of the Danish and Portuguese crowns also had a diplomatic aspect. Leyel wrote of a treaty that had brought great benefit to the Danish, who had been treated more favourably than the Dutch or the English.[77] The viceroy had also received orders to allow the Danish to trade within all Portuguese spheres of influence, including Macao. Leyel emphasised that he had goods stored at Dansborg, and that these should be transferred to Manila on a ship that would depart in May the following year, arriving in June and returning in November. From Manila, the Danish would transport silver to Macao, where Chinese goods could be purchased using the proceeds.[78] Indeed, this exchange had the potential to yield a high profit in Europe. If the ship eventually returned to Dansborg by February, a significant profit could be made in only ten months. For the journey between Manila and Macao, Leyel relied on the Danish–Dutch treaty, which allowed the Danish to sail freely between those two ports.[79]

One of Leyel's most difficult challenges was the relationship with his previous employer, the VOC. While he served as commander of the DEIC, he remained suspicious and cautious regarding the VOC. Indeed, his constant worries about the latter featured in all of his reports, and in 1646, he told his subordinates to ignore any gossip regarding the VOC and its affairs.[80] The VOC was a far bigger European player in the Indian Ocean, and during the first half of the century, it had successfully challenged the Portuguese to become the strongest European commercial power in the region. The VOC had capitalised on its power by acquiring exclusive rights in the spice trade, and to a large extent came to control the latter. On the Coromandel Coast, the VOC possessed a relatively large factory in Pulicat and a smaller trading post in Masulipatnam.[81] In the South of the Coromandel, the VOC used local brokers, although during the 1640s, they also tried to acquire permanent factories.[82] Indeed, the VOC took the retreat of the Portuguese on

100 *The vulnerability of being connected*

the Coromandel as a sign to increase their own presence, as Raychaudhuri has noted.[83] Thus, Leyel had to engage in a problematic relationship with a far bigger European rival. In several instances, Leyel commented upon the aggressive behaviour of the VOC. For example, in 1645, Leyel alleged that several VOC ships had encountered survivors of a DEIC shipwreck off the coast of Bengal, only to deliver the men into the hands of the "moors" of neighbouring Pipley, who had taken them prisoner.[84]

Soon after this episode, Leyel reported that VOC officials had arrived from Carical, which lay at a short distance from Dansborg. They were following orders from the VOC governor in Pulicat, Arnold Heussen, to obstruct trade and communication between the Danish and the Nayak. Leyel's suspicions turned out to be well founded, and he reported that the VOC was willing to pay the Nayak more than the DEIC. Luckily, for Leyel, the Nayak had decided to stay loyal to the DEIC, and rejected the overtures of the VOC. The VOC representative had showered lavish gifts upon the father of the Nayak, Regnade Naiq, but the Nayak had refused to have any further contact with the English or the Dutch. Leyel also stated that the VOC should not trespass on the lands of the Nayak of Tanjore, since this would harm the DEIC's trade. The DEIC had been trading in Negapatnam alongside the Portuguese for twenty-five years, and the Nayak had agreed to exclude the VOC, the EIC, and the French from his realm. Leyel attached great value to this exclusive access, having paid a large sum to the Nayak in order to establish the relationship.[85]

The VOC officials had also visited the Nayak's minister Tiagapule and his brother Regnapdopule in the hope of establishing trade relations. The Nayak himself had been in Tranquebar during Leyel's absence, in order to discuss the matters that had arisen from Tiagapule's attempt to confiscate money from the inhabitants of the town. The reason for this aggression was that Tiagapule had the right to tax certain regions in the Nayak's territory, and had decided to tax the inhabitants of Tranquebar. To Leyel, this was unacceptable. The DEIC had refused to pay, stating that their agreement with the Nayak of Tanjore exempted Tranquebar from Tiagapule's taxes. Tiagapule was furious, surrounded the town, and began to burn down houses. Nielsen, who at the time was the acting governor, had decided to open the fort, in order to provide shelter to the general population. According to Leyel, the VOC had assisted Tiagapule in his attack, which proved that it was willing to go to any lengths to damage the DEIC.[86]

The best way for Leyel to fight against the VOC was to partner up with local merchants. Leyel reported that the VOC continued to obstruct the DEIC in both Porto Novo and the territory of the Nayak of Sinces. For trade purposes, Leyel had entrusted business to one of his old partners, Malaio Chinene Cheti, who had thirty-five years of experience of trading in Pulicat and on the Coromandel Coast, and who enjoyed good relations with the local rulers. The VOC opposed the activities of DEIC and Malaio by obstructing their access to Pondicherry, Porto Novo, and Tegnapatnam. Leyel

The vulnerability of being connected 101

retorted that all trade was conducted in agreement with the local rulers, as brokered by Malaio. In 1645, Leyel remarked with reference to the latter: "I maintain correspondence and friendship with him because he is really capable, and can be of great help to us not only in relation to the King and the Nayaks, but also in our struggle against the Dutch." Leyel thus felt that his relationship with Malaio was significant, and that his collaboration with the DEIC was particularly valuable in competing against the VOC.[87]

Malaio belonged to the principal trading community of South India, the Chettis. During the seventeenth century, the latter were involved in many commercial enterprises, offering a combination of brokerage and moneylending. Remarkably, many Chettis originated from the same family. In particular, it is known that Malaio Chetti and his brother Chinanna Chetti were important shipowners and merchants.[88] It is difficult to pinpoint exactly to whom Leyel was referring, but, according to Dutch sources, Malaio Chetti had already died in 1634, prior to Leyel's appointment as commander.[89] It is thus more likely that Leyel was referring to Chinanna Chetti, who had considerable experience in Pulicat and connections to the VOC, having worked as the latter's chief broker in Pulicat.[90] Subsequently, the VOC put an end to their dealings with Chinanna, for reasons that remain unclear. However, Radika Seshan has suggested that the VOC feared losing control over their main broker, to the point that they had his family imprisoned in Pulicat. Chinanna had his revenge by besieging Pulicat and damaging the interests of the VOC on the Coromandel Coast. Subsequently, in 1657, he established a business in the Kingdom of Tanjore.[91] Leyel, emphasising his relationship to Malaio (Chinanna Chetti), demonstrates that the competing European powers were attempting to win the support of local rulers and merchants for their own ends.[92]

However, Leyel's relationship with the Dutch was not unremittingly hostile. In 1646, during a return voyage from Makassar, the ship *Christianshavn* called at Batavia to buy supplies. They discovered that at least since July, no ships had arrived from the Republic, and that the VOC was currently without a governor; Cornelis van der Lyn, an elderly council member, was occupying the position on an interim basis. Van der Lyn treated the DEIC well, and provided them with a new bookkeeper and materials for repairs. Some fifteen Danish employees from the VOC enlisted with the DEIC.[93]

In a letter dated 1 October 1645, Leyel instructed Poul Nielsen to maintain friendly relations with other Europeans, including the VOC. According to Leyel, there were VOC merchants who wished to trade with the DEIC in Tranquebar, and it would be prudent to conduct negotiations with them in private, so as to conceal the affair from the Nayak. Leyel was in favour of such trade, so long as the VOC agreed to pay the DEIC 20 per cent tax. Leyel also suggested that the English should be invited to participate in the trade with Tranquebar, through the medium of Calipa and Jayapa, Leyel's brokers, and in return for the same tax.[94]

The decision to allow certain VOC merchants to trade privately in Tranquebar gives a different picture of the relationship between the VOC and

102   *The vulnerability of being connected*

Leyel. Perhaps this was a desperate attempt to attract trade to Tranquebar, or a convenient way of doing business off the books. In the end, the DEIC could never fully compete with the VOC. However, these events demonstrate that Leyel used his local connections in order to at least resist the VOC supremacy in the region. In contrast to the Portuguese, the relationship with the VOC was more competitive. Indeed, it seems as if both the Portuguese and Leyel were similarly threatened by the VOC.

To summarise, Leyel had to balance competing and overlapping networks. The different types of relationships he had with the VOC underline the fact that the companies were run by people who had their own ways of doing business, especially in the local context. The relationship with the Portuguese demonstrates that Leyel was engaged not only with the *Estado* but especially with the merchants outside of the *Estado*. Such local connections were vital for Leyel, and it was largely through local merchants that he managed to develop business in Asia. Indeed, this highlights the importance of focusing not only on the business relationships between royal monopolies and trading companies but also on the merchants who operated outside of the states and companies. Their dependency on certain key individuals was a challenge not only for the companies but also for the employees representing them. In the end, Leyel proved better at balancing his connections with local merchants than with DEIC employees. In fact, Leyel's complicated balancing act demonstrates just how international, intertwined, and multifaceted social connections overseas were.

Carloff's ghost investments in Europe

During the overseas career of Henrich Carloff, several overlapping networks were brought into play as individuals established, maintained, and misused their business connections. This section focuses on the challenges that balancing between these connections posed for Carloff's Atlantic career. As discussed in the previous chapter, Carloff's room for manoeuvre diminished significantly as the SAC became increasingly attached to the Swedish elite, and this led Carloff to leave the SAC during the spring of 1657. In 1657, Carloff again switched allegiance, now offering his entrepreneurship to the Danish king, Fredrik III. In August, it was agreed that Carloff would undertake an expedition to West Africa in order to dislodge the SAC from its position, a task in which he succeeded. This expedition will be dealt with in Chapter 6. In this section, the focus is on how Carloff balanced between the political authorities and his financial supporters.

The contract of August 1657 with Denmark stated that Carloff should finance the attack on Carolusborg on his own account.[95] As such, he contacted a group of Amsterdam merchants for financial assistance: Jasper Vinckel, Jean le Vainqueur, Jan Vlasblom, Floris Elias, Cornelis Joosten Heyns, and Nicholas Pancras. Together, they agreed to provide a ship called the *Diamant*, which would be renamed the *Glückstadt*, and which would set

The vulnerability of being connected 103

sail from Emden to Glückstadt, and from there to Africa, before finally returning to Glückstadt.[96] The reason for this stopover in Glückstadt was that the ship would receive its official Danish documents from the factor of the city, and thus acquire institutional shelter.[97] During the voyage to the Cape Coast, Carloff was supposed to make another stopover in Sierra Leone and deliver a cargo to the local factor, Gerrit Bremer. Thus, the attack on the Swedish possessions was not the sole intention of the voyage.

The financing of the voyage was performed through what will be referred to here as *ghost investing*.[98] In principle, a ghost investor was someone who wanted to remain anonymous. This was because in the seventeenth century, countries did not allow their subjects to invest in foreign trading enterprises and ventures.[99] In practice, ghost investments were made through fake bottomry loans, in which the official freighter of the ship was a strawman for the real investors. As referred to in this chapter, bottomry loans (a contract based on a combination of credit and insurance) were usually made to skippers, who had also received foreign passports. The freighter of the ship could purchase a bottomry in advance of the voyage. If the voyage was successful, the freighter would pay back the creditor with interest, but if the voyage was not completed, the creditor would cover the losses. Basically, the bottomry loan revolved around the question of who the actual owner of the cargo was. In the passports, the skipper had the licence for the voyage and also appeared as the owner of the cargo. In the licences, there was nothing about bottomry contracts.

It would be almost impossible for inspectors and prosecutors to know who was providing or paying for the trading goods. Ghost investing was a widely used practice in Western Europe. For example, at the end of the 1640s, ghost investors from Amsterdam had already participated in African voyages that had set out from Glückstadt. Thielman Wilkens, Carloff's colleague during his time with the WIC on the Gold Coast, was officially running similar investments, in which the funding really came from Amsterdam.[100] Here, too, the aim was to circumvent the privileges of the WIC. This kind of ghost identity protected Dutch investors and previous employees of the WIC. Officially, Carloff ran the operations, but, in reality, much of the capital came from the Amsterdam investors.[101]

Carloff stated that he had invested money in the voyage himself. However, the real financial means were provided by Abel Verbeeck and Andries Sael. The reason why the latter chose to offer their support is unclear, but it would seem that Carloff did not possess enough capital. According to Carloff, the combined investors had invested a total of 50,000 guilders in the operation, and he was supposed to return their investment plus interest. His previous personal investments in the SAC had likely been a combination of his own capital, earned during his years as prosecutor, and similar *ghost investments*. Carloff himself claimed that he had used the money that he had accumulated as a WIC official.[102] However, the amount of capital invested was so large that it could not, I claim, have come from Carloff alone.

104 *The vulnerability of being connected*

In 1662, Carloff referred to this type of business as a "simulatie." Indeed, this reveals the intention to circumvent the privileges of the WIC. Carloff declared that there had not been a single Dane involved in the plans for the African voyages, even though the official head of planning was Marten Baers, a resident and factor of Glückstadt, whom Carloff knew very well.[103] In 1651 and 1656, the Danish king granted Baers licences for trade in Africa. The licence of 1656 was granted to three residents of Glückstadt: Henry and Marten Baers and Gerrit Bremer, the factor of the Amsterdam merchants in Sierra Leone.[104] Baers was involved in negotiating favourable terms for the Glückstadt merchants, for trade not only in Africa but also in the North Atlantic.[105] According to Carloff, Baers had no own capital invested, and it was merchants from Amsterdam who were footing the bill. Baers later complained that the investors had failed to pay for his services.[106] This complaint probably referred to the licence that Baers, his brother, and Bremer obtained in 1656. Notwithstanding, Baers and Bremer invested a considerable sum in the Glückstadt Company in 1661.[107] This was also a ghost investment. According to Carloff, the company ships *St Marten* and *Die Liebe* (previously *Stockholms Slott*) were covered by ghost investors. The company ships *Postellion von Venedig* and *Fredricus* were also financed by similar false bottomry loans. Apparently, the ship *Graaf Enno*, which was investigated on the Gold Coast by the WIC on suspicion of interloping, was also equipped and financed by the same people.[108]

Carloff's relations with the Amsterdam investors made him aware of the mechanism of ghost investing. Carloff later stated that he had heard from Jasper Vinckel that the bottomry loans between the investors and Baers were intended to avoid raising suspicion amongst WIC officials, who might encounter the *Glückstadt*.[109] This demonstrates that investors in Amsterdam, Dutch skippers in Glückstadt, and the royal factors in Denmark were all aware of the opportunities and risks that bottomries offered. The company offered a legal framework within which such individuals could pursue their business. Indeed, this was a quicker way to make a profit from the African trade than buying shares in larger companies and waiting for dividends.

Furthermore, Carloff served as the central node that connected the various different parties. It is worth noting that his knowledge of how to balance these different networks had been acquired during his years as WIC prosecutor on the Gold Coast. In particular, it was during this time that he learnt how shipping documents could be used for or against specific freighters and skippers.

When Carloff returned to Glückstadt on 8 June 1658, the Danish–Swedish war had resulted in heavy losses for Denmark. The peace treaty of Roskilde, signed on 26 February 1658, stated, amongst other things, that the Danish were to return all the captured forts to the Swedish, including Carolusborg. The Swedish representatives had heard what had happened in Africa, and wanted to have Carloff arrested. Carloff therefore fled from Glückstadt and hid abroad for several months.[110] However, his connection with the Danes

The vulnerability of being connected   105

remained intact. After the conflict between Sweden and Denmark had been resolved, in 1659, the Danes contacted Carloff in Groningen in the Dutch Republic. The Danish representative, Poul Klingenberg, offered Carloff and his companions trade rights in Africa under Danish protection. In May 1659, a new contract was signed. Carloff could keep the gold from the captured ship *Stockholms Slott*, and Carolusborg would become the property of the Kingdom of Denmark.[111] According to the agreement, Carloff and his associates would also be allowed to trade in Western Africa. The commanders of the fort would be servants of the king, but would also assist Carloff with trade.[112] Klingenberg, who represented the interest of the Danish crown, was an important connection for Carloff. Through this connection, he could balance his personal interest with that of his new patron, Fredrik III (1648–1670). The negotiations were held in Hamburg, where Carloff was represented by his business partner, Jan de Swaen.[113] Right after the agreement between Carloff and Klingenberg, on 20 May 1659, the Glückstadt Company was established, being destined to hold a monopoly over Danish trade in Africa for twenty-five years. Once again, a Nordic company with close links to an international maritime community had been established.[114]

According to Carloff, the plans for the company were largely developed by previous WIC employees Isaac Coymans and Gerard van Tets, in the course of discussions at the house of the Amsterdam merchant Jan de Swaen. According to Carloff, de Swaen was the largest investor in the Amsterdam network, making a profit of approximately 8,000 guilders on each successful trip, which represented a strong incentive for further investment. For Coymans, the motive to join the Glückstadt Company was the possibility of trading his personal goods on the coast.[115] The skippers of the ships *Die Liebe* and *St Marten* – Jorrien Schroeder and Joost Cramer, both previous SAC employees under Carloff – were also present.[116] According to Carloff, during the planning stage, it was suggested that the company should be based in Glückstadt, where investors and employees held burgher rights. Moreover, as was pointed out, this would require bringing Danish officials into the company in order to make it appear more Danish.

In a notarised statement from August 1660, Carloff declared that he had, on his patrons' behalf, given de Swaen, the factor of the Glückstadt Company, a bottomry loan in order to outfit the company ships *Die Liebe* and the *St Marten* for a cargo worth 20,000 guilders, to be transported from Amsterdam to the Gold Coast and from there back to Glückstadt. However, further ghost investing was required, partly because Carloff had returned to Amsterdam, and partly because, as a result of the privileges of the WIC, he could thus no longer invest in the Glückstadt Company. Instead, a new bottomry was transferred via Jacob del Boe, the director of the Glückstadt Company.[117] In another notarised statement, de Swaen stated that he owed Carloff 6,000 guilders, which he had borrowed to equip the *Die Liebe*. De Swaen had entrusted the ship to Jürgen Schröder (Jorrien Schroeder) as skipper, and had expected him to sail to the Gold Coast and São Tomé,

106 *The vulnerability of being connected*

before returning to Glückstadt. Upon arrival, de Swaen would repay Carloff his loan, plus 30 per cent interest.[118]

It is not surprising that these men planned the company. Based on their previous employment, they were well aware of the financial challenges that the WIC faced as a result of its numerous conflicts with Portugal in the South Atlantic. They also knew how to apply for shelter, which other previous WIC employees had already received in Glückstadt. Finally, they knew that there was a strong possibility of being able to access the profitable gold trade, particularly by offering their expertise to Nordic rulers in exchange for the right to operate the Nordic trade in Africa.

Things eventually took a surprising turn, to the extent that Carloff withdrew his power of attorney from de Swaen on 14 October 1659.[119] A month earlier, de Swaen had himself stated that he had learnt the true intentions of Carloff, and that he had already done more for Carloff than he was allowed to by power of attorney.[120] Carloff must have known of the risks and possible problems that foreign commissions entailed for the Amsterdam consortia. Indeed, Carloff's business partner Isaac Coymans was even convicted of treason. Letters from Coymans to the new governor of the Glückstadt Company, Joost Cramer, had been intercepted by WIC officials on the coast. In the letters, Coymans warned Cramer about a possible WIC attack against the Danish positions on the coast, and advised that Cramer ally himself with the Fetu caboceer in order to defend the Danish enterprise. The letters were useful to the WIC, which proceeded to use them in a court case against Coymans. After the case was opened in the Republic, the trial and the conflict between the WIC and the Danish Company were extensively debated in public.[121] In January 1662, Coymans was convicted of treason. His sentence was six years in prison, a fine of 20,000 gulden, and banishment from Amsterdam upon his release. In the end, Carloff avoided being charged, since he had turned himself in and had assisted the WIC in investigating and dismantling the network.[122]

As W.B. den Blanken has made clear, the main issue at stake was the responsibility of the WIC and the Danish Company vis-à-vis their respective states. Unsurprisingly, both parties questioned each other's rights on the Gold Coast. Den Blanken argues that Coymans' sentence was relatively mild, given that he had been convicted of treason.[123] Moreover, other business partners whose names were brought up in court were not even convicted. There are two reasons behind this. On the one hand, the Republic and Denmark were at that time neutral and even allies, and there was no desire on either side to provoke hostilities. Indeed, this meant that the WIC was largely impotent. On the other hand, some of the members of the jury were influential people from Amsterdam, including Nicholas Pancras. Thus, the same person who had financed Carloff's initial Danish operation was also on the jury charged with delivering a verdict on Coymans. Eventually, the conflict between the parties was resolved due to more urgent political issues, related to the outbreak of the Second Anglo-Dutch War. Overall, the conflict and the resultant court case reveal two interconnected points. First, individuals such as Carloff were able to challenge the existing organisational structures of the trading companies, since at this time the legal framework of the states vis-à-vis their external organs remained underdeveloped. Second, the close connection between Carloff and the elite of Amsterdam is obvious. Indeed, this demonstrates that the connections between individuals were fraught with complicated considerations of trust and loyalty.

Carloff stood at the intersection of several networks. On the one hand, there was a pool of Amsterdam investors, among them Jasper Vinckel, Jean le Vainqueur, Jan Vlasblom, Floris Elias, Cornelis Joosten Heyns, and Nicholas Pancras. Given that all these men held burgher rights in Amsterdam, they were covered by the WIC charter. However, they used Carloff to transfer capital, resources, and powers of attorney to de Swaen in Amsterdam. Consequently, if we are to understand the role played by Carloff and his fellow business partners, it is paramount to understand that many did not themselves finance overseas operations but rather represented networks looking to invest risk capital in new ventures. Overseas entrepreneurs were able to attract such investors because of their connections and expertise overseas, which increased the chance of a profitable return on any investment. In the end, ghost investments serve to highlight the complexity of the social relationships between the businessmen who supported overseas entrepreneurship. It was partly Carloff's own desire for profit but partly also his social connections that forced him to act. As the aftermath of his Danish service, he was thus never completely free to do as he pleased but rather compelled to balance various connections and to mediate between the interests of different networks.

Balancing relationships in Western Africa

By analysing the aftermath of Carloff's expedition in 1658, this section focuses on vulnerable local relationships and issues of trust. Of particular interest are Carloff's relationships on the Gold Coast. The correspondence that Carloff maintained with the WIC officials show that Carloff was not only serving the interest of the Danish king but also played a high-risk game in which he offered his services to several people, and then took advantage of his business partners in order to turn the conquest to the best possible advantage.

The relationship between Carloff and the WIC Director-Generals, Jan Valckenburgh and Casper van Heussen, was complicated, yet at the same time representative of the relationships that Europeans had with each other on the coast.[124] Some of the correspondence between Carloff and Valckenburgh suggests a close partnership, whereas other letters suggest frustration, and even bitterness. Initially, Carloff was friendly and suggested a mutually beneficial plan to maintain trade on the coast.[125] Carloff assured Valckenburgh that following the conquest of the SAC's assets, the SAC employees

108 *The vulnerability of being connected*

would swear an oath to him. Those who refused would be arrested and sent back to Europe. Among the men who had sworn allegiance to Carloff, Carloff chose Samuel Smidt as acting governor. He had previously been employed by the WIC and the SAC under the patronage of Carloff, and remained a reliable asset.[126]

Smidt was already close to Carloff prior to the conquest. Smidt stated that in 1657, he had been hired by Carloff to accompany him onboard the ship *Glückstadt* on a voyage to Guinea. The ship owners were Carloff, Mr Lavinckeur (Vaincquer), Mr Vinckel, and Mr van de Beecken. Smidt knew all three personally, since they had bought cargo for Africa together. Lavinckeur (Vaincquer) also accompanied Smidt to Friesland, in order to purchase cloth from the merchant Geert Oeges.[127] The cloth was delivered in Amsterdam to Vinckel and other shipowners, and then dispatched along with the rest of the cargo on the *Glückstadt*, which sailed to Guinea under Carloff's direct command.[128] Smidt's declaration demonstrates that he was well informed about Carloff's network of investors in Europe. Although only a junior partner, Smidt was well connected himself, and aware of Carloff's social and business relations in Europe.

Carloff's correspondence with Valckenburgh shed further light on his plan for the region. He envisaged the entire Gold Coast under one (European) ruler and made a proposal to this effect to the Directors of the WIC in Amsterdam. Carloff would also have appreciated a personal meeting with Valckenburgh. However, at that time, such a meeting might be seen as suspicious.[129] Considering the fact that the two companies were supposed to be competing, it was probably a wise precaution to avoid gossip that might call into question Carloff and Valckenburgh's motives.

In another letter, Carloff wrote that he was pleased that Valckenburgh had agreed to the idea of bringing the coast under one ruler.[130] Carloff had received confidential information from Coenrad van Beuningen, who at this time was the ambassador of the Dutch Republic in Denmark. Apparently, van Beuningen had recommended that the Danish crown turn over the management of the Swedish possessions to an ally of Denmark. The ally in question was of course the Republic, which had signed an alliance with Denmark in 1645. The connection to van Beuningen endured for a considerable time. Almost twenty years later, van Beuningen wrote a recommendation letter on behalf of Carloff to the States General, arguing in favour of appointing him governor of Suriname.[131] Indeed, Carloff was well connected within the diplomatic and political circles of the Republic.

Carloff added that he had already discussed the topic with Eduard Man, the director of the WIC in Amsterdam, who thought that it would be better to destroy the fort altogether. Man's suggestion to destroy Carolusborg arose because the WIC wanted to attract trade to Elmina instead, and to put an end to the use of Fetu merchants as middlemen (as has been discussed in earlier chapters). According to Carloff, Man did not understand coastal politics: demolishing the fort was impossible, because the locals would oppose it.

The vulnerability of being connected 109

In the event of such opposition, he believed, the fort would fall into the hands of the English, to the detriment of all parties concerned. As such, Carloff's plan was to raise the topic once again with the WIC. Carloff concluded his letter by requesting that Valckenburgh keep its contents a secret and, if necessary, burn the letter.

Carloff's letters to Valckenburgh highlight the events that occurred in Western Africa following the conquest of the SAC fort. The letters reveal a reality that was radically different to what had been envisaged in the contract (August 1657) between the Danish monarch and Carloff: in particular, it becomes clear that Carloff had never entirely severed his connections with the WIC. Although negotiating with WIC officials in Western Africa, he was at the time sailing under a Danish commission, financed with Dutch capital, and making use of his local African connections. Indeed, Carloff was entangled in several competing networks, and his individualistic behaviour eventually created trouble for his progress on the coast.

Upon his return to Europe, Carloff once again approached Eduard Man, suggesting an agreement between Smidt and the WIC.[132] Carloff suggested that the handing over of the fort should be done in Smidt's name. Thus, the Danish would not be able to accuse him of misconduct in the future. Indeed, Carloff did not wish to interfere with the agreement but merely to keep the gold and merchandise he had procured during the attack on the settlement. However, it is equally possible that Carloff wanted to remove any possible suspicion of wrong-doing in the event of any future collaboration with the WIC. In March, Carloff wrote to Smidt once again.[133] Here, he stated his suspicion that Klingenberg, Marselis, and other potential investors were planning to continue trading in Africa without him.[134]

Judging from the letter to Smidt, it seems that the Danish did not have a long-term plan for Carloff. Indeed, he may have used this fact as an excuse to justify the transfer of the fort to the WIC. Carloff continued his letter to Smidt by stating that the Swedish had made an agreement with the English to attack Carolusborg together. According to Carloff, it would thus be preferable for the Danes to voluntarily cede the fort to their Dutch ally. As such, Casper van Heussen should prepare a document preparing the surrender of the fort.[135] In other words, Carloff was almost ordering Smidt to surrender the fort to the WIC.

However, matters were more complicated than they appeared. After all, during the spring of 1659, without the knowledge of the officials of the WIC, Carloff was still negotiating with the Danes regarding the progress of Danish trade in Africa. At the same time, he entered into an agreement with representatives of the WIC chamber in Amsterdam. On 20 March 1659, it was agreed that Carloff would order Smidt to transfer the fort to the WIC. As a result, Smidt and Carloff would be treated with respect by the WIC. The agreement further stipulated that Carloff would be allowed to sell the goods that he had accumulated in Africa in Amsterdam. These goods would be transported to Amsterdam on WIC ships, under his name.[136]

110   *The vulnerability of being connected*

Eventually, Carloff changed his mind and sent a new letter to Smidt. All of a sudden, he no longer wanted to surrender the fort to the WIC but to the Danish crown instead. In Carloff's words, the situation had changed in Europe, due to the shifting political relationship between Sweden and Denmark. Once again, he had the chance to send ships to Western Africa, but Smidt would have to be patient. Smidt ought to be aware of the possibility of English ships coming to the coast, and to remain alert and suspicious towards the WIC and English merchants at all times.[137] As mentioned at the beginning of this section, in May 1659, an agreement had been made between Poul Klingenberg and Carloff (Jan de Swaen had represented Carloff in these negotiations). This agreement acknowledged that Carloff would surrender the fort to the Danish king, but that he was to be allowed to keep the gold from the ships. Furthermore, it was stated that Carloff and his business partners were to be allowed to trade in the regions that he had surrendered to the Danish crown. Carloff was to be respected on the coast, and the Danish officials should always assist Carloff.[138] The political context in Europe played an important role in how Carloff perceived his business opportunities. This demonstrates that Carloff was playing a high-risk game with two different parties. On the one hand, he was negotiating future plans for the Africa trade in Denmark. On the other hand, he was attempting to improve his relationship with the WIC by promising to surrender Carolusborg to the WIC.

However, Carloff's last letter to Smidt did not have the intended outcome. Unbeknown to Carloff, Smidt had already surrendered the fort to the WIC. In this regard, an official statement and a letter from Smidt to Carloff sheds light on how Smidt and Canter had justified the surrender of the fort to the WIC.[139] Smidt, Canter, and the others who had sworn an oath to Carloff had decided to transfer all the possessions to the WIC, because Carloff had not kept to his side of the bargain. Smidt went to great lengths to explain that it was Carloff's failure to send ships and payments that had damaged the relationship between the men on the ground and Acrosan. Smidt and Canter explained that Carloff had clearly lied, since the promised ships had never arrived. Acrosan's anger had been exacerbated by the fact that he had dismissed several Swedish ships, which had attempted to reclaim the Swedish possessions. According to the caboceer, the contract with Carloff was still valid, and he had full trust in his former partner, and, for that reason, he had not allowed the Swedish ships to land on the coast. However, Carloff's failure to appear had left Acrosan with no other option than to trade in gold with an English ship, even though he had forbidden the English to establish contact with the Danish. The reason why Carloff had failed to send ships was most likely that the Glückstadt Company had not yet fully taken form; the Danish King Fredrik III was busy with the peace negotiations that followed the peace of Roskilde in 1658, and, soon after the peace, war broke out once again. Acrosan was disappointed with the absence of ships that could be used for trade. Carloff had failed to deliver on his promises

The vulnerability of being connected 111

to Smidt, Canter, and Acrosan, and this had ultimately resulted in Carloff losing the trust of his local connections. For Carloff, the worst blow was the loss of Acrosan.[140]

Smidt and Canter felt that they had been abandoned by Carloff, a feeling that had been exacerbated by the fact that when the WIC ships *Eyckenboom* and *Coninck Salomon* had arrived on the coast, they carried no letters addressed to them. As such, they discussed the situation with their subordinates and concluded that transferring the fort to a friendly ally was the only possible solution. Remarkably, Smidt and Canter's arguments indicate that Carloff had not managed to win the loyalty of his subordinates. According to Smidt, the WIC had hired him to manage their trade on the coast. He was pleased with the fact that the WIC had chosen to offer him employment, despite his previous actions. Smidt had changed allegiance, and the way that he addressed Carloff was not the way to treat a trading partner. The relationship between Smidt and Carloff had thus changed dramatically. In this case, none of his contacts had shown any real sign of loyalty, since they all knew that loyalties could shift rapidly. In addition, the WIC officials had attempted to use the slow information flow between Carloff and Smidt to their own advantage. Indeed, it is likely that they confiscated letters sent from Europe and circulated malicious rumours and gossip.

However, it is important to consider the other motives behind the surrender. The contract had stipulated the transfer of the fort and lodges to the WIC.[141] The remaining gold in the fort was to be transferred to Carloff. All previous Danish employees who were willing to accept a new job offer would be entitled to do so, and those who wanted to return home could. Furthermore, the employees were allowed to keep or to trade their belongings, including slaves, who could be sold at a fixed price on the coast. The commander (Smidt) and the upper factor (Canter) were allowed to either take employment with the WIC or to wait for a suitable moment to depart for Europe. The WIC would cover their daily expenses on the coast while they awaited transport. Smidt and Canter were also offered a bonus for their favours to the WIC (Smidt 5,000 guilders and Canter 4,000 guilders). Canter returned to Europe late in 1659 with a significant quantity of gold, with which he meant to compensate Carloff for the surrender of the fort. However, Canter deposited the gold with the WIC, and the company released it to Carloff only after he had formally signed off the surrender of the fort.[142] In short, for Smidt and Canter, there were also financial and career motives behind the transfer. Employment in the WIC could provide them with new opportunities and potentially greater stability than that offered by Carloff.

In the autumn of 1659, still unaware of the transfer on the coast, Carloff tried to maintain his balancing act in Europe. Carloff wrote to the upper factor Johan Canter, stating that he wanted to know about the state of affairs there.[143] In another letter to Smidt, he wrote that he knew about four ships being equipped to sail to Guinea. According to Carloff, the WIC had received orders to treat Danish ships with respect.[144] These letters

112   *The vulnerability of being connected*

demonstrate that Carloff was not aware of the current state of business in Western Africa. However, he continued to try to reconnect with his subordinates. This highlights how challenging it was to maintain connections with people at a distance through ineffective modes of communication.

Matters were further complicated by Carloff's relationship with the caboceer Acrosan. In a letter to the representatives of the SAC dated May 1659, Acrosan claimed to have been mistreated by Carloff and his men.[145] In 1658, Carloff had promised that when he arrived on the coast, he would continue to improve trade with Acrosan and the Fetu. However, Acrosan had eventually understood that Carloff had broken his promises. Indeed, this was the reason why Acrosan had conquered the fort when it was transferred to the WIC. He wished to remain loyal to the SAC, and to allow only the Swedish company to enter the fort. He confirmed that Carloff's untrustworthy behaviour was the reason for his decision, and that he would hand over the fort to a Swedish representative if one appeared within a year. In the meantime, he would be in charge. If the SAC did arrive within the stipulated period, they would only have to pay the monthly tribute and other customary gifts for the time that Acrosan had taken care of the fort. Whether Acrosan would have been able to keep his promises is unclear, since the SAC was unable to send ships to the coast by the time of the deadline.

Finally, in October, the first Glückstadt Company ship arrived on the coast. In charge was Joost Cramer, the previous business partner of Carloff in the SAC, who was now employed by the Glückstadt Company.[146] Cramer soon realised what had happened in April and found himself unable to enter Fort Carolusborg. Cramer did not manage to claim Carolusborg for the Glückstadt Company but did receive Acrosan's permission to build another fort further east on the coast. Cramer tried to protest against the WIC but in vain. Over the subsequent years, the Cape Coast would remain a contested region.[147] The WIC remained a strong power on the Gold Coast, and the English and the Danish also managed to establish permanent settlements. The SAC also tried once more to establish itself, but eventually left the coast having had little success.

Eventually, Carloff realised that his opportunities on the Cape Coast had evaporated, and that even his former ally Acrosan had abandoned him. During a subsequent dispute between the WIC and the Glückstadt Company (1662–1665), Carloff took the side of the WIC and openly declared that the Glückstadt Company had been a sham. He was pressured to pick a side so as to avoid being accused of treason (at the time, he resided in Amsterdam). He even managed to keep the gold that he had stolen from the SAC. However, Carloff no longer returned to the Gold Coast.

This section has shown that Carloff ultimately failed to balance his connections. However, at the same time, it has demonstrated just how fragile these social connections were for all Europeans. Furthermore, the section has shown the ways in which the European political context had an impact on how individuals perceived business opportunities. In short, the relationship between competitors and collaborators on the coast could change almost overnight, with serious implications for the balance of business networks and, ultimately, for the trading companies themselves. Indeed, this made business uncertain, and even chaotic, a fact of which the individuals concerned were abundantly aware.

Conclusion

This chapter has explained why balancing different connections was important to overseas entrepreneurship. Leyel not only had to manage the accounts and books of the company. He also had to please local rulers and merchants in order to maintain effective trading relationships. He managed these connections by instructing company employees as well as local merchants who were directly or indirectly involved with the DEIC. Through Leyel, several overlapping business networks became intertwined. The experiences of Leyel and Carloff demonstrate the necessity of relationships with local rulers and merchants. Local business relationships were built upon the promise of selling goods at low prices in the local market, paying tributes, offering lavish gifts, and obeying local rulers. As such, the local relationships of individuals were key to the success of the companies they served.

Carloff's involvement in ghost investing shows how the interests of individuals alternately coexisted and conflicted with those of the trading companies. Study of the investments made through the Glückstadt Company demonstrates how complex systems were devised in order to circumvent the privileges of chartered companies (in this case, the WIC). These systems operated through both individuals and interest groups. As noted, in the Nordic context, overseas entrepreneurship required coexistence between the trading companies and individuals, on an almost equal footing. In addition, the interests of individuals were important both within and in relation to the local trading systems and networks in which they operated.

Carloff, who balanced between his own interests and those of the Danish, the Swedish, and the Dutch, provides a good example. Through close study of the challenges that such individuals faced, it becomes apparent that these connections were extremely uncertain and vulnerable. The ruthlessness of seventeenth-century overseas business stemmed from the way in which relationships could be transformed almost overnight. Without good relationships with local rulers, European merchants and employees were at the mercy of their rivals. In this regard, the difference between Leyel and Carloff was that Leyel was more isolated, and thus forced to survive with only a few men, with whom he ultimately failed to reach a mutual understanding. His relationships with the Nielsens and Hansen demonstrate this well: one day, he appointed them as acting governors or factors, and the next, they conspired to overthrow him. The explanation for this is that Leyel represented the interests of the king, and simultaneously collaborated with

114 *The vulnerability of being connected*

local merchants, both of whom were disliked by the other company employees. Carloff, on the other hand, moved back and forth between Europe and Africa, and was more closely connected to his European networks. In the end, Leyel remained loyal to the king, whereas Carloff switched his allegiance multiple times. Leyel hoped that his loyalty would bring him upward social mobility, whereas Carloff was in a different position, and demonstrated no enduring loyalty to any monarch or, indeed, to anyone at all.

Leyel and Carloff often chose to act in an individualistic fashion. In particular, they were unable to maintain any inner coherence in their social relationships within the companies. The fact that both men had problems with the companies they worked for suggests, on the one hand, that they failed to develop their social connections within the companies effectively. On the other hand, it suggests that the companies were not harmonious enterprises but were rather riven by conflicts of interest between the various employees.

Choosing the right business associates is crucial for an individual entrepreneur. Indeed, this choice says much about the individual's capacity to interpret his social environment. The choice of connections is based on the individual's evaluation of the potential benefits, which again indicates the individual's intentions. If the intention is understood, it becomes clearer why individuals choose to connect with some and not with others.[148] This approach can shed new light on the concepts and uses of trust and loyalty. When Leyel and Carloff faced questions regarding the loyalty and trust of others, they unconsciously signalled that they too were subject to chains of trust and loyalty. The people involved in overseas trade were aware of how quickly loyalty could shift, and knew that trust was a vague, rhetorical matter. In the end, Leyel and Carloff ultimately failed to balance the networks they were supposed to connect. Leyel was overthrown in a mutiny, and Smidt handed Carolusborg over to the WIC just as Carloff had decided that the fort should not be transferred to them after all. Trust was fluid and negotiable, as was the line between loyalty and betrayal.

Finally, although people in the seventeenth century did not use the term "networks," they were nonetheless aware of the different sets of connections that linked them personally to others. As such, the management and optimal balancing of connections were crucial to career opportunities and economic success. Business and exchanges, in Europe and overseas, included several competing, overlapping, and collaborating networks, which could change rapidly if their participants decided to enter, leave, support, or even betray them.

Notes

1 Müller, *The Merchant Houses*; L. Kooijmans, *Vriendschap*; L. Kooijmans, "Risk and Reputation; Lesger and Noordegraaf," *Entrepreneurs and Entrepreneurship in Early Modern Times*.
2 Discussion on networks and hierarchy, see Walter Powell, "Neither Market nor Hierarchy: Network Forms in Organization," in *Markets, Hierarchies and Networks: The Coordination of Social Life*, ed. Grahame Thompson (London:

The vulnerability of being connected 115

SAGE, 1991), 265–276; Ylva Hasselberg, Leos Müller, and Niklas Stenlås, "Åter till historians nätverk," in *Sociala nätverk och fält*, ed. Håkan Gunneriusson (Uppsala: Historiska Institutionen, 2002), 7–32.

3 RAC, DK, B 246 A, Leyel to the directors 22.11.1644.

4 Pessart had for the last years been in favour of abandoning Dansborg and moving the headquarters to Masulipatnam where the Northern textile trade was more profitable.

5 RAC, DK, B 246 A, Leyel to the directors 22.11.1644.

6 RAC, DK, B 246 A, Leyel to the directors 22.11.1644; RAC, DK, B 246 A, Sentence declaration over Pessart, 28.06.1644.

7 Emeldy and the coast of Zinzley are in the Golconda kingdom.

8 A local merchant boat used in the Indian Ocean. RAC, DK, B 246 A, Leyel to the directors 22.11.1644.

9 Today, it is located in the southern part of the city of Chennai, on the Coromandel Coast.

10 RAC, DK, B 246 A, Leyel to the directors 22.11.1644.

11 RAC, DK, B 246 A, Copy of the letter from Leyel to J. Stakenborrig, 18.11.1643, Masulipatanam.

12 RAC, DK, B 246 A, The fort council's reply to Leyel 12.06.1644.

13 I will return to Simão D'Almeida later in this chapter.

14 RAC, DK, B 246 A, Leyel to the directors 22.11.1644.

15 "gud folade hannem som saa skammeligen haffue udset woris nations gode naffn og rokte udi disse land," RAC, DK, B 246 A, Leyel to H. Knutsen, 1.07.1644.

16 RAC, DK, B 246 A, Sentence declaration over Pessart, 28.06.1644.

17 RAC, DK, B 246 A, Leyel to P. Nielsen, 20.10.1645.

18 RAC, DK, B 246 A, Letter to the king, 18.10.1645.

19 RAC, DK, B 246 A, Leyel to P. Nielsen, 20.10.1645.

20 RAC, DK, B 246 A, oath to serve acting governor P. Nielsen, 18.10.1645.

21 RAC, DK, B 246 A, Leyel to the directors, 12.12.1645.

22 RAC, DK, B 246 A, Leyel to P. Hansen, 1.02.1647.

23 RAC, DK, B 246 A, A. Nielsen to Leyel, 10.02.1648.

24 RAC, DK, B 246 A, petition from the people of the town Tranquebar to Leyel, 26.07.1645; RAC, DK, B 246 A, Leyel to the directors, 22.11.1644. More extensively about the two priests see Bredsdorff, *The Trials and Travels*, 106–119.

25 RAC, DK, B 246 A, J. Lauridsen to Leyel, 30.01.1645; RAC, DK, B 246 A, Leyel's reply to J. Lauridsen, 30.01.1645.

26 RAC, DK, B 246 A, Leyel to the directors, 22.11.1644.

27 RAC, DK, B 246 A, Sentences over N. Udbyer and C. Sturm, 8.10.1645.

28 RAC, DK, B 246 A, Mutiny document, unknown author, most likely the mutineers, 31.12.1648.

29 RAC, DK, B 246 A, P. Hansen to Willem Leyel, 8.01.1646.

30 RAC, DK, B 246 A, Leyel to P. Hansen, 31.07.1647.

31 RAC, DK, B 246 A, Leyel Report, 6.10.1643.

32 RAC, DK, B 246 A, Mutiny document, unknown author, most likely the mutineers, 31.12.1648. Bredsdorff on the mutiny, see Bredsdorff, *The Trials and Travels*, 167–171.

33 Roberto White (in some sources Roberto Blanco) and Antonio Carvalho were mentioned as the local intermediaries.

34 RAC, DK, B 246 A, Leyel to the directors, 12.12.1645; Bredsdorff, *The Trials and Travels*, 134.

35 RAC, DK, B 246 A, Leyel to the directors, 22.11.1644.

36 Guido Meersbergen van, "The Dutch Merchant-Diplomat in Comparative Perspective: Embassies to the Court Aurangzeb, 1660–1666," in *Practices of*

116   *The vulnerability of being connected*

Diplomacy in the Early Modern World c.1410–1800, ed. Tracey Sowerby and Jan Hennings (New York: Routledge, 2017), 147–165.

37 Martha Chaiklin, "Elephants and the Making of Early Modern India," in *The Indian Ocean in the Making of Early Modern India*, ed. Pius Malekandathil (New York: Routledge, 2017), 457–475, 459–460.

38 Frans Birkenholz, "Merchant-Kings and Lords of the World: Diplomatic Gift-Exchange between the Dutch East India Company and the Safavid and Mughal Empires in the Seventeenth Century," in *Practices of Diplomacy in the Early Modern World c.1410–1800*, ed. Tracey Sowerby and Jan Hennings (New York: Routledge, 2017), 219–236.

39 In the original document, *"forsækrings kostnader,"* RAC, DK, B 246 A, Leyel to the directors 12.12.1645.

40 RAC, DK, B 246 A, Leyel to the directors 12.12.1645.

41 RAC, DK, B 246 A, Leyel to the directors, 12.12.1645.

42 The attack is discussed more in detail in the previous chapter. RAC, DK, B 246 A, several letters: 8.03.1645–25.03.1645.

43 RAC, DK, B 246 A, Leyel to the directors, 12.12.1645.

44 RAC, DK, B 246 A, Leyel to the directors, 22.11.1644.

45 From 1527 to 1658, a series of conflicts occurred between the Portuguese and the Kingdom of Ceylon, which was under the rule of Candy. The VOC often intervened in these conflicts, especially between 1639 and 1658, usually allying itself with Candy. The conflict thus became a part of the Portuguese–Dutch rivalry in the East. Eventually, the alliance between the Candy kingdom and the VOC broke down, and all parties declared war against each other. See George Davison Winius, *The Fatal History of Portuguese Ceylon: Transition to Dutch Rule* (Cambridge, Mass: Harvard University Press, 1971).

46 RAC, DK, B 246 A, Leyel instructions to A. Jacobsen, 26.07.1644.

47 RAC, DK, B 246 A, Leyel to the directors, 15.11.1646.

48 RAC, DK, B 246 A, Leyel to the directors, 22.11.1644.

49 Tapan Raychaudhuri, *Jan Company in Coromandel, 1605–1690: A Study in the Interrelations of European Commerce and Traditional Economies* (Gravenhage: Martinus Nijhoff, 1962), 7.

50 RAC, DK, B 246 A, Instructions to frigate *Ellefant*, 16 April 1644.

51 RAC, DK, B 246 A, Leyel to the directors, 12.11.1645.

52 RAC, DK, B 246 A, instructions to Adrian Jacobsen, 27.07.1644; RAC, DK, B 246 A, Leyel to A. Nielsen, 1.02.1647.

53 RAC, DK, B247 B, Leyel instruction to S. Charstenson and W. Mouridsen, 19.09.1645; 21.09.1646.

54 Subrahmanyam, *The Political Economy of Commerce*, 167.

55 The *St Michael* made several business voyages to the Malayan peninsula, RAC, DK, B247 B, Leyel instruction to S. Charstenson and W. Mouridsen, 19.09.1645; 21.09.1646; RAC, DK, B247 B, Leyel instructions to Torstenson, 19.02.1645; Bredsdorff, *The Trials and Travels*, 149.

56 Luis Felippe Ferreira Reis Thomaz, "The Indian Merchant Communities in Malacca under the Portuguese Rule," in *Indo-Portuguese History: Old Issues, New Questions*, ed. Teotonio de Souza (New Delhi: Concept Publishing Company, 1985), 56–72, 57–62 .

57 RAC, DK, B247 B, Leyel instructions to Torstenson, 19.02.1645; RAC, DK, B247 B, Leyel instruction to S. Charstenson and W. Mouridsen, 19.09.1645.

58 RAC, DK, B 246 A, Instruction to Jakob Andersen on Wahlby 5.11.1646 and instruction on J. Hansen Christianshavn 19.02.1647.

59 RAC, DK, B 246 A, Passport to ship Trangabara, 28.08.1644.

60 Leonard Y. Andaya, "The 'Informal Portuguese Empire' and the Topasses in the Solor Archipelago and Timor in the Seventeenth and Eighteenth Centuries," *Journal of Southeast Asian Studies* 41, no. 3 (October 2010): 391–420;

Stefan Halikowski Smith, *Creolization and Diaspora*; Anthony Disney, *The Portuguese in India and Other Studies, 1500–1700* (New York: Routledge, 2009); Maria Augusta Lima Cruz, "Exiles and Renegades in Early Sixteenth Century Portuguese India." *The Indian Economic & Social History Review* 23, no. 3 (1986): 249–262.

61 Subrahmanyam, *The Portuguese Empire in Asia, 1500–1700: A Political and Economic History* (Chichester: John Wiley & Sons, 2012).

62 Winius, "The 'Shadow Empire'," 83–101.

63 RAC, DK, B 246 A, Leyel to the directors, 22.11.1644.

64 Readers familiar with the historiography of the Indian Ocean might wonder whether the local Portuguese were Topazes (mixed-race, European-Asian Christians, who were not necessarily connected to the official Portuguese authorities). Based on the sources at hand, it is difficult to say one way or the other.

65 RAC, DK, B 246 A, A. Nielsen to Leyel, 11.10.1644.

66 RAC, DK, B 246 A, Leyel instructions to A. Nielsen, 4.09.1644.

67 RAC, DK, B 246 A, Leyel to the directors, 22.11.1644.

68 Raychaudhuri, *Jan Company*, 114. Confirmed by Leyel. RAC, DK, B 246 A, Leyel to the directors, 22.11.1644.

69 RAC, DK, B 246 A, Leyel to the directors, 12.12.1645.

70 RAC, DK, B 246 A, Leyel to N. Samson, 24.05.1647.

71 His salary was 4 *pardous*, which was a considerable amount in the Danish context. Poul Nielsen, the acting governor, had a monthly salary of 10 *pardous*. RAC, DK, B 246 A, Instructions to P. Nielsen, 20.10.1645.

72 RAC, DK, B 246 A, Instructions to P. Nielsen, 20.10.1645.

73 RAC, DK, B 246 A, Instructions to P. Nielsen, 20.10.1645.

74 "wi corresponderer meget med huarandra," RAC, DK, B 246 A, Leyel to the directors, 15.11.1646.

75 Raychaudhuri, *Jan Company*, 98 and 113.

76 RAC, DK, B 246 A, Leyel to J. Hansen, 24.05.1647.

77 It is unclear to which treaty Leyel was referring. Future research might focus on Danish foreign policy towards Portugal, but this is of little importance to this book, which concentrates on entrepreneurship. Nevertheless, it is important to stress that in the first half of the seventeenth century, there was no centralised Danish foreign policy. Responsibility for foreign relations was divided between the Danish Chancery and the German Chancery, and the relationship between the two chanceries was diffuse. Throughout the 1640s, Denmark's main concern was the venomous relationship with Sweden and particularly the situation in the Baltic. Even during the Thirty Years War, Denmark tried to maintain an equal standing in relation to the continental powers but eventually failed due to its diminished position in the Baltic. From this perspective, it is plausible that Denmark aimed at maintaining a good relationship with the Portuguese king. From the Portuguese end, after gaining independence from Spain, the Portuguese crown had concluded an alliance with Sweden in 1641. Considering the numerous overseas battles between the Dutch Republic and Portugal, including in the Indian Ocean, it would not be surprising if the Portuguese crown had been open to the possibility of a diplomatic arrangement with the Danish, who were fellow competitors against the Dutch.

78 Although the trade was still under monopoly control, silver was the main currency, and therefore crucial to successful trade in China.

79 RAC, DK, B 246 A, Leyel to the directors, 15.11.1646.

80 RAC, DK, B 246 A, Leyel to H. Ekman, 21.09.1646.

81 Seshan, *Trade and Politics*, 24; In Masulipatnam, the VOC did not have a fortification, Subrahmanyam, *The Political Economy of Commerce*, 168.

82 Subrahmanyam, *The Political Economy of Commerce*, 168.

118 *The vulnerability of being connected*

83 Raychaudhuri, *Jan Company*, 2–3.
84 Poul Nielsen was eventually sent to rescue the survivors, in which he succeeded. See Bredsdorff, *The Trials and Travels*, 134–135.
85 RAC, DK, B 246 A, Leyel to the directors, 12.12.1645.
86 Ibid.
87 "jeg holder goed correspondent og wennskab med hannom eptersom hand meget for maar. Baade hoss formentioned kong ogh naiquerne ogh hand kand oss megit were behuelpelig imod hollenderne," RAC, DK, B 246 A, Leyel to the directors, 12.12.1645.
88 Seshan, *Trade and Politics*, 62–64.
89 Malaio Chetti, also known as Astrappa Chetti, Coolhas, ed., *Generale missiven*, deel 1, 1610–1638, 7.03.1631, 298; Subrahmanyam also confirms this, *The political Economy of Commerce*, 307.
90 Chinanna Chetti, also known as Malaio Chinene.
91 On the career of Chinanna, see Ibid., 307–314.
92 Brenning has discussed the importance of the Malaya family as key brokers in the Coromandel trade. See Brennig, "Chief Merchants," 323–329.
93 Ibid.
94 RAC, DK, B 246 A, Leyel instruction to P. Nielsen, 1.10.1645.
95 RAC, TKIA, Diverse akter vdr. Det ostindiske kompagni og Guinea, Contract between Carloff and Fredrik III, 1.08.1657; Justesen, *Danish Sources*, 1–3
96 In 1662 Carloff was forced to declare the events around 1659 because the WIC had pressed charges against the Glückstadt Company and Carloff would otherwise have been accused of treason. Via the declaration he received immunity for the charges; Sieveking, "Die Glückstädter Guineafahrt," 37; NL-HaNA, Staten-Generaal, 1.01.02, inv.nr. *12572.41*, Carloff declaration, 12.10.1662; Carloff's declaration printed in De Roever, "Twee Concurrenten."
97 On institutional shelter, see Chapter 2.
98 A similar concept has been discussed by Filipa Ribeiro da Silva, who has referred to investors involved in these kinds of activities as silent or passive investors, Filipa Ribeiro da Silva, "Private Businessmen in the Angolan Trade, 1590s to 1780s: Insurance, Commerc and Agency," in *Networks and Trans-Cultural Exchange: Slave Trading in the South Atlantic, 1590–1867*, ed. David Richardson and Filipa Ribeiro da Silva (Boston/Leiden: Brill, 2014), 90.
99 NL-HaNA, Staten-Generaal, 1.01.02, inv.nr. *12572.41*, Placaten of the WIC 1624, 1632, and 1657.
100 SAA NA: 2278, fol.63, 25.10.1650.
101 Christian IV also made similar arrangements when financing the first DEIC. See Chapter 3.
102 NL-HaNA, Staten-Generaal, 1.01.02, inv.nr. *12572.41*, Carloff declaration, 12.10.1662; De Roever, "Twee Concurrenten," 200; Dahlgren, *Louis de Geer*, 348; Porter, *European* Activity, 378.
103 In 1625 Baers became a resident in Glückstadt. Glückstadt, Das Stadtarchiv, Bürgerbuch, Baers Bürger rights, 6.01.1625; NL-HaNA, Staten-Generaal, 1.01.02, inv.nr. *12572.41*, Declaration by Carloff 12.10.1662, Carloff's declaration printed in De Roever, "Twee Concurrenten."
104 Nørregård, *Danish Settlements*, 13.
105 Glückstadt, Das Stadtarchiv, urkunden 12, 16.05.1651; Nørregård, *Danish Settlements*, 12.
106 NL-HaNA, Staten-Generaal, 1.01.02, inv.nr. *12572.41*, Carloff declaration, 12.10.1662; Carloff's declaration printed in De Roever, "Twee Concurrenten."

The vulnerability of being connected   119

107 Nørregård, *Danish Settlements*, 22.
108 De Roever, "Twee Concurrenten," 216.
109 NL-HaNA, Staten-Generaal, 1.01.02, inv.nr. *12572.41*, Carloff declaration, 12.10.1662; Carloff's declaration printed in De Roever, "Twee Concurrenten."
110 Henrich Sieveking, "Die Glückstädter Guineafahrt," 30; The diplomatic negotiations have been extensively dealt with by Granlund, *En svensk koloni i Afrika*, 32; Nováky, *Handelskompanier*, 205.
111 Sieveking and Nörregård give different dates. Here the dates by Nørregård are followed.
112 Nørregård, *Danish Settlements*, 23.
113 SAA NA: 1128, fol.272-273, 15.03.1659.
114 Nørregård, *Danish Settlements*, 47–55; Feldbæk, *Danske Handelskompagnier*, 355–363.
115 De Roever, "Twee Concurrenten," 216.
116 NL-HaNA, Staten-Generaal, 1.01.02, inv.nr. *12572.41*, Carloff declaration, 12.10.1662; Carloff's declaration printed in De Roever, "Twee Concurrenten." Glückstadt municipal archives state that the captain of the *St Marten* was Cornelis Janssen, who had been born in Voorburg (in the Netherlands), had received burgher rights in Glückstadt, and had been granted a licence to travel to Guinea. Glückstadt, Das Stadtarchiv, Bürgerbuch 23 April; 1660.
117 SAA NA: 1134, fol.143, 3.08.1660. "bodemerijgeld with opgeld."
118 NL-HaNA, Staten-Generaal, 1.01.02, inv.nr. *12572.41*, de Swaen signed the declaration, 3.07.1659; FC, N8, 183.
119 NL-HaNA, Staten-Generaal, 1.01.02, inv.nr. *12572.41*, Henrich Carloff to Jan de Swaen, 15.03.1659 (the withdrawal was added to the power of attorney document 4.10.1659); FC, N8, 171–173; De Roever, "Twee Concurrenten," 214.
120 NL-HaNA, Staten-Generaal, 1.01.02, inv.nr. *12572.41*, Jan de Swaen to Carloff, 14.09.1659; FC, N8, 193.
121 Pamflet Knuttel 8905A, remonstrantie aen de Ho: Mo: Heeren de Staten-Generael der Vereenighde Nederlanden: Overgegeven den Junij 1664 Bij de Heeren de Bewint-hebberen van de Geoctroyeerde West-Indische Compagnie der Vereenighde Nederlanden. Opende jegens Verscheyde Memorien van den Heer Resident Charsius, wegens de (gepretendeerde) Deensche Africaensche Compagnie, aen haer Ho: Mo: overgegeven (Amsterdam 1664).
122 For more about this event, see Brieven, confessie; mitsgaders, advisen van verscheyden rechtsgeleerden in de saeck van Isaac Coymans gegeven; als mede de sententie daer op gevolgt (Rotterdamn 1662); Den Blanken, "Imperium in Imperio."
123 Den Blanken, "Imperium in Imperio," 52–63.
124 Valckenburgh was the Director-General of Elmina 24.01.1656–27.04.1659 and Casper Van Heussen 27.04.1659–7.04.1662.
125 NL-HaNA, Staten-Generaal, 1.01.02, inv.nr. *12571.38.1*, Henrich Carloff to Jan Valckenburgh, 15.02.1658, FC, N8, 41–43.
126 NL-HaNA, Staten-Generaal, 1.01.02, inv.nr. *12571.38.1*, Henrich Carloff to Jan Valckenburgh, 15.02.1658, FC, N8, 41–43.
127 At the time, cloth was one of the primary European products on the Western African market.
128 NL-HaNA, Staten-Generaal, 1.01.02, inv.nr. *12572.41*, Declaration by Samuel Smidt, at Elmina, 22.07.1659; FC, N8, 184.
129 NL-HaNA, Staten-Generaal, 1.01.02, inv.nr. *12571.38.1*, Henrich Carloff to Jan Valckenburgh, 15.02.1658, FC, N8, 41–43.

120 *The vulnerability of being connected*

130 NL-HaNA, Staten-Generaal, 1.01.02, inv.nr. *12571.38.1*, Henrich Carloff to Jan Valckenburgh, 16.02.1658, A copy of the letter from 16.02.1658 also in, NL-HaNA, 1.01.02, inv. nr. *12572.41*; FC, N8, 43–44.
131 NL-HaNA,Verspreide West-Indische Stukken, 1.05.06, inventarisnummer *1178*. Van Beuningen recommendation letter on behalf of Carloff, Undated document.
132 NL-HaNA, Staten-Generaal, 1.01.02, inv.nr. *12571.38.1*, Carloff to Man, 11/21.01.1659, FC, N8, 166.
133 RAC, Tyske Kancelliet Udenrigske Afdelning (TKUA), Nederlanderne: akter vedr. Det poltiiska forhold, 1660–1665, 70-14-70-1, Henrich Carloff to Samuel Smidt, 2/12.03.1659; FC, N8, 169–170.
134 Carloff must be referring to the Klingenberg family. On the Klingenberg and Marselis family, see John Lauridsen, *Marselis konsortiet: en studie over forholdet mellem handelskapital og kongemagt i 1600-talets Danmark* (Copenhagen: Jysk Selskab for Historie 1987); Sieveking, "Die Glückstädter Guineafahrt," 24; Nørregård, *Danish* Settlements, 11 and 15.
135 RAC, TKUA, Nederlanderne: akter vedr. Det poltiiska forhold, 1660–1665, 70-14-70-1, Henrich Carloff to Samuel Smidt, 2/12.03.1659; FC, N8, 169–170.
136 NL-HaNA, Staten-Generaal, 1.01.02, inv.nr. *12572.41*, Contract: Henrich Carloff – WIC, 20.03.1659, FC, N8, 175.
137 NL-HaNA, Staten-Generaal, 1.01.02, inv.nr. *12571.36*, Henrich Carloff to Samuel Smidt, 13.04.1659; FC, N8, 178–179; NL-HaNA, Staten-Generaal, 1.01.02, inv.nr. *12572.41*, Henrich Carloff to Samuel Smidt, 26.09.1659, FC, N8, 185.
138 RAC, TKIA, Diverse akter vdr. Det ostindiske kompagni og Guinea. Contract between Poul Klingenberg and Henrich Carloff, 28.03.1659 and 10.05.1659, The date from March indicates that this negotiation had started already in March.
139 RAC, TKUA, Nederlanderne: akter vedr. Det poltiiska forhold, 1660–1665, Samuel Smidt & Johan Canter to Dirck Wilree 18.04.1659; Copies of the declaration, NL-HaNA, Staten-Generaal, 1.01.02, inv.nr. *12571.38.1*, 22.08.1662; NL-HaNA, Staten-Generaal, 1.01.02, inv.nr. *12572.41*, 27.06.1664; NL-HaNA, Staten-Generaal, 1.01.02, inv.nr. *12572.41*, Samuel Smidt to Henrich Carloff, 31.09.1659; FC, N8, 189–191; FC, N8, 205–206.
140 Acrosan was the richest and most powerful man not only in the Fetu Kingdom but on the entire Gold Coast.
141 This is a combination of capitulations from three different sources. NL-HaNA, Staten-Generaal, 1.01.02, inv.nr. *12571.38.1*; NL-HaNA, Staten-Generaal, 1.01.02, inv.nr. *12571.36*; NL-HaNA, Staten-Generaal, 1.01.02, inv.nr. *12572.41*; FC, N8, 201–202.
142 Porter, *European Activity*, 397; Brieven, confessie; mitsgaders, advisen van verscheyden rechtsgeleerden in de saeck van Isaac Coymans gegeven; als mede de sententie daer op gevolgt (Rotterdamn 1662).
143 Carloff sent the letter with Joost Cramer on the *St Marten* to the coast.
144 NL-HaNA, Staten-Generaal, 1.01.02, inv.nr. *12572.41*, Carloff to Canter, 1.10.1659; FC, N8, 198; NL-HaNA, Staten-Generaal, 1.01.02, inv.nr. *12572.41*, Carloff to Smidt, 6.10.1659.
145 NL-HaNA, Staten-Generaal, 1.01.02, inv.nr. *12571.38.1*, Jan Claessen (Acrosan) to the directors of the SAC, 29.05.1659; FC, N8, 215.
146 NL-HaNA, OWIC, 1.05.01.01, inv.nr. *13A*, Joost Cramer to Casper Van Heussen, 11.10.1659, 461–465 (scans 463–467); FC, N8, 221–222.
147 NL-HaNA, OWIC, 1.05.01.01, inv.nr. *13A*, Joost Cramer to Casper Van Heussen, 11.10.1659, 461–465 (scans 463–467); FC, N8, 221–222; NL-HaNA, OWIC, 1.05.01.01, inv.nr. *13A*, Casper Van Heussen to Joost Cramer, 22.10.1659, 466–475 (scans 468–477); FC, N8, 223–225.
148 Mark Casson, *Entrepreneurship*, 24–26.

5 Knowledge and overseas business

Introduction

This chapter focuses on the importance of the accumulation of knowledge for overseas business. During the early modern period, the Dutch Republic was a centre for information and knowledge circulation regarding overseas trade. From a knowledge point of view, the Dutch overseas trade thrived through various travel journals and merchant manuals. Several travellers wrote journals from all parts of the globe, and these remained an important source of knowledge for both contemporaries and modern historians alike.[1] The different manuals, descriptions, and journals varied greatly from each other, and no definite protocol was followed. In addition, it was common to borrow freely from others' works and to embellish previous descriptions of distant regions. Many travellers made notes while they travelled and completed their manuscripts only upon return. These manuscripts were turned into books for a growing public of readers interested in the overseas world. Indeed, by the seventeenth century, the Republic and especially Amsterdam had developed an entire industry of knowledge and information circulation.

Dutch cartographers such as Willem Jansz Blaeu, Cornelis Claesz, and Johannes Vingboons led the world as mapmakers. Burghers of the city read newspapers, news from Asia and the Atlantic circulated widely among Dutch entrepreneurs, and it is thus no wonder that Amsterdam became a central entrepôt for knowledge circulation.[2] Indeed, this is also why so many aspiring Nordic merchants and public officials studied at Dutch universities, which placed a strong emphasis not only on merchant skills but also on a broad education in "overseas affairs," including languages, religions, and cultures.[3] Combining overseas travel and knowledge was common among educated men. For example, Philippus Baldaeus travelled with the VOC to Asia and wrote extensively on Malabar, Coromandel, and Ceylon. He had previously studied oriental languages and theology in Groningen and Leiden. Similar to Baldaeus, Abraham Rogerius travelled with the VOC to Asia and wrote widely on the Indian people and their culture for a Dutch audience.[4] In the Atlantic context, travellers like Olfert Dapper and Arnout Leers authored wide-ranging studies of the regions and cultures of West Africa.[5]

122 *Knowledge and overseas business*

From a knowledge perspective, there was a lively scene for both publishing and reading about the overseas world. However, although there was no shortage of information from overseas, the question of how to apply information in business practices was a different matter. During the seventeenth century, all European business enterprises faced the challenge of how to access and process scarce and irregular flows of information between Europe and overseas. Due to reasons characteristic of transcontinental trade, such as long distances and uncertain sailing conditions, there was a pressing need for the local knowledge of the men stationed overseas. The later were crucial for the perception and planning of business in Europe, since they had the most up-to-date knowledge of local business rhythms and patterns. Such individuals were also responsible for conducting business in practice, which meant that they needed an understanding of how to trade with both non-European merchants and European competitors, in environments that were remarkably different from those at home.

This chapter focuses on two interlinked topics. On the one hand, it studies the ways in which individuals translated accumulated information into knowledge. On the other hand, it examines how they applied this knowledge in order to strengthen their entrepreneurship.

Knowledge of overseas trade

This chapter revolves around the questions of overseas experience, information, and knowledge. Although these were interconnected and overlapping, they were not equivalent but rather mutually constitutive. Together, information and experience constituted knowledge of overseas business. Knowledge of overseas business was accumulated through the individual's experience, presence, and active participation in business conducted overseas, as well as his capacity to access and translate business information, both for his own benefit and for that of the trading enterprises for which he worked. This can be summed up as *knowledge of overseas trade*, which, for an individual with an entrepreneurial mindset, was something worth pursuing, particularly in order to demonstrate an aptitude for entrepreneurship to the directors of the companies in Europe.

Here it is chosen to use the concept *knowledge* rather than that of *know-how*. The reason for this is that although practical skills in conducting trade (*know-how*) are included within the more general term *knowledge*, the latter extends far beyond the merely practical sphere of the former. Thus, business know-how is a subordinate aspect of the larger concept of knowledge.

Of special interest for this chapter is the word "experience," which played a crucial role in the activities of both Leyel and Carloff. The concept of experience refers to the accumulated practices of long-term service overseas, as well as the capacity to navigate different zones of social and economic interaction. Here, experience refers to an individual's continuous presence in a physical space, as well as his capacity to process learning by doing

Knowledge and overseas business   123

(in this case, business and administration). Simultaneously, experience refers to the understanding of the local context, including its various actors, competitors, political entanglements, and cultural and social constraints. Experience can thus be understood as the understanding of multiple settings, through continuous visits and relational trial and error. In the long run, the successful management of experience resulted in a more effective adaptation of oneself and use of available means, in a process that transformed experience into usable knowledge. Overseas, not everyone was able to translate experience into knowledge, either due to personal limitations, such as a lack of literacy or cultural adaptability, or due to environmental constraints, for instance, difficulties in surviving in inhospitable environments. Entrepreneurial-minded individuals such as Leyel and Carloff were among those who successfully managed to convert experience into knowledge.

The accumulation of knowledge was as dependent upon experience as it was upon the capability of acquiring and managing information. Donald Harreld emphasises the companies' need for up-to-date information regarding market conditions. In the case of the early modern period, information flowed slowly due to long distances and infrastructural constraints. As Harreld stresses: "Very large joint-stock companies, like the East India Companies, relied most heavily on their individual functionaries abroad to provide market information."[6] In a similar fashion, Ann Carlos and Santhi Hejeebu argue that such overseas agents "were the vital generators of information that oiled the wheels of transcontinental commerce."[7]

In the overseas context, information comprises two factors. First, access to information refers to the capacity for gathering and accumulating information about overseas trade. Second, based on their previous experience, individuals knew how accumulated information could be used, for example, to exploit rumours and reports in order to influence the overseas trading situation, or to promote their career and social advancement in Europe. Ann Carlos and Stephen Nicholas propose that during the early modern period, international markets were characterised by uncertainty and asymmetric information. Trading companies did their best to decrease transaction costs by collecting, processing, and coordinating information on tastes, commodities, and prices.[8] The source of this information was the employees and local agents. For that reason, companies devised ways to supervise their personnel, in an attempt to reduce risk and to increase the opportunities for profit.[9]

The importance of accessing and controlling flows of information is generally referred to in economics as the "principal–agent problem." The relationship between the principal and the agent can become complicated when the agent makes decisions on behalf of his principal, and the principal does not have access to the same information as the agent. This becomes problematic, especially when the agent is motivated by his own self-interest and might thus be tempted to harm the interest of the principal. The main

124   *Knowledge and overseas business*

reason for such problems is the asymmetric access to information, which means that the agent has more up-to-date knowledge, for instance, of local markets and trading customs. Instead of focusing on how the companies (principals) managed to control their employees (agents), this chapter discusses the principal–agent problem from the standpoint of employees.

The importance of relevant information for the companies has also been noted by Mark Casson, who points out that information was not freely accessible to everyone, and, for that reason, individuals holding privileged information had an advantage in intervening either in the company or in the wider marketplace. Indeed, this is the main reason for which Casson considers information, when transformed into knowledge, as an important element in entrepreneurship and an asset for entrepreneurs. This is why, in the seventeenth century, knowledgeable individuals became so crucial for companies and investors. As Casson puts it, experience, information, and knowledge are highly localised, and only people on the ground are able to make full sense of them, since they are the only ones who observe the actual events.[10]

In practice, agents, who possessed crucial information regarding market conditions, had an extensive knowledge of the availability of products, of foreign competitors, and of suppliers, and thus held a competitive advantage compared to their counterparts.

Leyel and knowledge in the Indian Ocean

Ludovicus de Dieu, a scholar in oriental languages at Leiden, provided a contemporary account of Willem Leyel's early years in Asia. In his introduction to *Historia Christi*, he explains that:

> I owe it to the Danish merchant Willem Leyel, who now is the director of the Danish East India Company, to confess that the information that this man, raised above the ordinary spirit of commerce, though no scholar, while he still lived in Persia, learned to speak, read, and write the Persian language, passed on to me, when he spent some time in Leyden, has been very useful.[11]

This quotation demonstrates that Leyel, like many other young Nordic officials, had studied at Leiden. Thus, Leyel had participated in the knowledge accumulation culture for which the Republic was renowned. The text also suggests that Leyel learnt Persian during his employment with the VOC. Indeed, the letters and fragments amongst his papers confirm this suspicion. Bredsdorff has concluded that Leyel's interest in learning Persian is an exception to a commonly held image of the Danish merchant:

> The men who conducted the business of buying and selling in the distant Danish possession, are usually viewed as sitting with their noses

Knowledge and overseas business 125

buried in their accounts, longing for the day *when* they could return home with a large store of gold pieces in the bottom of their chests. Men who evinced no interest whatsoever in the magnificent culture of the East, in its history or literature, if only they could make a good profit.[12]

Bredsdorff's view of Leyel may be accurate, and it is possible that Leyel was fascinated by non-European cultures. However, it ought to be added that the reason for Leyel's eagerness had more to do with his business ambitions. During the period of Mughal rule, Persian was the administrative language of the empire, and was commonly used in Asia as a language of business.[13] The same could be said of Portuguese, which, during the seventeenth century, was the *de facto* overseas business language in both the Indian and the Atlantic arenas. Thus, learning Persian and Portuguese would have been extremely prudent, if not absolutely necessary, for Leyel.

Leyel accumulated experience during his earlier years in the service of the VOC. Travelling through multiple ports in the Indian Ocean, developing a command of the major trading languages, practising different customs of trade, and entangling his interests with those of local merchants all resulted in a certain degree of adaptation to the social and cultural world of the Indian Ocean. When Leyel entered DEIC employment, he was thus able to translate the acquired experiences into knowledge, which he attempted, not always successfully, to apply in practice.

The historian Steven Harris has shown that company employees "were bound by both written and unwritten rules of conduct, and corporate leaders had at their disposal mechanisms for the social and cognitive training and disciplining of members."[14] Leyel was required to report to the directors of the company in Copenhagen, and was accountable for DEIC business in Asia. His reports were supposed to provide the directors and the king with sufficient information about the state of the company in India.[15] In the DEIC, the person responsible for reporting to Europe was the commander, so the directors in Copenhagen had high expectations of this person.

From early on, Leyel sought to create the impression of being the right man for the position. One of his strategies was to exploit the information he was able to gather for his own benefit. He often began reports by underlining the bad conduct of fellow employees, especially Pessart, thus making his own actions appear in a good light. In other words, he presented himself as the man who was in the right place at the right time to save the company. To emphasise his importance, after the siege and subsequent inspection of Fort Dansborg, he reported that all matters regarding the company were in a desperate state, that the whole affair was embarrassing, and that it endangered Danish respectability in the eyes of other Europeans.[16]

Another recurring theme in Leyel's reports was his complaints regarding his colleagues' heavy alcohol consumption. "Here more than anywhere else in the world, opportunities for drinking and loose behaviour abound."[17] To reinforce his role as saviour of the company Leyel drew an association

126 *Knowledge and overseas business*

between the immoral behaviour of other employees and administrative difficulties. This became a convenient way for Leyel to send signals about who was to blame for the bad management of the company in Asia. The fault lay with his nemesis Pessart and his companions, whom Leyel referred to as rebels, rhetorically placing them outside of the orderly and morally superior space of the company.[18]

Leyel continued to cultivate his image as the only person capable of securing the best interests of the company. For example, he informed Copenhagen that trade in Makassar was about to collapse, largely because of Pessart's unpaid debts. Had Leyel not made the journey there, the entire factory would have been lost to other Europeans, and the DEIC would have faced great losses, since Makassar was the place in which it made most profit. He promised the directors that within one year, he would repay the outstanding debts and continue to expand trade.[19]

Furthermore, Leyel portrayed himself as the only trustworthy employee in the East. He complained that he had no one else he could trust, and, for that reason, he had been forced to appoint Anders Nielsen as the acting governor at fort Dansborg, so that he could travel in order to sort out the problems that had been caused by his predecessor.[20] However, what he failed to report was that this travelling often involved trading for his own benefit.

Leyel also insisted on demonstrating his knowledge of local customs to the directors in Europe, particularly by explaining how gift-giving was an essential part of his duties, and how well he performed it, particularly in relation to the Nayak. He also compared his own skill in these matters to that of his predecessor Crappe, a man who was much admired by the company directors in Denmark.[21]

From Leyel's reports, a director in Copenhagen, without access to any other information, could easily believe that the company was in trouble, and that forceful measures were needed. By blaming his co-commander for everything that had gone wrong with the company, Leyel justified his decision to take charge of the DEIC in Asia.[22] For Leyel, it was important to protect the image of his own superior judgement. Indeed, this was probably why Leyel's communiques were so personal, disclosing only the vaguest information about the details of business.[23]

In a separate report addressed to the King of Denmark, Leyel described what had happened in India since he had arrived. In general, the information was the same as that which he gave to the directors. However, in the letter to the king, one gets the impression that Leyel emphasised his own importance even more strongly. He stated to the king that he had done his utmost to improve trade in India, and that he would demonstrate his success in his subsequent reports.[24] Leyel perhaps saw an opportunity to send divergent information to the directors and to the king, and to thus manipulate the situation to his own advantage.[25] Indeed, this would have been quite feasible, given the monopoly that Leyel held over information.

Knowledge and overseas business 127

Among the things that Leyel omitted from his reports to the directors and the king was the fact that he was allowing the Dutch and the English to trade at Tranquebar, provided they kept their flags hidden.[26] Similarly, he made no mention of the fact that he was providing employment to local merchants, or that he was extending credit to other DEIC employees. In his reports, Leyel gave the impression that he was operating alone in India, whereas in reality he depended upon a multiplicity of different networks (as has been demonstrated in the previous chapter).

One way in which Leyel conveyed his own importance was to give detailed explanations of how he had improved trade. In particular, Leyel wanted to give the impression that he had made Tranquebar a more attractive venue for trade by stabilising exchange rates. In addition, Leyel was keen to emphasise that security had improved since the construction of the fort, and that new houses had been built using materials from Emeldy, Japara, and Makassar.[27] Leyel went to great lengths to demonstrate how he had saved the position of the Danish in Asia. His reports especially underlined the role of knowledge: Leyel understood what was needed and demonstrated his knowledge regarding competitors, the challenges of business, and, most importantly, the measures required to improve trade. After all, he was on a royal mission. "I would prefer to leave India, but I would be ashamed of doing so before I have, with the help of God, developed trade for the better, and before the king has sent someone else to relieve me."[28] Leyel felt that he was a valuable asset for the company and stressed his importance by accentuating the burden of serving in Tranquebar.

As discussed in Chapters 2 and 4, the company relied on only a few men in India. Therefore, an experienced overseas employee like Leyel was invaluable. Nothing in his appointment suggests that the other directors doubted his capabilities. However, despite the lack of critical voices, the other directors might not have been pleased with Leyel's personal appointment by the king. It was, after all, against the original charter of the company, and it was difficult to know who Leyel was really representing: the king or the company. His appointment in India was perhaps a relief for the other directors, since it seemed that he was representing the king's interests foremost.

In his reports, Leyel also gave the impression of being knowledgeable. He took the liberty to present his vision of how trade should be conducted in practice. As an example, Leyel claimed that it was absolutely necessary that the directors send additional ships to India, preferably large ships, along with several newly recruited men. If this could not be done, Leyel suggested hiring people from other companies, especially officers, carpenters, and smiths. Alternatively, he suggested that seasoned India trade veterans could be hired in Europe and sent out to serve under the DEIC.[29] He often returned to his request for ships, of between 120 and 150 lasts, which would be deployed in the intra-Asian trade. With these ships, it would be possible to sail continuously from the Coromandel Coast to Ceylon, Sumatra, and Java.[30]

128 *Knowledge and overseas business*

In addition to his request for equipment and ships, Leyel also demanded men and women. The men should be trained up to become employees of the company, while the women would serve to sustain the continuity of the settlement. This suggests that Leyel planned to embed the company in the intra-Asian trade by fostering a more permanent DEIC settlement. Also, in his report to the king, Leyel demanded further reinforcements. He stated that he hoped to send the *Christianshavn* back to Copenhagen with a handsome profit, but that he currently could not spare the ship and its crew without risking the Danish position in the intra-Asian trade. He suggested imitating the strategy of the Portuguese in Goa, who carried their goods under the flags of other companies but maintained forts and settlements as property of the king.[31]

Leyel had yet more suggestions. Since reinforcements from Europe had failed to arrive, he proposed allowing other Europeans to handle the shipping between Europe and Tranquebar. He envisaged a non-Danish country or institution assuming the costs and the risks of transport, paying a recognition fee to the DEIC, but retaining the profits from the sale of the goods in Europe. This controversial proposal illustrates the dire straits that the DEIC was in. However, at the same time, it shows Leyel's ability to adapt to a difficult situation.[32]

Leyel's suggestions extended into the diplomatic realm as well. He was in favour of a diplomatic treaty with Portugal, as a means of reciprocating the royal decree that had granted the Danish access to Macao, as well as to all the other places within the Portuguese sphere of influence. He concluded that, ultimately, the Portuguese had been friendlier and more accommodating than the English or the Dutch. Leyel's enthusiasm for entering Macao was driven by his desire to connect the Spanish American-Manila trade with Macao, and consequently with China. He had a vested interest in the transport of goods from Dansborg to Manila in exchange for silver, which he wanted to trade in Macao for Chinese products, which would in turn bring a high profit upon their sale in Europe. If the deal was timed well, Leyel argued, significant profits could be obtained within ten months. However, in order to fulfil his plan, Leyel needed the Danish crown to finalise yet another diplomatic treaty, this time with the Dutch, so as to secure passage through the Straits of Malacca (the only route to Manila).[33] To facilitate DEIC access to the markets in Manila, Leyel also insisted on a treaty with Madrid. In sum, such references to European diplomacy was yet another way for Leyel to demonstrate his own knowledge and expertise to the king. At the same time, these efforts reveal Leyel's vision of the world, in which trade in Asia was deeply intertwined with politics in Europe and vice versa.

Given the lack of contact with Copenhagen, there was another problem that Leyel needed to face, namely the proliferation of unreliable information through rumours and gossip. Leyel had no choice but to depend upon such sources to obtain information from Europe. For example, in his first report, Leyel noted that he had heard rumours from Dutch merchants regarding

Knowledge and overseas business 129

the arrival of a ship from Glückstadt at Cutiara, in Ceylon.[34] However, in a letter to Anders Nielsen dated 1644, Leyel admitted that he possessed no detailed information about that ship, and ordered Nielsen to investigate and report the crew and the merchant responsible as soon as possible.[35]

Second-hand information also played another role. News from Europe was often received through rumours. In a letter to Poul Hansen dated 1646, Leyel wrote that in Bantam, he had heard from the Dutch that Denmark had concluded peace with Sweden. In the same letter, he also repeated the rumour that the VOC would send 6,000 men to Batavia that year, a measure that had become necessary since the Dutch company had lost 500 men in Ceylon, whilst fighting against the King of Candy.[36]

Leyel also gathered information from newspapers. For example, on one occasion, he reported that seven ships had arrived from Portugal in Goa, carrying newspapers. Through the latter, he had learnt that in 1646, the Dutch had sent seventy ships to the West Indies in order to fight the Spanish Atlantic fleet.[37] The arrival of newspapers from Portugal in Goa, and from England in Madras, was again mentioned in letters to Poul Nielsen and Jørgen Hansen dated December 1646. Through these newspapers, Leyel had been able to reconstruct political developments back in Europe. He was keen to stress the growing tensions between the Dutch Republic and England, and between the former and the Portuguese.[38] He was also astonished by the fact that the King of England had been defeated by the Parliamentarians in the Civil War, and had fled to a castle in Scotland. He was afraid of what would happen in England in the future, and mourned the fact that he had received "no news from home or from Holland."[39]

News finally arrived from home in a letter from Leyel's son, Hans, and his wife Ellenor Leyel, dated 28 December 1646. After several incidents in the service of the DEIC, Hans had ended up in England. He explained to his father that the Danish king was planning to create a new company, as soon as the court official Corfiz Ulfeldt returned to Copenhagen. Meanwhile, some non-company Danish ships were being prepared to set sail to India.[40] In a subsequent letter, Hans informed his father that Johan Braem, Jakob Mickelsen, and Roeland Crappe, the veteran directors of the DEIC, had all died.[41]

Rumours, gossip, personal correspondence, and newspapers were thus the sources of information at Leyel's disposal. These different sources varied as to their reliability. In practice, Leyel had to decide how to deal with the existing information, which news to trust, which to disseminate, which to withhold, and which to "adapt" in order to advance the interests of the DEIC, to secure the loyalty of its employees, or to further Leyel's own personal ambitions.

Carloff and knowledge in the Atlantic

Steven Harris has shown that trading companies needed to recruit reliable employees, and to send them overseas in order to develop business and to

130 *Knowledge and overseas business*

provide up-to-date correspondence and intelligence reports. The success of these information circuits varied greatly between the different companies.[42] However, all companies attached great importance to them, which meant that the companies were the preferred employers for men with more or less sophisticated writing and reading skills. Therefore, the contribution of individuals was absolutely essential for the companies, regardless of their organisational structure or economic success.[43]

In this regard, Robert Porter has written about the importance of hiring men with extensive experience on the Gold Coast. According to Porter, the English were particularly fortunate in managing to secure the services of Arent de Groot for their first expedition to the Gold Coast. As Porter put it:

> De Geer made an even more spectacular catch, for he was able to engage as Director-Commandant of the Swedish company the man who was perhaps the most energetic, enterprising and experienced of all the WIC officials on the Gold Coast – the fiscal, Hendrick Carloff.[44]

For Henrich Carloff, his accumulated knowledge was the starting point for his employment with the SAC. Carloff's 1646 mission to São Tomé, while in the employ of the WIC, had enabled him to become acquainted with the island, its population, and its mode of sugar production. This was essential knowledge for the SAC, since Louis de Geer's argument for founding a company in Sweden had been precisely in order to tap into the sugar trade with São Tomé. According to Louis de Geer, this had the potential to become as lucrative as the Asian trade.[45] Although sugar was an important motive, the SAC would eventually focus on the gold trade on the Gold Coast. For Queen Christina, hiring Carloff was a means to reach the King of Fetu, with whom she wished to establish good relations.[46] After all, it was through the Fetu that Europeans could buy gold from the hinterland. From an entrepreneurial point of view, these two events demonstrate how Carloff's overseas knowledge was the reason for his hiring and the consequent establishment of the SAC. De Geer and the queen believed that employing Carloff would improve the prospects for Swedish trade in Africa. However, when de Geer presented his plans for a Swedish Africa Company, he met with a cold response from the Royal Council, something which can be explained by reference to internal power struggles rather than by any specific opposition to the plan. Indeed, this was one of the reasons for which de Geer approached the queen in person. Unlike the council, she agreed to his proposal.

A second occasion on which Carloff's knowledge was specifically mentioned as a motive for hiring him was his entrance into the French West India Company (FWIC) (1664–1674).[47] The company operated on the Slave Coast in Western Africa and hired Carloff on 8 February 1665.[48] Even if a contract was signed between the FWIC and Carloff, it was his brother-in-law, Jean Andre Wolzogen, who represented him in the negotiations in Paris.[49] Wolzogen became his representative in France partly because of

Knowledge and overseas business 131

their family connection, but first and foremost because he belonged to an Austrian noble family, spoke French, and was acquainted with French court culture. He facilitated Carloff's access to the French overseas networks and helped him during the process of naturalisation in France.[50] Wolzogen's role was thus surely important for Carloff's entrance into the French company. However, more decisive was Carloff's knowledge of African trade. He was hired to take command of all the outposts and factories, illustrated in Figure 5.1, that would be established in the Kingdoms of Luanda, Congo, and Angola, and any other region between the Equator and the Cape of Good Hope, for a period of six years. His contract also bound him to carry slaves to the French West Indies.[51] In Carloff's contract, Angola likely referred to the whole Central West African coast, specifically the Luango Coast, and possibly Benguela.[52]

Even if many of the places mentioned in Carloff's French contract related to areas controlled by Portugal, the geographical terminology implied that the French company were using Carloff to forge a link with the Portuguese in the South Atlantic.[53] The Portuguese already controlled the Luanda

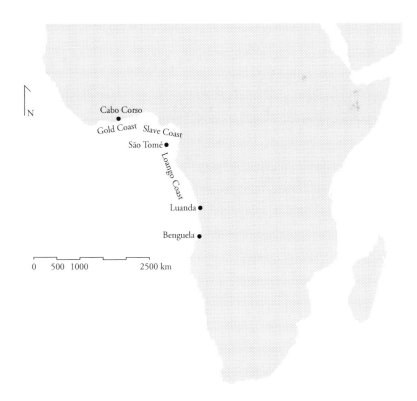

Figure 5.1 Map of the region of Western Africa in which Carloff was active.
Source: Map drawn by Panu Savolainen.

132 *Knowledge and overseas business*

trade, and, for this reason, Northern European slave traders tended to resort to other regions of Central Western Africa. However, even in the Luango, Northern Europeans could easily buy slaves from African traders without Portuguese intervention. In other regions, such as in Benguela, it was not uncommon for Northern Europeans to interlope Portuguese slaving fleets, with the active support of Luso-African merchants on the coast.[54] These activities were not unknown to Carloff. He had an extensive knowledge of the Portuguese sphere of influence, by virtue of having acted as a mediator in São Tomé between the local Portuguese administration and the WIC, and through his service in Dutch Brazil. His contract also specified that he was to be allowed to buy or capture slaves to supply the Caribbean market. This is remarkable, since capturing slaves was not a common European practice on the Gold Coast. However, the Portuguese had been doing it for decades in Central Western Africa.[55]

The contract between the French company and Carloff was atypical, since he was not officially put on the company's payroll. Carloff was free to sell slaves on the Caribbean islands, on the condition that the French company had first pick of 7 per cent of the slaves. The return cargoes of sugar that Carloff would receive in the West Indies should then preferably be transported to La Rochelle or Dunkirk. If that was impossible, he should make use of other French ports. The company would pay all import duties and expenses incurred in the unloading of the cargo. Any exports from Guinea to France would earn Carloff a recognition fee of 7 per cent. Finally, Carloff was allowed to fly the company's flags on all his ships.[56] With this contract, Carloff thus moved from being an entrepreneur in Africa to being an entrepreneur in the Atlantic, and shifted his focus from trading in Africa (as had been the case during his time with the SAC and the Glückstadt company) to trading with Africa.

During a time of increased interest in the slave trade, Carloff was by no means the only one to sign a contract with the French company. A similar contract was drawn up and signed by a man called Jacquet, who became director of commerce in Senegal, in an outpost that he had himself established.[57] Carloff was in a position where he knew that his experience and knowledge was valued in France. The contract with the French company shows that he did not only offer companies knowledge of how to operate in Western Africa, but also used that knowledge to convince rulers in Europe to grant him the opportunity to personally profit from Africa through trade.

The contract with the French company was important in other ways. The moment that Carloff signed this new agreement was prior to the Second Anglo-Dutch War, in which France also played an important role. Carloff, who had ceased to trade on the Gold Coast after the skirmish of 1659, was looking for a new outlet. The first step was to become naturalised as French, since the French company did not officially allow the participation of foreigners. In this sense, Carloff's naturalisation as French was similar to his ennoblement in Sweden in 1654.[58]

Knowledge and overseas business 133

James Pritchard has stated that the biggest obstacle for French overseas commerce was the limited demand for colonial goods, a situation that also existed in the Nordic kingdoms, where Carloff had served previously. The French chartered companies, such as the West India Company (1664), the Senegal Company (1674), the Guinea Company (1685), and the Saint-Domingue Company (1698), provided services to the state rather than being commercial enterprises. By 1668, foreign trade was forbidden in French colonies and all trade officially monopolised by the companies.[59] For Pritchard, these companies were not economic success stories. However, certain individuals nonetheless profited from overseas trade, even if they were not necessarily the investors of the companies. As Mims has demonstrated, private merchants were able to challenge the monopoly of the company, among them Dutch smugglers, who profited greatly from the French plantations.[60] Like the Dutch, Carloff benefitted by establishing a private enterprise, while continuing to assist in the development of company trade. This is why his contract cannot be considered either a typical labour contract, or a proof of property (in shares or bonds) in the FWIC. The following section will focus on the impact that Carloff and his knowledge had within the French company.

The *Journal du voyage du Sieur Delbee* provides a unique contemporary account of the accumulation of knowledge, and particularly Carloff's knowledge of Western Africa.[61] According to Stewart Mims, the French Navy captain, François Delbée, wrote about Carloff with great respect, stating that he had considerable experience in the African trade and an impressive knowledge of local practices.[62]

> Mister Carolof, who has traded for a long time in this country, has retained great knowledge of it ... [thus] it would not be right if what he has done were to be forgotten, since it has the potential to help those who will conduct similar enterprises in the future. Moreover, his knowledge will be useful and agreeable to the public.[63]

Unlike Leyel, Carloff thus had someone else to sing his praises, a fact that served only to increase his reputation in the eyes of others.

Carloff arrived at Offra in the Kingdom of Ardres (a coastal area in present-day Benin) on 4 January 1670 aboard the *La Justice*.[64] His task was to negotiate a favourable trading location for the French company. To this end, Carloff had a first meeting with the *Fidalgo* (the chief or governor), who was responsible for the commercial affairs of the kingdom. Carloff made an official request to meet the king and, at the same time, sent a personal envoy to the king on his own initiative. Carloff hoped for a quick reply, but none came for four days. In his message to the king, Carloff had reminded him of the fact that they had previously drank the *Bocca á Bocca* together.[65] Finally, a messenger arrived on 16 January, bearing the reply that the king had not forgotten his long relationship with Carloff. Considering this relationship,

134 *Knowledge and overseas business*

he did not require the French company to present him with gifts in advance of an audience, as was customary when receiving Europeans. In addition, the king promised the French the same trading rights as other Europeans in the region. The favour the king showed towards the French thus arose from his personal relationship with Carloff.[66] As a result, the company obtained unconditional access to the local market and permission to establish a permanent factory. For a recently established company, Carloff's knowledge of the market and negotiating practices were indeed a valuable asset.

However, the historian Eberhart Schmitt has claimed that Carloff could not have been the person who had previously drunk *Bocca á Bocca* with the king. According to Schmitt, Carloff had previously worked on the Gold Coast, and not in Offra.[67] Nevertheless, Carloff did have access to information regarding local customs, and thus had the knowledge required for this type of operation. Having only the account of Delbée to go by, it is not possible to establish whether or how Carloff exploited the information that Delbée had reported. It is known, however, that the latter – who was greatly respected in France – had decided to report on the establishment of trade connections in Western Africa based on the knowledge of Carloff. Carloff's knowledge of the Slave Coast was based on his previous experience, prior to joining the French company. In 1662, Carloff had sailed with a Dutch licence to Angola, in order to buy slaves from the Portuguese.[68] It is entirely possible that Carloff visited the King of Ardres during this trip, since many ships stopped there while heading to Angola. At the same time, during Carloff's employment with the WIC, the company made several exploratory voyages to the Kingdom of Ardres, and, according to Robin Law, the SAC and the Glückstadt Company also traded there during the 1650s, at a time when Carloff was on their payroll.[69]

However, not all of Carloff's knowledge was used for the benefit of the trading companies. He also used his knowledge of the Western African trade and, in particular, the slave trade. Between 1580 and 1674, the Dutch slave trade was mainly organised through private entrepreneurs in Amsterdam. This was because in 1662, the Spanish had sold the Asiento (licence/contract) to Genoese merchants, who had in turn subcontracted to private merchants in Amsterdam. Thus, in the first half of the century, it was not the WIC that was the main Dutch carrier of slaves but rather private merchants from Amsterdam. Carloff swiftly tapped into this line of business.[70] According to the Transatlantic Slave Trade Database (TSTD), illustrated in Table 5.1, in 1662, Carloff owned the *St Joris*, which completed a successful Atlantic voyage around that time.[71] The ship departed from Texel (in the Dutch Republic) for Luanda, where 373 slaves were purchased. It then sailed for Cayenne and Guadeloupe, where the slaves were sold. In January 1665, the ship returned to La Rochelle, with captain Volkert Claas Roem. Den Heijer has mentioned this voyage, and has stated that Carloff was the captain of the ship. However, he was not an experienced sailor, and had thus hired Volkert Claas Roem to pilot the vessel.[72] There are methodological

Knowledge and overseas business 135

Table 5.1 Slave trade voyages involving Carloff

Commission/ company	Time period	Route	Ship	Cargo	Captain
Amsterdam	1662– 1665	Texel/Luanda/ Cayenne/ Guadeloupe	*St Joris*	373 slaves	Roem Volkert, Carloff: owner
French West India Company	1665– 1666	La Rochelle/West Africa/French Caribbean	*St Joris*	Slaves	Carloff: merchant
French West India Company	1666– 1668	Texel/Congo North/French Caribbean	*Tijdsverdrijf*	316 slaves	Carloff
French West India Company	1669– 1670	Le Havre/Offra/ Martinique	*La Justice*	750 slaves	D'Elbée
French West India Company	1671– 1672	Le Havre/Offra/ Guadeloupe	Unknown	450 slaves	Carloff

Source: www.slavevoyages.org/voyage/.Voyage nr: 11389, 21561, 44266 and 21560; Marcel Delafosse, "La Rochelle et les Iles au XVIIe siécle," *Revue d'histoire des colonies*, 36, 127–128 (1949), 238–281.

problems with the names used in the TSTD and their function within a ship, as has been pointed out by Silva and Sommerdyk: "Often captains, pilots, freighters and ship owners performed various tasks and roles related not only with sailing but also to business. Their tasks often included operating as accountants in charge of commercial transactions on board the ships and on the coast, where they would conduct trade with local traders whether they were African, Euro-African or European."[73] Whatever the position attributed to him in the TSTD, Carloff's participation in yet another business in Africa demonstrates his flexibility and wide-ranging knowledge.[74]

Quirijn Spranger, the director of the colony at Guyana, reported that on 9 April 1664, Carloff had arrived aboard the *St Joris*. The papers of the ship confirmed that Carloff was sailing under a commission from Amsterdam.[75] He had received this commission, it would seem, on the condition that he would not approach the Gold Coast.[76] However, Carloff was not the only Amsterdam resident involved in such slave trade voyages; men such as Henrique Mathias, Jan Foullon, Isaac Coymans, Cornelis Hendricksen, and Dirck Gerloffsen were also involved in similar enterprises, and some of them, like Carloff, were also previous WIC employees.[77] The slave trade that emanated out from Amsterdam was not a new business.[78] While Carloff had been prosecutor on the Gold Coast, a Portuguese merchant residing in Amsterdam, Samuel Lumbroso, declared that in 1646, he had been aboard the *De Eendracht* as a passenger, and had sailed to Guinea, where the ship had purchased two hundred slaves.[79] The previous skipper of de Geer, Arent Gabbesen, had also traded slaves in Western Africa towards the end of the

136 *Knowledge and overseas business*

1650s.[80] In 1671, Thielman Wilkens declared that he and Claes Janssen had been employed by the WIC as merchants on the Gold Coast and the Slave Coast in 1659, in 1660, and in 1663. There, they had traded in gold, ivory, and, above all, slaves.[81] In other words, many previous WIC, SAC, and Glückstadt Company employees had been involved in the slave trade. This involvement marked a transition away from trading primarily in gold and underscores the importance of entrepreneurial adaptation and versatility.

Carloff executed a new voyage immediately after his contract with the FWIC. In March 1665 he departed from La Rochelle intended to purchase slaves in West Africa and sell them in the French Caribbean. The ship returned in spring 1666. This was his first voyage sailing under the French flag and was owned by the FWIC. When a new voyage began in 1666, Carloff was captain of the *Tijdsverdrijf.* He departed from Texel and sailed to Western Africa, where he purchased 316 slaves, who were then sold at an unspecified French Caribbean port. Carloff eventually returned to Zeeland in 1668.[82]

Among Carloff's various slave trading voyages, particularly worthy of mention is an expedition that he made under the French flag with Captain Delbée in 1669. During this voyage, Carloff transported 750 slaves to Martinique.[83] Two years later, in 1671, he set sail from Le Havre, heading for Whydah,[84] where he bought 450 slaves, who were then transported across the Atlantic to Guadeloupe. He lost about one hundred of them in the middle passage; a great loss of life, and earnings.[85] Indeed, the number of casualties during this voyage demonstrates the sheer cruelty of this type of trade. Thus, Carloff accumulated experience in the slave trade during his employment with the WIC, the SAC, and the Glückstadt Company, as well as with the French. The experience that he and others gained during such company service could then be transferred into new forms of business.

Knowledge was accumulated not only through experience but also through the ability to access information about how trade was being developed and conducted between Europe, Africa, and the Americas. Indeed, Carloff had both. For the SAC, the Glückstadt Company, and the FWIC, having someone capable of making the connection between various networks and markets was a valuable asset.

Carloff's knowledge was of obvious value to his contemporaries. The governor of Guadeloupe, Du Lion, wrote to Jean-Baptiste Colbert on 18 July 1670 that Carloff had completed a successful slave voyage and had received payment for his human cargo.[86] He also praised Carloff for his excellent knowledge of trade in gold, ivory, and slaves.[87] Indeed, his appreciation of Carloff's know-how was such that Du Lion agreed to grant Carloff land close to Grand Cul-de-sac, for the purpose of building a plantation. Together, he reported, they had plans for building a church, a sugar mill, and a warehouse. In the letter that followed, Du Lion continued to praise Carloff for his knowledge of Africa and requested Colbert's approval for their joint plans. He also mentioned that Carloff had been offered jobs by the English and the Dutch, but

Knowledge and overseas business   137

that he had declined.[88] Later, Du Lion reported that Carloff had returned to the island with yet another 350 slaves.[89]

Du Lion was not alone in praising Carloff's knowledge. In October 1670, the governor of the island Marie-Galante, Jacques De Boisseret, reported that he had been selling slaves on Carloff's account.[90] In these reports, Carloff was represented as a trustworthy source of information, a regular supply of slaves, and knowledge. The letters by Du Lion and De Boisseret were appreciative of Carloff's knowledge of the Africa trade, meaning primarily the slave trade. However, they also reflected Carloff's transformation into an Atlantic businessman, with access to plantations and the associated trade in cash crops.

The importance of the circulation of overseas knowledge was also apparent in Carloff's communiques to the French Company regarding the slave trade, and especially local trading practices. His understanding of daily practices, the need for gift-giving and tributes, and personal connections, which he had acquired whilst in WIC employment, culminated in the writing of a manual for French captains of slave ships.[91] The manual was included as an appendix to the journal of Delbée. In the manual, Carloff transferred his knowledge to the French company, providing privileged and detailed information about the slave trade. For instance, he recommended hiring canoers from the Gold Coast to navigate the waters of the Slave Coast for the benefit of European slave traders.[92] Indeed, the lack of natural harbours on the Slave Coast hindered the landing of European ships and forced entire fleets into dangerous bays on the Guinea Coast. The use of canoers was thus a practical solution to a long-standing challenge.

Carloff's manual offers a unique opportunity to understand the importance of his access to information combined with his previous service. The first part of the instructions dealt with the voyage prior to arrival on the Slave Coast. Captains should be careful after having passed the latitude of Cape Verde, because of the currents surrounding the islands. Indeed, it was not uncommon for ships to be seized by these currents and swept onto sandbanks. After reaching the Western African coastline, Carloff recommended sailing close to the land, since local merchants would probably have their canoes loaded and ready to come on board. He further suggested that Gran Sestre would be a good place to trade iron for malagette (pepper).[93] The next stop should be at the river of Saint Andre, to pick up water and firewood. However, he warned that the locals there were hostile and might try to attack the ships. After taking in provisions, captains should then advance towards the shoreline. Locals would probably try to sell ivory, but prices would be prohibitive. After the cape of Three Points, the voyage should continue with smaller sails, and captains should be aware of the rocks at Takorari. At Ante, captains should anchor the ship and buy a canoe, since these were absolutely necessary in Ardres.

A canoe should have between sixteen and twenty rowers, and should be paid for with muskets, the only object of barter accepted in the area.

138 *Knowledge and overseas business*

According to Carloff, captains would need approximately fifty muskets for each canoe. Once aboard the canoes, captains should continue the four-day journey to Ardres. They were also advised to ask the carpenter on board to acquire wood to strengthen the canoe.[94] The Gold Coast canoes were usually dug out from a single tree trunk, and were thus unsuitable for the Slave Coast, and required modification.[95] Upon arrival in Ardres, captains should delegate the canoes to the *Commis General*. The General was then responsible for the loading of the merchandise brought from Europe into a boat, which should cross the water where the dangerous currents began. The goods should then be returned to the canoes, which should then be entrusted to the local agent, who would know how to navigate the waters. When enough slaves had been purchased, the expedition should depart.[96]

The final part of the manual was devoted to the crossing of the Atlantic. From Fernand Po, where the wind was usually very strong, skilled captains should reach Cabo Lopo. Once there, captains should provision their ships with plenty of water and wood, because these could be easily obtained there. After setting out from Cabo Lopo, captains would face the challenge of manoeuvring into the open Atlantic, or risk being thrown back to where they had departed from, where they would then have to wait for another month or so. If this happened twice, provisions would be exhausted, and the ship would be forced to anchor at *São Tomé*.[97] If the right course were taken, ships should then head to Annabon Island, where provisions for the sailors and slaves could be obtained cheaply. Once the ships were provisioned, captains should head for the southeast or risk being delayed for months. This leg of the journey would be the greatest test for any captain.[98] The southeast winds would be favourable to the crossing of the Atlantic, reaching in the first instance Penedo São Paulo, and from there the Caribbean.[99] At this point, Carloff ended his instructions, stating that the remaining voyage was already well known. This last part of the instructions reveals Carloff's knowledge of navigation in Western Africa and the Atlantic, particularly through the vivid and detailed descriptions.

The travel journal of Olfert Dapper shows that the usage canoes was already known before Carloff's journal. In his more detailed account, Dapper explained in detail the role of canoes in the region. His book was published in 1668, thus prior to Carloff's journal. Dapper never personally visited the places he described but rather wrote from Amsterdam. In his book on Africa, he must have read previous journals, and was probably in touch with travellers who had been to Africa. Knowledge was usually transferred in chains, and Dapper's work provides a good example of this. Indeed, Dapper was probably also influenced by the work of Arnout Leers, who already in 1665 had published a travel journal of West Africa.[100]

After all, Amsterdam was a central hub for information exchange, and travel journals were bought and read by many of its inhabitants. The prevalence of travel accounts and maps attests to the growing market for

Knowledge and overseas business   139

geography, history, and culture. Travel journals were not only an Atlantic phenomenon. Indeed, Philippus Baldaeus wrote extensive travel journals on the people and cultures of the East Indies. He also wrote about the DEIC, concluding that its operations in Asia were limited, and wondering why the Danes did not do more to encourage trade in Asia.[101] During the 1670s, Baldaeus' book was also translated into English, German and French. This demonstrates that such journals also circulated outside the Republic. Thus, it is unlikely that Carloff presented anything fundamentally new. However, he was able to benefit from existing information and translate it for his own benefit. It is also worth noting that Délbee considered it important to include Carloff's manual in his own journal, thus underlining the substantial knowledge that Carloff possessed.

Carloff's manual was a rich source of information for French captains unfamiliar with the African waters and with the slave trade. The fact that he provided detailed and accurate information implies that this was by no means a new subject for him. He was able to give advice on how to sail, how to purchase goods and provisions, and how to avoid the pitfalls of the journey. His information also provided a good overview of the challenges, risks, and uncertainties associated with this type of trade. However, although Robin Law has noted that Carloff was the first to recommend the use of canoers from the Gold Coast for slave purchases on the Slave Coast, it seems likely that this was already an established practice.[102] Nevertheless, from an entrepreneurial point of view, Carloff disseminated a great deal of important knowledge to the French and others.

Conclusion

This chapter has argued that experience and access to information were entrepreneurial assets that resulted in knowledge. They were utilised by Leyel and Carloff to enhance their importance to the companies they served. The starting point for this chapter was an analysis of the principal–agent problem from the point of view of the agent rather than the principal. Instead of looking at how companies tried to control their employees, this chapter has demonstrated how employees used informational asymmetries within the companies to their own advantage.

Studying the principal–agent problem from a reversed perspective shows that information became an important asset for individuals and thus created competition for those positions that involved channelling information to Europe. Aiming to accumulate as much knowledge as possible, individuals often overstated their own importance, which further complicated the channelling of information. In this sense, it cannot be argued that individuals solved principal–agency problems, but rather changed their form.

From an entrepreneurial point of view, Jari Ojala and Leos Müller have demonstrated that asymmetries in the distribution of information were certainly beneficial for individuals. As they put it, "The bigger the information

140 *Knowledge and overseas business*

asymmetry, the greater the advantage and the potential profit for the well-informed actor."[103] In line with these findings, this chapter has shown that individuals with exclusive access to information were tempted to use their position to further strengthen such asymmetries and to hinder companies from developing new information-gathering strategies. In short, this would ensure that the individuals concerned would remain indispensable. Information asymmetry was a source of profit. It allowed individuals to mobilise their experience, to gather information, to translate it into knowledge, and to channel it in the way that most benefitted themselves personally, and in some instances also the companies they served.

During the seventeenth century, individuals who possessed the right type of knowledge were valuable assets. However, they were also a threat. Directors in Europe simply did not have the information that these men had. Companies could never be sure about the information their agents transmitted. Leyel did send extensive reports back to Europe and represented himself as the saviour of the company. However, whether his plans were actually implemented at the meetings of the directors is unclear. Around the time of the mutiny, the Danish king Christian IV had died (1648), and what would happen to the company remained unknown. Eventually, the company was restructured, and continued to operate, with various additional restructurings, well into the mid-nineteenth century. Carloff provided the French company with useful knowledge about how to engage with the local rulers on the Slave Coast, and also about how to participate in the slave trade. Even if the results of their reports are not entirely clear, they do at least demonstrate the importance of the knowledge they had accumulated.

Knowledge was based on the accumulation of two things, namely the experience of being stationed locally, and the reading of previous travel journals. Knowledge was demonstrated through the written word. Reports, correspondence, instructions, manuals, and narratives remained central to the production of knowledge. Leyel and Carloff both sought to control the distribution of information, and this suggests that they were aware of the value of the knowledge they possessed. Nonetheless, for this knowledge, Leyel and Carloff depended on their own physical presence in trading zones, their access to local information and practices, their capacity for mobility and travel, their acquaintance with local trading cultures, and, as discussed in the previous chapter, simply knowing the right people. Indeed, Leyel and Carloff went even further: they translated information into knowledge – a skill that not everyone possessed. In this sense, the exclusivity of knowledge, and not just information, constituted an important entrepreneurial asset. In practice, such individuals were indeed gatekeepers of overseas knowledge, a fact that gave them a considerable competitive advantage.

Notes

1 See R.M. Dekker, "Van 'grand tour' tot treur-en sukkelreis', Nederlandse reisverslagen van de 16e tot egin 19e eeuw," *Tijdschrift voor Historische en Kunstwetenschappen, in Opossum* 4 (1994), 8–25.

2 On Dutch cartography, Djoeke van Netten, *Koopman in kennis, De uitgever Willem Jansz Blaeu n de geleerde wereld (1571–1638)* (Zutphen: Walburg pers 2014). On Dutch newspapers and the Atlantic, see Michiel van Groesen, *Amsterdam's Atlantic – Print Culture and the Making of Dutch Atlantic* (Philadelphia: University of Pennsylvania Press, 2016).

3 Ewert Wrangel, *De Betrekkingen tusschen Zweden en de Nederlanden op het gebied van letteren en wetenschap* (Leiden: Brill, 1901).

4 Abraham Rogerius, *De open-deure tot het verborgen heydendom: ofte waerachtigh vertoogh van het leven ende zeden; mitsgaders de religie, ende gods-dienst der Bramines, op de Cust Chormandel, ende de landen daar ontrent* (Leiden 1651); Philippus Baldaeus, *A True and Exact Description of the most Celebrated East-India Coasts of Malabar and Coromandel and also of the Isle of the Ceylon* (Amsterdam 1672).

5 Olfert Dapper, *Naukeurige beschrijvinge der Afrikaensche gewesten, van Egyten, Barbaryen, Libyen, Biledulgerid, Negroslant, Guinea, Ethiopiën, Abyssinië getrokken uit verscheyde hedendaegse lantbeschryvers en geschriften van bereisde onderzoekers dier landen* (Amsterdam 1668); Arnout Leers, *Pertinente Beschryvinge van Afrika* (Rotterdam, 1665).

6 Donald Harreld, "An Education in Commerce: Transmitting Business Information in Early Modern Europe," in *Information Flows: New Approaches in the Historical Study of Business Information*, ed. Leos Müller and Jari Ojala (Helsinki: SKS, Finnish Literature Society, 2007), 63–83, 67.

7 Ann Carlos and Santhi Hejeebu, "Specific Information and the English Chartered Companies, 1650–1750," in *Information Flows*, ed. Müller and Ojala (Helsinki: SKS, Finnish Literature Society, 2007), 139–69, 140.

8 Ann Carlos and Stephen Nicholas, "Theory and History: Seventeenth-Century Joint-Stock Chartered Trading Companies," *The Journal of Economic History* 56, no. 4 (1996): 916–924, 916.

9 Ann Carlos and Stephen Nicholas, "Agency Problems in Early Chartered Companies: The Case of the Hudson's Bay Company," *The Journal of Economic History* 50, no. 4 (1990): 853–875, 858.

10 Casson, ed., *Entrepreneurship*, 9.

11 Bredsdorff, *The Trials and Travels*, 19; the quote is a translation by Bredsdorff from Niebuhr's study. "Jeg skylder, siger han, den Danske kjöbmand Wilhelm Leyel, som for nærvarende Tid er Kgl. dansk Direktör for den ostindiske Handel, at tilstaae: at de Oplysninger, som denne Mand, der, ophöjet over den almindelige Kjöbmansaand, endskjöndt ingen Videnskabsmand, medens han opholdt sig i Persien, har lært at tale, læse og skrive det persiske Sprog, har meddeelt mig, da han tilbragte nogen Tid hos os i Leyden, har været mig særdeles nyttige." Niebuhr, "Nogle efterretninger om Wilhelm Leyel," 147. On de Dieu, see W.M.C. Juynboll, *Zeventiende-eewsche Beoefenaars van het Arabisch in Nederland* (Utrecht: 1931), 200–204.

12 Ibid., 19–20.

13 Ibid., 20.

14 Steven J. Harris, "Networks of Travel, Correspondence and Exchange," in *Networks of Travel, Correspondence and Exchange: Volume 3, Early Modern*

142 *Knowledge and overseas business*

Science, ed. Katharine Park and Lorraine Daston (New York: Cambridge University Press, 2006), 341–364, 357.

15 RAC, DK, Diverse kongelige ekspeditioner det Ostindiske Kompagni vedkommende, Instructions to the commander, undated, but related to the First DEIC.

16 RAC, DK, B 246 A, Leyel to the directors, 22.11.1644.

17 "eptersom her giffis meehre leylighed till druekenskab og losagtighed end paa nogen stadre i warden," RAC, DK, B 246 A, Leyel to the directors, 22.11.1644.

18 RAC, DK, B 246 A, Leyel to the directors, 22.11.1644.

19 RAC, DK, B 246 A, Leyel to the directors, 12.11.1645.

20 RAC, DK, B 246 A, Leyel to the directors, 22.11.1644.

21 RAC, DK, B 246 A, Leyel to the directors, 12 December 1645.

22 RAC, DK, B 246 A, Leyel to the directors, 22.11.1644.

23 Similar argument by Casson. See Casson, *The Entrepreneur*, 42.

24 RAC, DK, B 246 A, Leyel to the king, 12 December 1645.

25 RAC, DK, B 246 A, Leyel to the directors and the king, 12 December 1645.

26 RAC, DK, B 246 A, Leyel to P. Nielsen, 20.09.1645.

27 RAC, DK, B 246 A, Leyel to the directors, 12 December 1645.

28 "jeg will hemskt gierne begire at forlodis naff India. Mens jeg skammer mig at giörre det. Indtill jeg med guds hjelp haffuer braegt alting ude een god status og nogen merelhlig thienste for hands majestet og faderlander aff mig skiber her," RAC, DK, B 246 A, Leyel to the directors, 22.11.1644.

29 RAC, DK, B 246 A, Leyel to the directors 12 December 1645; RAC, DK, B 246 A, Leyel to the king 12 December 1645.

30 Ibid.

31 Ibid.

32 Ibid.

33 RAC, DK, B 246 A, Leyel to the directors, 15.11.1646.

34 RAC, DK, B 246 A, Leyel to the directors 22.11.1644.

35 RAC, DK, B 246 A, Leyel to A. Nielsen, 6.11.1644.

36 RAC, DK, B 246 A, Leyel to P. Hansen, 8.08.1646.

37 RAC, DK, B 246 A, Leyel to P. Hansen and J. Hansen, 16.11.1646.

38 RAC, DK, B 246 A, Leyel to P. Hansen and J. Hansen, 15.11.1646.

39 "jeg haffue indted nyt udaff wore land eller udaf Holland," RAC, DK, B 246 A, Leyel to J. Hansen, 24.05.1647.

40 RAC, DK, B 246 A, H. Leyel to W. Leyel, 28.12.1646.

41 Ibid.

42 Harris, "Networks of Travel, Correspondence and Exchange," 341–664, 357–358.

43 Regarding the importance of individuals and their knowledge, see Miles Ogborn's work on English East India Company employees, Miles Ogborn, *Indian Ink: Script and Print in the Making of the English East India Company* (Chicago: University of Chicago Press, 2008).

44 Porter, European Activity, 290.

45 Nováky, *Handelskompanier*, 91; Dahlgren, *Louis de Geer*, 336; Granlund, *En svensk koloni i Afrika*, 7; S. Bergh, ed., *Svenska Riksrådets Protokoll*, 1649 (Stockholm: Norstedt & Söner, 1912), 6.12.1649.

46 RAS, LA, 82, The power of attorney by the queen, undated; Granlund has transcribed and translated the letter. Granlund, *En svensk koloni i Afrika*, Appendix 2.

47 Compagnie Française des Indes occidentales.

48 Regular trade on the Slave Coast was established in the seventeenth century, but the Portuguese had begun to trade slaves in the region already around 1550. See Robin Law, *The Slave Coast of West Africa 1550–1750: The Impact of the Atlantic Slave Trade on an African Society* (Oxford: Clarendon Press, 1991), 117–121; A Ly,

Knowledge and overseas business 143

La Compagnie du Sénégal de 1675 à 1696 (PhD dissertation, Bordeaux: Université de Bordeaux, 1955), 94–95; Mims, *Colbert's West India Policy*, 117.

49 Archives Nationales (AN), Minutier central des notaires de Paris (MN), AN/MC/ET/VI/527, Commercial treaty, 28.08.1665; Mims, *Colbert's West India Policy*, 117.

50 Mims, *Colbert's West India Policy*, 117.

51 However, there are problems with the place names in the contract. Filipa Ribeiro da Silva and Stacey Sommerdyk have stated with reference to the slave trade in Central Western Africa that "the definition of Angola's location and size differs from one group of European traders to the next, and shifts significantly over time." Filipa Ribeiro da Silva and Stacey Sommerdyk, "Reexamining the Geography and Merchants of the West Central African Trade: Looking behind Numbers," *African Economic History* 28 (2010): 77–105, 78.

52 Ribeiro da Silva and Sommerdyk, "Reexamining the Geography," 77–82.

53 During the period 1660–1675, there was a significant increase in the Dutch slave trade in Western Africa. At the same time, there was a decline in the Portuguese slave trade. See Ribeiro da Silva, *Dutch and Portuguese*, 250–254.

54 Concerning the structure of Central Western African trade and the decline of Luanda trade, see Ribeiro da Silva, *Dutch and Portuguese*, 200; Roquinaldo Ferreira, "Transforming Atlantic Slaving: Trade, Warfare and Territorial Control in Angola, 1650–1800" (PhD dissertation, Los Angeles: University of California, 2003), chapter 1; On the importance of Luango and Benguela, see Mariana Candido, "The Formation of a Colonial Society in the African Coast: Benguela and the Atlantic World, 1600–1780," in *Seaports in the First Global Age Portuguese Agents, Networks and Interactions (1500–1800)*, ed. Cátia Antunes and Amelia Polónia (Porto: Uporto Edições, 2016), 197–219, 209–210; Arlindo Caldeira, "Angola and 17th Century. South Atlantic Slave Trade," in *Networks and Trans-Cultural Exchange: Slave Trading in the South Atlantic, 1590–1867*, ed. Filipa Ribeiro da Silva and David Richardson, (Boston/Leiden: Brill, 2014), 101–142, 113.

55 Candido, "The Formation of a Colonial Society," 206–207.

56 The contract has been transcribed by Ly and translated by Mims, *Colbert's West India Policy*, 118.

57 Mims, *Colbert's West India Policy*, 117.

58 See Chapters 3 and 4.

59 James Pritchard, *In Search of Empire: The French in the Americas, 1670–1730* (Cambridge/New York: Cambridge University Press, 2004), 191.

60 Wim Klooster has also studied such cross-imperial actions, Wim Klooster, "Curaçao as a Transit Center to the Spanish Main and the French West Indies," in *Dutch Atlantic Connections, 1680–1800: Linking Empires, Bridging Borders*, ed. Gert Oostindie and Jessica Vance Roitman (Boston/Leiden: Brill, 2014), 25–51.

61 Francois Delbée, Journal du Voyage du Sieur Delbee, Commissaire General de la Marine aux Isles, dans la Coste de Guinee pour l'etabblissement du Commerce en ces Pays en l'annee 1669 (Paris, 1671).

62 Mims, *Colbert's West India Policy*, 165.

63 "Sier Carolof, qui ayant long-temps trafiqué en ce pais, y avoit conserve beaucoup de connoissance & d habitude: cette pensée me paroissant d'autant plus raisonable, qu'il ne seroir pas juste que ce qu'il a fait demeure comme ensevely dan l'oubly, puis qu'il peut server de regle á ceux qui formeron á l'avenir de pareilles entreprises & sa connoissance est aussi utile qu'agreable au public." Delbée, *Journal du Voyage du Sieur Delbee*, 387–388.

64 The kingdom has various spellings: Ardrah, Ardres, Adra and Arrada. The present-day name is Allada. Offra was a sea port region controlled by the inland

144 *Knowledge and overseas business*

Kingdom of Ardres. The region was famous for its slave trade; present-day name: Benin.

65 A cultural ritual, to show respect towards each other.

66 Mims, *Colbert's West India Policy*, 168–169.

67 Eberhard Schmitt, "Die Französiche Westindienkompanie Verhandlet mit dem König von Ardrah wegen einer Befestigten Handelsstation und Der Guinea-Küste 1670," in *Der Aufbau Der Kolonialreiche*, ed. von Matthias Meyn, Manfred Mimler, and Anneli Partenheimer-Bein (München: Otto Harrassow- itz Verlag, 1987), 193–203, 197.

68 Heijer, "Een dienaar," 171.

69 Law, *The Slave Coast*, 124.

70 Cátia Antunes, Filipa Ribeiro da Silva, "Amsterdam Merchants in the Slave Trade and African Commerce, 1580s–1670s," *Tijdschrift voor sociale en econo- mische geschiedenis* 9, no. 4 (2012): 3–30.

71 Slave trade database, search profile: captain, name: Carloff, www.slavevoyages. org/voyage/search (TSTD) Voyage number: 11389; Issues considering the usage of the slave trade database, Julie M. Svalastog, *The Transatlantic Slave Trade Database: Qualitative Possibilities and Quantitative Limitations* (M.A. disserta- tion King's College London, 2012).

72 Heijer, "Een dienaar," 171.

73 Ribeiro da Silva and Sommerdyk, "Reexamining the Geography," 96.

74 On the different roles onboard these ships, see Ibid.

75 SAA NA: 3188, fol.386, 25.12.1665.

76 Heijer, "Een dienaar," 171.

77 Several notary entries show this: SAA NA: 1117, fol.191, 16.06.1656, SAA NA: 604, fol. 193, 12.12.1651; SAA NA: 2118, fol. -, 1.08.1657.

78 On the role of Amsterdam merchants in the Africa trade, see the works by Antunes and Ribeiro Da Silva, "Cross-Cultural Entrepreneurship," *Itiner- ario* 35, no. 1 (April 2011): 49–76; Filipa Ribeiro da Silva, "Crossing Empires: Portuguese, Sephardic, and Dutch Business Networks in the Atlantic Slave Trade, 1580–1674," *The Americas* 68, no. 1 (2011a): 7–32.

79 SAA NA: 1690, fol. A/1009, 9.06.1648.

80 SAA NA: 1899, fol. 173, 3.10.1657.

81 SAA NA: 3589, fol. 258, 15.09.1671.

82 TSTD, Voyage number: 44266.

83 Schmitt, "Die Französiche Westindienkompanie," 195.

84 It is possible that Whydah here refers to Offra.

85 Schmitt, "Die Französiche Westindienkompanie," 194; TSTD, Voyage number: 21561.

86 France (FR), Archives nationales d'outre-mer (ANOM), Secrétariat d'État à la Marine – Correspondance à l'arrivée en provenance de la Guadeloupe, C7A1 F 253; 18.07.1670. Du Lion to Secrétariat d'Etat à la Marine; "Inventaire détaillée" accessible online: http://anom.archivesnationales.culture.gouv.fr/ark:/61561/be1 85yuxvuo (accessed 8 January 2020).

87 FR ANOM C7A1 F° 275, 25.07.1670. Du Lion to Secretaria d'Etat a la Marine.

88 FR ANOM C7A1 F° 279, 28.07.1670. Du Lion to Secretaria d'Etat a la Marine.

89 FR ANOM C7A1 F° 46, 7.03.1672. Du Lion to Secretaria d'Etat a la Marine.

90 FR ANOM C7A1 F° 371, 3.10.1670. Jacques de Boisseret to Secretaria d'Etat a la Marine.

91 Manual by Henrich Carloff to the French Ship Captains printed in, Delbée, *Journal du Voyage du Sieur Delbée*, 475–494.

92 Law, *The Slave Coast*, 126 and 149.

93 Delbée, Journal du Voyage du Sieur Delbee, 478.

Knowledge and overseas business   145

94 Ibid., 483.
95 Law, "Between the Sea and the Lagoons," 226.
96 Delbée, *Journal du Voyage du Sieur Delbee*, 484.
97 Ibid., 487–488.
98 Ibid., 490.
99 Ibid., 491.
100 Dappert, *Naukeurige*; Leers, *Pertinente*.
101 Baldaeus, *A True and Exact*, 652.
102 Law, "Between the Sea and the Lagoons," 225.
103 Leos Müller and Jari Ojala, "Information Flows and Economic Performance Over the Long Term: An Introduction," in *Information Flows*, ed. Müller and Ojala (Helsinki: SKS, Finnish Literature Society, 2007), 14–28, 21, 140.

6 The sea was a violent place to work

Violence in seventeenth-century maritime trade

In the history of maritime business and entrepreneurship, the primary focus has conventionally been on trade. In contrast, the role of violence has been dismissed as counterproductive, in that it increased uncertainty and risk, thereby heightening costs. Indeed, studies of entrepreneurship have been almost completely silent regarding the relationship between trade and violence. However, Sanjay Subrahmanyam has argued that individuals involved in overseas trade often behaved like warriors as well as merchants.[1] Similarly, historians such as David Parrot, Jeffrey Fynn-Paul, Marjolein 't Hart, and Griet Vermeesch have recently developed the concept of military entrepreneurship, demonstrating how such entrepreneurs supplied the state with the means to wage war. However, their approach focused on those men who developed the war industry, rather than those who used violence for social or economic gain. Unlike the large war contractors of the European states, Leyel and Carloff's main concern was neither logistics nor supply. Instead, they received the means of violence from the companies they served, and used them to advance their own entrepreneurial projects. Although only remotely connected to overseas business, the concept of military entrepreneurship can be fruitfully applied to the relationship between business and violence.[2] As such, this chapter discusses overseas business and entrepreneurship from the perspective of violence.

Although there have been relatively few explicit studies of the relationship between violence and entrepreneurship, the wider historiography of early modern trade has often touched upon the question of violence. According to the Swedish historian Jan Glete, "The sea was a violent place of work."[3] The maritime world offered many incentives for ship captains, pilots, sailors, and merchants to use violence; attacking and plundering ships was a good source of income, a means for political engagement, and a way for states to assert their sovereignty.[4] During this period, states themselves were the largest purveyors of maritime violence. The seventeenth century witnessed the expansion of navies, through which commercial companies and convoy systems could maintain an immense apparatus of violence, particularly for purposes of overseas expansion. For example, the studies of Erik Odegard, Henk den Heijer, Michiel de Jong, Gerrit Knaap, Han Jordaan, and Victor Enthoven have convincingly demonstrated the way in which the Dutch trading companies were, to a certain extent, developed in order to participate in wars (WIC) and to have the capacity to engage in naval battles (VOC).[5] In this chapter, however, the aim is not to study the companies as instruments of war but rather to acknowledge that such commercial enterprises had a violent side.

The Indian and Atlantic Oceans were zones of opportunity, and violence was a natural means of pursuing the latter, giving the sea the character of a frontier, on which trade and violence were intertwined. The sources and the nature of violence were often unclear: states sponsored some acts and forbade others, violence was performed by private entrepreneurs, and the dividing line between the state and private violence was often unclear. Rulers offered individuals opportunities for privateering, a decision that entailed several consequences. First, at least in theory, states became stronger as privateers used violence in their name. However, violence often backfired, especially in Asia. Second, privateering was a means of upholding mercantilism, since attacks on foreign ships were in keeping with this ideology. Third, rulers used privateering licenses as a means to distribute privilege and power among specific social groups, in an attempt to win support for the mounting expenses that maritime expansion entailed. Fourth, states provided a cover of legitimacy for violence by private parties. Indeed, this can be referred to as the "nationalisation" of violence, this being part of the process of the monopolisation of violence that was inherent to modern states. Finally, violence at sea during times of peace was a way of maintaining a constant preparedness for war.

At the time, the definition of legality and illegality was a question of political power. States, companies, and individual traders defined the borders of legality in accordance with their own interests. This made overseas business different from business in Europe. Investigating ships suspected of illegal practices provided a means to earn a living, and here, too, violence played a crucial role. The line between trade, privateering, and piracy was blurred, and became increasingly so the further one was from Europe.[6]

Adam Clulow has argued that the reality of Asia was often very different from the discussions regarding the use of violence that took place in Europe. In his words,

> company agents on the ground in Asia tended to pile a number of ideas on top of another with little thought to connection or consistency, or to rely on the more basic notion that force was essential to doing business in Asia.[7]

Either way, maritime violence was an integral part of overseas business. Indeed, an act of violence such as privateering was potentially very

148 *The sea was a violent place to work*

profitable. However, it could also be ineffective: instructions to fleets were written by people lacking specific knowledge of the areas concerned, often the wrong ships were captured, captains and crews risked their own lives as well as those of those on board the ships they sought to capture, and there was a possibility that some of these captains and crews would overstep the limits specified by the original commissions, turning from privateers into pirates.[8]

For individuals, the sea brought both opportunities and risks, in both legal and illegal settings. The risks included premature death, illness, shipwreck, and accidents on board, all of which risks were increased by violent attacks at sea. However, since violence was used for aggression and for protection, delimitation and justification of violence were performed in contracts, charters, commissions, and treaties. Lastly, violence could be justified as a means to improve trade. In this sense, Jan Glete has suggested that violence was one of the skills acquired by seamen in pre-modern times. He has further stated that long-distance trade tended to be controlled by those groups that used violence most efficiently at sea.[9] Violence thus played a crucial role in early modern expansion and trade. To paraphrase Carlo Cipolla, during the early modern period, guns, sails, and empire were closely intertwined.[10]

Needless to say, not all overseas entrepreneurship involved violent behaviour. There were in fact several merchant groups who did business without violence, and even condemned the use of it by others. Nonetheless, at least in the Nordic companies, violence was often present. This does not mean that individuals always chose violence in order to make profit, but rather that they were prepared to use violence if necessary to secure new opportunities for profit. Thus, violence was not necessarily a priority but rather an option. Unlike most of those studied in historical accounts of entrepreneurship, overseas entrepreneurs did not shy away from deploying violence if necessary. From a short-term perspective, one could profit from privateering or pillaging settlements. However, from a long-term perspective, violence was seldom successful, because it created potential enemies and weakened the capacity of the workforce overseas.

In order to illustrate the role of violence in early modern overseas entrepreneurship, this chapter will discuss Leyel's use of violence as a means to break the social hierarchy of the Danish settlement at Tranquebar, as well as his use of violence against local ships in the Bay of Bengal. In the case of Carloff, the focus will be on how violence was used to disrupt the hierarchy of the Swedish settlement at Carolusborg (1658), as well as in the course of a maritime campaign in the Caribbean (1676). These events were related to the maritime world of trade, business, and violence, even if some of them occurred on land. Violence was common in the overseas context, and Leyel and Carloff were not only willing to use it for purposes of business but also internalised it as an essential feature of overseas entrepreneurship.

Violence in the Indian Ocean trade

In 1628, Leyel was appointed captain in the Danish navy, a fact which suggests that he was deemed ready to engage in combat. The task was, however, short-lived, since the king, Christian IV, left the Thirty Years War only one year after Leyel's appointment.[11] As commander in Asia, Leyel immediately resorted to violence upon his arrival in 1643, specifically during the siege of Fort Dansborg. In his correspondence with Governor Jakob van Stakenborrig and Chaplain Niels Andersen Udbyneder Leyel threatened to use violence if he was not allowed to enter the fort.[12] When he was refused entry on 21 June, he justified his recourse to violence as part of his mission to rescue the DEIC. He was assisted in this endeavour by Simão D'Almeida, his Portuguese contact in Negapatnam. On 22 June, Leyel arrived at Tranquebar with seventy soldiers, both European and local.

In the town, he met three DEIC employees, who had left the fort, and who informed him that the people inside would not resist in the case of an attack. According to Leyel, the inhabitants of Tranquebar saw his troops as liberators from the tyranny of Pessart and Udbyneder. Soon after that, Leyel, assisted by the people of Tranquebar as well as the firepower of the *Christianshavn*, took over the fort, meeting with little resistance.[13] Although he may have exaggerated the local response to his arrival, violence proved an excellent means of achieving his aims. Violence was thus deployed not only as a means to make a quick profit but also as a way to demonstrate who was in charge of the company. In this sense, violence provided a means to maintain order and to reinforce the hierarchy of the business enterprise.

The instructions and rules devised to punish company employees indicate that physical violence was not exceptional. Rigorous discipline was expected of all DEIC employees. For example, the crews had to participate in daily prayers. The punishment for failing to obey this rule was being tied to the mast. The crew was punished severely for misconduct; the captain could cut their wages, meals, and drinks; and corporal punishment was not uncommon. The person receiving the punishment could be tied to the mast, stabbed with a knife through the hand, or even keel-hauled.[14] In the case of an attack on a commander, captain, or merchant, the assailant was punished with death.[15] Throughout Leyel's rule in Asia, he deployed violence as a means to maintain control within the settlement. Thus, it is important to stress that not all violent behaviour was directed towards other companies and competitors. Indeed, within the companies themselves, violent acts were often used to punish deviant behaviour, as we have seen in the example of the siege of the fort and the subsequent punishment of its employees. Such harsh discipline and punishments demonstrate that men like Leyel and Carloff were constantly surrounded by violence. As such, it is not surprising that violence was also an integral part of trade. To paraphrase Jan Glete, maritime trade was indeed a violent workplace, particularly overseas.

150 *The sea was a violent place to work*

The violence that arose from attempts to control assets (forts, factories, castles, etc.) and people (discipline) serves to partially explain the blurring of the line between legitimate and illegitimate violence. Furthermore, raiding as a means to destroy competitors was a common feature of European activities in the Indian Ocean. Leyel's participation in privateering raids against Bengali ships in the Bay of Bengal provides an example of this. Although the DEIC was involved in such activities, the latter were not typically associated with the trading companies. For her part, Kathryn Wellen has raised the question of why such a small company would choose to attack one of the largest powers in the world through acts of privateering.[16] In response, she has suggested that the motive was to profit from the seized ships, especially since the Mughals, with their almost non-existent navy, were hardly capable of resisting the DEIC at sea.

European naval advantage has long been understood by historians, and Wellen goes to great lengths to account for the DEIC's raids, presenting her argument from the company's perspective. In my view, Leyel's participation in the raids in Bengal can also be explained from an entrepreneurial point of view: in short, the circumstances and the opportunity to make a profit coincided. The administration in Europe hardly knew what was going on in the Indian Ocean. This was different from the case of the VOC and EIC, whose directors were aware of the situation in the Indian Ocean and occasionally intervened to stop privateering and to keep profit-driven agents at bay.[17]

Violence at sea included pirates, privateers, corsairs, and buccaneers.[18] Privateering was an activity in which ships belonging to private owners and sailing under state commission (the so-called "letter of marque") seized enemy vessels and cargoes. This meant that privateering was confined to periods of war. On the other hand, piracy was an act of maritime robbery. The main difference was that a privateer acted under the authority of a state.[19] While a privateer would share his "prize" with the state, a pirate, if caught, would be hanged.[20] The word "privateering" as used here is based on the seventeenth-century justification of violence at sea. As the representative of the king in Asia, Leyel used his authority to justify privateering, so as to avoid accusations of piracy back in Europe. However, for their part, local merchants and rulers probably saw such violent attacks as a clear-cut case of piracy.

After studying the privateering campaigns in the Gulf of Bengal, Kay Larsen, Gunnar Olsen, and Kathryn Wellen have concluded that these began with the loss of the DEIC ship *St Jacob* in 1640. The ship was sailing from Makassar to Masulipatnam, but a storm forced it to seek shelter on the coast. The local authorities refused assistance and the ship was wrecked, the crew imprisoned, and the cargo seized. The crew was eventually freed, but the cargo was not returned. As a result, Pessart, commander at the time, declared a naval war on the Bengalis, using the *St Jacob* and its treatment by the local authorities as his *casus belli*.[21] The violence against the Bengali ships continued when Leyel arrived. However, in his case, privateering took

The sea was a violent place to work 151

on a more organised form, becoming an important source of income and business, especially during the years when Copenhagen failed to support the company. On 24 August 1644, Leyel wrote a document in Portuguese justifying the use of violence against the Bengalis.[22] He provided a detailed overview of events dating back to 1625, while using strong language and doing everything in his power to vindicate his own actions. The five-page document concluded by stating that the Danes had been forced to cease trading in some places due to acts of robbery and tyranny committed by the Bengalis.[23] For Leyel, the aim was to justify acts of violence as a morally legitimate reaction to the injustices of the locals, even if such violence was technically illegal.

Kathryn Wellen has demonstrated that early modern European justifications of violence were often built upon complex narratives. According to Wellen:

> company agents wrote complicated, and sometimes convoluted, arguments to justify their use of violence. Often, they compiled long lists of grievances, made assumptions about who was responsible for losses incurred, and supplemented these with accounts of unsuccessful attempts at obtaining compensation.[24]

In his reports to the directors, Leyel stated that he had intervened against the Bengalis because they had seized a Danish frigate, which had been carrying four elephants intended for the governor in Masulipatnam.[25] However, he also acknowledged that Danish raids were a means to improve the difficult state of the company and to increase the wealth of its employees. Leyel also wrote of how the *Wahlby* and the *Christianshavn* had raided the Bay of Bengal, capturing several ships with valuable cargoes.[26] In 1644, the company continued with these actions, seizing both smaller and larger ships, some as big as 250 lasts.[27] Leyel explained that between September and January, he had developed a patrolling system to detect Bengali ships, and as a result would be able to seize up to thirty-five ships of various sizes during the winter months. During the raids, the cargo was seized, and the confiscated ships came under company authority. The growing organisation of the raids proves that Leyel had no intention of ending these attacks. However, such continuous raids did not necessarily mean that Leyel was planning a full-scale war against the Mughals.[28] In this case, maritime violence remained primarily a short-term solution to the problem of accumulating sufficient capital to sustain and expand the Danish trade in Asia.

Towards the end of 1645, Leyel commented on the prospect of ending the privateering raids. The Prince of Bengal had declared his willingness to negotiate with the DEIC, and Leyel was also willing to negotiate, on the condition that the prince would send ambassadors to Tranquebar.[29] However, he complained that the VOC would oppose this plan, since the prospective treaty would entitle the DEIC to enter the Bay of Bengal legally and

152   *The sea was a violent place to work*

to establish a factory there, which was against the interests of the VOC.[30] Privateering and violence had thus given Leyel a way into trade in the Bay of Bengal. Curiously, when writing to the king, Leyel does not mention the privateering raids, despite the fact that he usually provided detailed information about events on the coast and further afield in Asia. The reason for this silence was probably his concern about the king's reaction, especially if the latter were to discover that these raids had been committed under royal authority. Even when Leyel did relay some information about the privateering raids, he tended to associate these with trading endeavours, particularly the purchase of rice on the coast of Zinzley in Bengal.[31]

Tales of violence were far more evident in local correspondence.[32] This stemmed from Leyel's need to defend his actions, to show resilience, and to command respect from others. In an instruction to skipper Simon Charstenson and pilot Willem Mouridsen of the *St Michael*, Leyel ordered them to be on the alert for the Bengalis, since the latter were everyone's "worst enemies." As such, he explained, attacking Bengali ships was a "fair deed."[33] In 1646, Leyel continued to assert that the Bengalis had severely mistreated the Danes, and even condemned them for murdering Danish company employees. In Leyel's mind, this meant that his subordinates ought to attack them at all costs, and he wished them: "God be on your side and bring plenty of success."[34]

Leyel also disclosed some practical information about the raids in his correspondence with his subordinates. He advised his men to embark upon these raids without hoisting the company flag, in order to avoid unpleasant reactions from the EIC or the VOC.[35] He also ordered the captains to head for the coast of Bengal during the night, and to harass and attack as many Bengali ships as possible.[36] Having seized the ships, Leyel made an inventory of what they carried and to whom they belonged. One of his most reliable sources of information in this regard was his local Portuguese connections.[37] The availability and organisation of this information enabled Leyel to estimate the value of the cargo on board, and to intimidate local rulers into compliance by threatening to attack their ships. How many of the raided ships and goods became assets of the company and how many went to enrich Leyel and his employees personally remain unclear.

Several unsuccessful attempts were made to re-establish peace. Unable to reach an agreement with Leyel, Mughal officials pressured other Europeans to serve as a buffer between the DEIC and their merchant shipping in the Bay of Bengal.[38] However, VOC officials replied that they would not take measures against the Danish. On the one hand, this underlines the degree of toleration for such actions. On the other hand, it also shows that the companies wished to avoid confrontation with one another. The Mughal requests were thus to no avail; privateering continued throughout the seventeenth century. Indeed, this was unsurprising, given that it was one of the best ways for the company personnel to make a profit.[39]

Under Leyel's command, the DEIC was involved in continuous and extensive raids against Bengali ships. Wellen has pointedly argued that the

The sea was a violent place to work   153

success of the DEIC stemmed from its technological superiority in ships and weapons. In addition, I would suggest that these raids also provided a solution to the problems that arose from the lack of support from the home country. The fact that Leyel went to such great lengths to justify his actions suggests that he was aware that many of these raids were unacceptable. Leyel claimed that the root of the problem lay with the attacks by the Mughals and projected a direct correlation between those events and the raids. Since Leyel was appointed to represent the interest of the king, it was not difficult for him to politically justify his privateering. However, it is probable that the locals saw the latter as nothing more than piracy.

Violence and entrepreneurial opportunities in Western Africa

In February 1657, Carloff informed the directors of the SAC that he was leaving the company. The directors were aware that Carloff had traded for his own benefit and had thus harmed the company interest. However, they still wanted him to continue as either co-director or governor in Africa.[40] Carloff was thus simultaneously a liability and an asset for the company. Even though the Swedish elite had become increasingly interested in the revenues that could be had from overseas trade, they were not willing to get their own hands dirty, and thus preferred to hire others to act on their behalf. In 1656, the president of the SAC, Christer Bonde, tried to persuade Carloff to stay, although to no avail.[41]

Nováky has suggested that the main reason for Carloff's departure was his weakened position within the company.[42] In a letter to Bonde, dated 1657, Carloff protested that he had been excluded from the administration of the company, and that the directors had neither paid his dividends from past ventures nor followed his suggestions for restructuring the company.[43] In a subsequent letter to the Danish king, Fredrik III, Carloff further elaborated on his decision to leave the SAC, stating that the directors had refused to refund his initial investments, and that he was disappointed with the re-structuring of the company, which he felt had diminished the power of the de Geer family and himself. Furthermore, Carloff added that the company was now administered by incompetent men.[44] Indeed, Nováky has noted that the influence of the de Geer family had remained untouched after the re-organisation, and that Carloff's own position had thus probably been weakened.[45]

The letter to Fredrik III represented another attempt by Carloff to demonstrate his entrepreneurial capacity. This time, he emphasised his proficiency in the systematic use of violence. First, Carloff explained how he had begun his career in the WIC in Brazil, and how he had participated in the endemic state of war that characterised the Dutch presence there. While still on the payroll of the WIC, he had then participated in the conquests of Luanda (Angola) and São Tomé. His participation in these conquests was not described in detail, and he probably overemphasised his role, since he

154   *The sea was a violent place to work*

had still been a low-ranking company soldier, at least in Brazil. Stressing his military past, Carloff proposed sailing to Africa under a Danish commission in order to attack the Swedish possessions there. Nothing regarding the establishment of permanent Danish trade in Africa was mentioned in the letter.[46]

On 1 August 1657, Carloff and Fredrik III signed a contract.[47] It was hardly a coincidence that Carloff had approached the Danish king exactly at the moment when Denmark was once again at war with Sweden in Europe. Approaching the Danish king in such a combative manner was thus an efficient way for Carloff to win support for his plans. The commission, which Carloff received, can therefore be considered a "privateering commission." For Carloff, however, a privateering commission meant entrepreneurial opportunity, and he lost no time in turning the use of violence into an entrepreneurial strategy. For the Danish king, offering Carloff a commission was a way to attack Swedish possessions overseas. Secondly, around 1657, the Danish crown had initiated a series of attempts to establish an organised trade between Denmark and Africa, and Carloff's proposal was a necessary first step in that direction.

The contract between Carloff and Fredrik III must also be understood as a mechanism through which to challenge Swedish interests in Africa at a relatively low cost. In the contract, Carloff acknowledged that King Fredrik III had granted him a commission to attack Swedish possessions and property on the Gold Coast, but only under six conditions. The first was that he should equip, supply, and arm the ships at his own expense. He could then dispose of any seized goods and ships as he saw fit, so long as he first brought them to Glückstadt. The second condition was that if Carloff captured Fort Carolusborg, he was to be responsible for holding onto it until the negotiations between the Danish crown and himself were concluded. If the king decided to start a company, Carloff was to be allowed to invest in it, and he would also become one of the directors, receiving a fixed percentage of the dividends. If the king decided not to start a company, Carloff was to be allowed to transfer the fort to whomever he wished, so long as this was not a hostile power. The third condition was that if Carloff failed in his mission, or if he had to rely on the assistance of Africans or other powers on the coast, he would be obliged to pay the king every tenth "pfenning" of whatever he obtained during the expedition. The fourth and the fifth conditions were that Carloff committed himself to confiscating and plundering the cargoes of Swedish ships. The sixth condition was that he had to allow all ships from Denmark and its provinces to come and go freely on the Gold Coast. From a violence perspective, the contract was a way for Carloff to demonstrate that he was capable of mastering Western Africa, including through the use of violence. For Fredrik III, it was simply a means to attack the Swedes.

Carloff's unusual position and the conditions of the contract resulted from the fact that this project required a large amount of capital. As stated

The sea was a violent place to work 155

in the contract, Carloff had to acquire the latter; the king did not want to invest in this expedition. However, equipping a ship, purchasing the outbound cargo, and paying the salaries of a crew were not cheap. In Chapter 4, the way in which Carloff financed the expedition was discussed. In return for investments, Carloff had promised the investors gold from Africa. The overlap between the interests of the investors in Amsterdam, Carloff's entrepreneurship, and the political struggle between Sweden and Denmark had created a considerable economic opportunity.

On 25 January 1658, the ship *Glückstadt* arrived in Western Africa. The ship first landed in Jumoree, after which it continued to Axim, where Carloff received additional support from the WIC. In particular, the Dutch officials provided Carloff with four cannons and forty-six local soldiers. A few days later, Carloff approached Fort Elmina and negotiated with the WIC regarding his intended attack.[48] Much like Leyel, Carloff received local support and managed to take over the fort without hardly any resistance.

Our information regarding the campaign in Africa is mostly drawn from a travel journal by Johan Müller, as well as a memoir written by the SAC governor, Johan Philip Krusenstierna, who was overthrown by Carloff.[49] Müller had visited Gold Coast right after the attack, was an eyewitness, and other sources largely confirm his version of events. As he put it:

> One morning in 1658, between five and six o'clock, this castle was captured by stealth by Henrich Carloff; for Carloff had gone to Guinea in the service of His Royal Majesty the king of Denmark and Norway etc. in order to seize control of some Swedish places and forts, insofar as occasion arose; and his wish came true. He landed unsuspected at night with several people, and at Cape Coast he met his good friend Acrosan or Johann Classen, who had been friendly and well inclined towards Carloff when the latter was still in Swedish service. Carloff revealed his intention to Acrosan and sought his approval, which he immediately obtained.[50]

Consequently, the attack took only a few hours and succeeded without serious resistance. This was unsurprising, since Carloff's troops far outnumbered the SAC employees of the fort. After the fort was captured, part of the garrison, consisting mostly of Germans and Dutchmen, decided to turn to Carloff for employment; the rest were imprisoned and then sent to Glückstadt. Moreover, the attack on Carolusborg also resulted in the seizing of the Swedish vessel *Stockholms Slott*, which had been anchored outside. It was loaded with gold and was taken as a prize. The rest of the Swedish possessions at Takorari, Anomabo, Jumoree, and Orsu were soon seized too.[51]

A letter from Carloff to the Dutch governor, Jan Valckenburgh, reveals how Carloff had managed to convince the caboceer: in particular, Carloff stated that he and Acrosan had a long-standing personal relationship. For the sake of their relationship, Carloff promised to forgive Acrosan's debts

156   *The sea was a violent place to work*

to the Swedish company, a promise that may have increased the caboceer's willingness to strike an agreement.[52] However, Nováky has argued that forgiveness of debts was probably not a strong enough reason to bind Acrosan to Carloff, since the SAC lacked the means to collect the debts anyway. Most likely, Carloff had also promised lavish gifts and better prices for African goods.[53] However, Nováky's interpretation can be further nuanced through consideration of a letter from May 1659. Here, Acrosan told the SAC directors that he had been under the impression that when Carloff had returned to the coast in 1658, he had still been in the service of the SAC. Carloff had supposedly told him that the reason for the attack was an internal struggle between the SAC officials. Acrosan further stated that he had made a personal agreement with Carloff to support and assist him when necessary, and had only later realised that Carloff had deceived him. His disappointment was such that he reaffirmed his loyalty to the SAC.[54]

Carloff's attack on Carolusborg also needs to be analysed from the point of view of the Fetus, since this episode relates to the importance of balancing between different local groups, as discussed in Chapter 4. Carloff's personal relationship with the rulers and merchants shows how crucial this network was. The Fetus supported Carloff even after the takeover of Carolusborg. In the aftermath of the conquest, two SAC ships arrived at Cape Coast. The ships attempted to attack the fort but were repelled by Carloff's men and his Fetu allies.[55] It is likely that this type of support was forthcoming because Carloff had managed to portray himself as a man who could deliver European goods, such as gunpowder, alcohol, and textiles, at lower prices than others. He seemed to have connections all over Europe, and this was certainly valued by the African merchants. Conversely, he also fulfilled a function in the African market.

Carloff's entrepreneurship was equally important to the other Europeans on the coast. The success of the attack resulted from Carloff's personal connection to Acrosan, the internal struggle within the SAC, and the support of the WIC. Even though the attack was carried out with both WIC and African support, it benefitted from the fact that the SAC was internally divided between those loyal to the company, such as Krusenstierna, and those loyal to Carloff, such as Samuel Smidt and Joost Cramer. In effect, this means that Carloff had supporters waiting for him on the coast. These men had been working with him for a long time, and Carloff had managed to maintain a firm relationship with them.[56]

After the takeover, Carloff summoned all SAC officials (with the exception of Krusenstierna, who was arrested immediately), and offered them the chance to join his service, on the condition that they swore him a personal oath. Carloff was uncertain about what to do with the Swedish employees, but most of them rejected his offer anyway. By contrast, most Dutch and German officials were willing to join Carloff. These included Samuel Smidt, who had joined the SAC in 1649, and also Abraham Heintzel, Johan Cornelesen, Sigmund Jeunisch, and Johan Christiansen Canter. The rest of the personnel were arrested.[57] The internal tension between the factions thus became a part of Carloff's strategy. After the conquest of the fort, he decided that he would get rid of those employees who had previously defied him. As Robert Porter argues:

> Carloff's greatest asset was his knowledge of the coast and its people. He was able to use this to full advantage as he proceeded – so much that this operation may be taken as a textbook example of how Gold Coast forts could be captured with very limited resources.[58]

Carloff's successful conquest earned him gold and changed the balance of power between the Swedish, Dutch, and Danish interests on the Gold Coast.

Violence in the Caribbean Sea

A second set of events also illustrate Carloff's use of violence, namely his activities in the Caribbean following his return to Dutch service. In 1676, a squadron was dispatched by the Admiralty of Amsterdam, under the command of Vice-admiral Jacob Binckes, who was assisted by Captains Jan Bont and Henrich Carloff. Their mission was to attack the French possessions in the Caribbean and to rebuild the Dutch settlement in Tobago. The initial attack was successful, but in 1677, the French retaliated in force, and the Dutch were forced to abandon the conquered islands and regions. This marked the end of the Dutch interest in this region, and their focus now shifted towards the island of Curaçao, to Suriname, and to Essequibo and Demerara.[59] Between 1674 and 1676, however, the Atlantic arena provided another opportunity for Carloff to use violence in furtherance of his career. While the attack of 1676 might not have brought tangible benefits, its motive, and the way in which it was performed, provide support for the argument that violence was a key means of overseas entrepreneurship.

The contract that Carloff had signed with the French West India Company in 1665 had bound him to serve his French masters for six years.[60] In 1671, the contract expired, and Carloff's interest in French trade declined; the FWIC was no longer appealing enough, and he now looked for new opportunities. He also knew of the challenges faced by the WIC: in 1674, it was facing bankruptcy. Indeed, the early 1670s were generally challenging for the Republic, which was again at war, first with England, and then with France. For Carloff, political events such as the Third Anglo-Dutch War and the Franco-Dutch War represented a source of entrepreneurial opportunity.

In 1676, the most important overseas arena for Carloff was the Caribbean, especially the island of Tobago and the city of Cayenne (in present-day French Guiana). With regard to the latter, the French had seized Cayenne from the Dutch in 1664. Cayenne was an important port, and its possession was contested by the European powers. For its part, Tobago had been successively occupied by the English, the French, the

158 *The sea was a violent place to work*

Dutch, and the Courlanders over the course of the seventeenth century. Its strategic location was important, since it offered a good anchoring point for slave-trading ships travelling from Western Africa to the Caribbean. Furthermore, its climate and soil were favourable for Europeans. In 1650, a Dutch family, the Lampsins, had received permission from the States General to establish a settlement on Tobago. In 1654, a large group of Zeeland settlers had arrived. The island had gradually prospered, annually harvesting crops of tobacco, dye, indigo, sugar, and cotton. The Lampsins had also allowed a large number of French planters to settle on the island, and both the Dutch and the French co-operated with the Courlandian settlers. Surprisingly, and for unknown reasons, Cornelis Lampsins then approached Louis XIV to request protection for the settlement. The Dutch historian Cornelis Goslinga has suggested that Lampsins perhaps believed that French support would improve his own position on the island. In 1662, Lampsins received the requested protection and would eventually become a member of the French aristocracy, with the title of Baron of Tobago.[61] The main result was that the island now fell into both the French and the Dutch spheres of interest.

For Carloff, a new entrepreneurial opportunity once again arose from the European political context. On the eve of the Second Anglo-Dutch War, the English conquered the island for a short period. It was also offered to the Courlanders, but, in the peace treaty of Breda, Tobago was restored to the Dutch. However, the French and the Courlanders remained interested in the island. In 1672, the English conquered Tobago. According to Goslinga, this was the first Caribbean action in the war between the Dutch Republic, England, and France.[62] James Pritchard has concluded that the Caribbean wars of 1672–1678 made France a stronger power in the West Indies. He has further argued that it was through naval action that the French managed to exclude the Dutch from their Caribbean colonies, rather than through commercial competition.[63] However, as will be demonstrated, before 1676, the French were still weaker in the West Indies than the Dutch. Due to events in Europe, the French believed that the Dutch were too tied down to be able to act effectively in the West Indies, and Colbert therefore devised a plan to expel all Dutch forces from the region. In August 1673, the Dutch planned to conquer the French islands with the aid of their Spanish allies. In Europe, the situation for France worsened in 1674, when England ended its alliance with France, and Charles II signed a separate treaty with the Dutch at the peace of Westminster. This gave the Dutch an opportunity to expel the French from the Netherlands, since France also had to defend its Atlantic and overseas possessions.[64]

The Westminster treaty thus put an end to the Second Anglo-Dutch War. However, the conflict between the Dutch and the French continued. At the peace treaty, the Dutch had once again acquired Tobago. Now, the Lampsins sold the island to the states of Holland, and it was placed under the authority of the Admiralty of Amsterdam. As such, the newly founded second WIC (1674–1792) was excluded from the administration of the island.[65]

From 1674 to 1675, at the time when Cayenne was in French hands and Tobago was offered to the states of Holland, Carloff approached Hiob de Wildt, the secretary of the Admiralty, with a new scheme, again involving violence. In consultation with Gaspar Fagel, the Grand pensionary (*Raadspensionaris*), an expedition to the Caribbean was planned.[66] It was no coincidence that Carloff approached the Board of the Admiralty at precisely that moment. During his service in the FWIC, Carloff had already sailed to the Caribbean and had sold slaves in Cayenne and Guadeloupe.[67] He had up-to-date knowledge of the French colonies and trade in the Caribbean, was familiar with the region, and was thus well equipped to take advantage of the complex political situation there. He wanted to attack the French possessions in the Caribbean, and to set about rebuilding Tobago. He had experience in the deployment of violence, and it was thus only logical that he contacted the Admiralty. Since his relationship with the WIC had deteriorated following the events of 1659, this new arrangement would give him a means to continue trading in the Atlantic while bypassing the company. Hiob de Wildt presented Carloff's plan to the Admiralty. Such an attack in the Caribbean could potentially provide a quick source of revenue, through seizure of enemy ships and confiscation goods, and Carloff thus expected to be rewarded with a governorship or a plantation afterwards.[68]

The timing of Carloff's approach made sense. During the previous years, the conflicts between the French, the English, and the Dutch had left the settlements in the Caribbean in a vulnerable position. Many forts had been severely damaged, and defences were weak in many places. Privateering in the archipelago had harmed shipping and trade, and previous attempts to take over the French islands, for example Martinique in 1674, had weakened the French defences.[69] At the time, France was also practically incapable of sending reinforcements to the West Indies. At the beginning of the war, one of the reasons for French weakness in the West Indies was that the French navy was relatively new compared to its English and Dutch counterparts. As such, it lacked experience.[70] Indeed, this was in keeping with what Carloff had experienced on the FWIC's ships.

Based on Carloff and de Wildt's proposal, the Admiralty decided to dispatch a squadron to the Caribbean, with Binckes as commodore. During the expedition, illustrated in Figure 6.1, Carloff was supposed to act as "commissioner general" and "second in command in the war council," and would later be appointed "governor of the island of Tobago."[71] For his part, Binckes already had considerable experience in the region. Together with Cornelis Evertsen, he had led an expedition in the Caribbean in 1673, seizing French and English ships around Guadeloupe and Cul de Sac. However, these attacks had been more concerned with quick revenue through plunder rather than with territorial conquest.[72]

160 *The sea was a violent place to work*

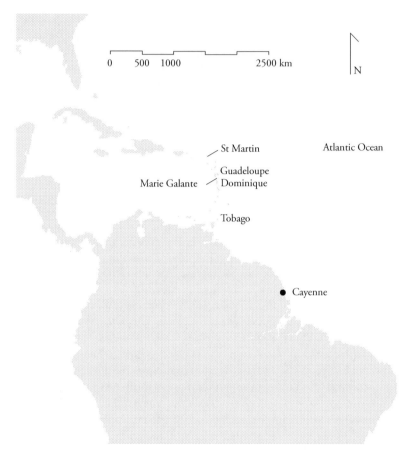

Figure 6.1 Map of the attacks in the Caribbean Sea.
Source: Map drawn by Panu Savolainen.

The attack

The expedition of Binckes, Bont, and Carloff arrived at Cayenne on 4 May 1676. The squadron landed with nine hundred men prepared to fight. The French offered no resistance and surrendered, and, within a few days, the entire settlement was under Dutch control.[73] After the attack on Cayenne, the squadron sailed on to the French island of Marie Galante, which they quickly captured and plundered. Many French planters on the island accepted Binckes' offer to join the Dutch and to settle in Tobago instead.[74] The next destination was Guadeloupe, where the Dutch squadron arrived on 16 June 1676. There, however, they had to abandon their plans of conquest, as they encountered a French squadron. Thereafter, Binckes sailed to St. Martin, an island inhabited by French and Dutch settlers, where he met

The sea was a violent place to work   161

with heavy French resistance, which he overcame only with great difficulty. As soon as the squadron left, the island was retaken by the French.

After departing from St. Martin, Binckes divided the squadron in two. Binckes himself led one part of it to Hispaniola and Puerto Rico. The purpose of this voyage remains unclear, but James Pritchard has suggested that Binckes attempted to convince the planters of Saint-Domingue, the French part of Hispaniola, to revolt against their French masters.[75] The other part of the squadron, under the command of Bont, headed towards Tobago.[76] Bont was accompanied by Carloff, more than a hundred newly recruited settlers from Marie Galante, and a few hundred slaves. However, events soon took an unexpected turn, when Bont decided to leave the rest of the squadron and disappeared.[77] This naturally weakened the Dutch forces but also left Carloff in charge. After calling at Hispaniola, Binckes' part of the squadron set sail towards Tobago, arriving in September 1676.[78] They immediately began to construct defences, since they were expecting a new attack by the French, which in fact took place only one year later.

The French fleet, under the command of Vice-admiral Jean Déstree, defeated the Dutch at the Second Battle of Tobago in December 1677. Binckes was killed in battle.[79] Thus, the final outcome was a failure for the Dutch: they had to settle for only Suriname and Curaçao, and the ambitious plan for Tobago was abandoned. A peace between the French and the Dutch was signed on 10 August 1678. This mainly concerned the war as fought in Europe, but there was also a clause that stipulated that the French would receive Tobago, Cayenne, and the Island of Gorée in Western Africa. The French also signed peace treaties with Spain and the Holy Roman Empire. Collectively, these treaties are known as the peace of Nijmegen (1679).[80]

In the light of these events, it is clear that the Caribbean was a contested region, and a great deal is already known about the imperial competition between Europeans. However, less is known about the private motives of the individuals who participated in such expeditions. In a recent biography of Binckes, Jan de Vries has concluded that the prospect of plundering French possessions and ships was more attractive than that of actually colonising the islands. Indeed, this insight can certainly be applied to Carloff.[81]

When the private motives of Carloff and Binckes are compared, the conflicting interests behind the expedition become clear. The squadron arrived at Cayenne on 4 May 1676, a date confirmed by both Binckes and Carloff. In many other regards, however, their respective reports to the Grand pensionary diverged. According to Binckes, he sent a trumpeter to the fort to demand the French surrender. Carloff, on the other hand, states that it was he who sent the trumpeter, along with his son Andreas, to the fort to negotiate. Even prior to the landing of the troops, Carloff had stated that he had sent his son on a reconnaissance mission to investigate the conditions of the fort.[82] Both men attempted to take credit for the successful attack. However, Carloff did at least acknowledge Binckes in his reports, whereas the latter completely ignored Carloff.

162　*The sea was a violent place to work*

After the attack, Carloff reported to Grand pensionary Fagel that the fort's defences had been weak. He had found only twelve soldiers and about three hundred slaves, although the fort itself was in good order, despite still bearing the marks of the previous attacks by English ships. However, Carloff explained that he had had an idea about how to improve the settlement. He requested that the Grand pensionary send two to three thousand soldiers as a deterrent against possible slave revolts, and in order to provide defence against French attacks. Carloff explained in detail the infrastructure of the settlement and promised to provide maps and accounts from the fort. There were nineteen sugar mills, producing good quantities of sugar, and cassava had also been planted. The settlement was inhabited by 400 slaves, 1,000 cattle, but only a few horses. The great strength of the settlement was its sugar production, whereas cotton, tobacco, and indigo did not grow well. Towards the end of the letter, Carloff argued that the islands of Guadeloupe and Saint Christoffer (Saint Kitts) ought also to be brought under Dutch authority, something that could easily be accomplished with a little extra assistance and effort.[83]

The attacks offered Carloff an opportunity to envision how he would restructure the settlements. He also emphasised that further Dutch expansion was desirable, and acknowledged the importance of support from Europe, both against possible French attacks and against slave revolts. According to the initial plan, Carloff would become governor of Tobago, and it was therefore understandable that he offered his opinions regarding plantations and trade. The fact that he discussed the development of the plantations and their labour force suggests that he had developed an interest in combining slave trading with the Caribbean plantations. Carloff wanted to position himself as a person capable of taking charge, but who also cared about business. In order to achieve his goal, he was not averse to using violence.

Binckes did not share Carloff's view. In his letter to Fagel of 13 May 1676, Binckes focused on his own role in the attack on Cayenne. He described the strategy of the attack, and how he had mobilised the troops.[84] In his letters, he did not mention Carloff, being more concerned with the naval side of the expedition. Binckes also wrote an instruction letter to Carloff's son, Andreas Carloff. The latter was to deliver secret missives to Grand pensionary Fagel, and to return home to The Hague. Above all else, he was to avoid all contact with the French.[85] It is unclear why Binckes sent Carloff's son on this voyage. One could speculate that Binckes did not want to have father and son working together, since this might have created difficulties for Binckes himself. Hence, sending Andreas to Europe was a convenient solution.

Carloff later reported that after the attack on St Martin, Binckes had decided to send a smaller squadron to take over Tobago – the second squadron mentioned above.[86] Carloff arrived on 4 August, and Binckes with his squadron on 29 September. According to Carloff, the population of the island had received them well. Having arrived, Binckes and Carloff immediately began repairing the fort, while waiting for instructions from home. Eventually, in November 1676, the tensions between the two men escalated, and Binckes had Carloff arrested, arguing that he had compromised his position. Indeed, Carloff's appointment had created problems for Binckes. According to Binckes, they were both working under the instructions and orders of the Admiralty. However, Carloff had become too confident of his own position, and had refused to follow orders from Binckes' staff. Binckes explained that he had great respect for Carloff, but that he had endangered the expedition. Furthermore, Binckes claimed that Carloff had conspired with other captains and had spread lies regarding Binckes' actions during the expedition. For example, Carloff had accused Binckes of plundering the island of Marie Galante for his own personal benefit. Thus, Binckes claimed that Carloff had tried to harm his reputation and had thereby endangered the entire expedition.[87] In a subsequent letter, other members of the council of war (*krijgsraadt*) agreed that Carloff had tried to destroy Binckes' reputation through false accusations and therefore ordered Carloff's arrest.[88]

In a notarised statement from 1677, Elias Pietersen, Hendrik de Verwer, and Adrian Martensen – all crewmembers of the *Poppiesbergh*, captained by Pieter Stolwijk – declared that in June 1676, Commander Binckes sailed straight past a French fleet in the waters between Dominique and Guadeloupe, without offering resistance. Indeed, several captains complained of Binckes' passivity.[89] In November 1676, however, the same captains had testified against Carloff.

Carloff's violent displays in the Caribbean primarily served the interests of the Admiralty of Amsterdam. However, deployment of violence had opened up new opportunities for Carloff himself, especially in the slave trade, the acquisition of plantations, and the possibility of becoming governor of Tobago. In the historiography of the events of 1676, most scholars agree that Carloff's behaviour was individualistic, narcissistic, and opportunistic, being a source of considerable problems for Binckes.[90] However, Carloff's motives were different from those of Binckes, and for Carloff, it had already become a habit to portray himself as competent and indispensable to the expeditions. Indeed, promoting this image of himself was crucial to his attempts to advance his own precarious career. The letters from Binckes and Carloff attest to the confusion that prevailed in the Caribbean. Although it is impossible to know who was telling the truth, the letters nonetheless show that attacking possessions and plundering islands was seen as an effective way to profit from expeditions. As such, these expeditions were not only a long-term attempt to establish plantations and to expand the frontiers of empire but also a short-term quest for profit. To people like Carloff and Binckes, numerous wars and conflicts led to instability, which in turn opened up opportunities for profit, such as through conquest and plunder.

The attacks in Western Africa and the Caribbean were similar, in the sense that in both cases, Carloff had first approached rulers or administrators in Europe who could offer support for his violence. In both cases,

164   *The sea was a violent place to work*

violence had taken on an entrepreneurial dimension – there was a prospect not only of making profit but also of improving social status. In the attack on Carolusborg in Western Africa, Carloff took charge, while in the Caribbean, he might easily have become governor of Tobago, in charge of the sugar plantations, and having a share in the slave trade.

Carloff approached European states during times of war or political conflict. Taking prizes, confiscating ships, and handing over forts and settlements could yield a large profit, as the plundering of the SAC's ship and fort demonstrate. In both campaigns, Carloff chose locations and targets based on his own previous knowledge of a region. Hence, knowledge and violence were complementary.

The confiscation of the gold reserves from the SAC possessions on the Gold Coast certainly yielded a quick profit. However, while Carloff thus benefitted in the short term, it is unclear whether the attacks really benefitted him in the long run. Arguably, by expanding Danish trade in Western Africa, Carloff indirectly sought to maximise the return on the bottomry loans that he had investing in this trade. Thus, there was a connection between the attack and the making of profit after the attack.

In the Caribbean context, there was a similar motive to use violence. From a short-term perspective, the prospect of plundering French possessions was economically attractive. From a long-term perspective, attacks on Cayenne and Tobago provided a means of demonstrating one's aptitude for violence and thus asserting one's supremacy in the region. It seems as if Carloff's idea was to convince his patrons in Amsterdam that he would be a good choice for governor of Tobago, since he would be capable of defending the settlement. In hindsight, it is known that he did not succeed in his plans. Nonetheless, his behaviour demonstrates that there was an entrepreneurial idea behind his violent acts. From a short-term perspective, whether Carloff actually wanted to become governor is unclear – it is possible that he was more interested in the prospect of making a fortune from privateering, as Binckes had done before him. In such an uncertain world, and given his life experience, he probably hoped for both. In sum, when we study the connection between entrepreneurship and violence, we should not focus only on the value of the cargo looted or the gold stolen, but also on the usefulness of violence in developing new business.

Conclusion

Leyel and Carloff lived in a world in which violence and coercion were omnipresent; in particular, wars and conflicts between European states opened up business opportunities overseas. In this way, politics and business became intertwined, and the deployment of violence became a means to entrepreneurial gain. While abroad, men were accustomed to interloping, piracy, competition with fellow Europeans, and violent forms of commerce such as the slave trade. In this context, it is understandable that individuals like Leyel and Carloff saw an opportunity to make profits through coercive means. Both men chose to use violence, even if they could have chosen differently (many others did not engage in violence). However, the two cases studied here demonstrate that violence was common in the European overseas ventures, and highlight the fact that that for men like Leyel and Carloff, violence was often a viable policy.

In the Indian Ocean, Leyel had lost contact with the rest of the administration of the company and thus found himself in a precarious position. Lacking reinforcements from Europe and being embroiled in a dispute with his predecessor, he turned to attacking ships in the Bay of Bengal as a means to keep business afloat. Leyel participated personally in these privateering voyages, although he also issued passports to other skippers for the same purpose. Furthermore, Leyel justified his actions through complex descriptions and arguments, which were typical of the time. In the Atlantic context, Henrich Carloff used violence in Western Africa and the Caribbean. The violent attacks on Fort Carolusborg, and on Cayenne and Tobago, occurred overseas, although they stemmed from European wars on the old continent.

Violence also materialised in the form of *threats*. As the conquests of the various forts suggest, it was not always necessary to actually engage in violence in order to achieve one's goals. Indeed, the mere threat of violence was often sufficient, and this served to make threats commonplace. For Leyel and Carloff, violence and coercion had very practical aims, and were often a matter of choice. Indeed, they helped to pay salaries, to pay rents and tributes to local rulers, and to generate quick profits. Furthermore, violence could also be justified politically, which made the transition from regular methods of trade into sanctioned or unsanctioned violence easier. In this sense, violence was as much about making profit as it was a political instrument in the struggle between states and empires. For the state, deploying men like Leyel and Carloff was a way to exercise power. If an undertaking such as Carloff's attack were successful, the state could claim a share of the success and profits. If it failed, the ruler could attribute the failure to a private enterprise. Yet again, the interests of rulers and private entrepreneurs overlapped.

Because of the type of business activities in which Leyel and Carloff were engaged, the results of violence were often difficult to predict. Indeed, it is not surprising that little is known about the actual value of the goods that were plundered and confiscated. In this chapter, it has been shown that Leyel's privateering gave him a personal advantage, in terms of both personal profit and the acquisition of means to keep the DEIC afloat. For his part, Carloff eventually obtained gold from the attack in Western Africa. In the Caribbean context, the prospect of becoming a plantation governor was reason enough to engage in violence. While striving after this goal, Carloff could at the same time carry out privateering raids against French ships. Whatever the monetary value of such entrepreneurship, it clearly demonstrates how closely connected violence and entrepreneurship were, at least in an overseas setting.

166   *The sea was a violent place to work*

The central conclusion of this chapter is that the prospect of making a profit through coercive means was often linked to a specific political context. In other words, individuals could benefit from the competition and conflict between different political powers. Men such as Leyel and Carloff were important cogs in the machinery of violence, offering a means to convert both private and public money into violence overseas. On the ground, they attempted to appropriate as much power, money, and resources as possible. In sum, by seizing ships, privateering, capturing forts, and negotiating with local rulers, such men acted as *brokers of violence.*

Notes

1 Subrahmanyam, "Introduction," in *Merchant Networks in the Early Modern World*, vol. 8, xiii–xxiii, xiii (London/New York: Routledge, 1976).
2 Jeff Fynn-Paul, Marjolein 't Hart, and Griet Vermeesch, "Entrepreneurs, Military Supply, and State Formation in the Late Medieval and Early Modern Periods: New Directions," in *War, Entrepreneurs, and the State in Europe and the Mediterranean, 1300–1800*, ed. Jeff Fynn-Paul (Boston/Leiden: Brill, 2014), 1–13; David Parrott, *The Business of War: Military Enterprise and Military Revolution in Early Modern Europe* (New York: Cambridge University Press, 2012).
3 Jan Glete, *Warfare at Sea, 1500–1650: Maritime Conflicts and the Transformation of Europe* (New York: Routledge, 2000), 40.
4 The literature on the topic is too extensive for one footnote. However, some examples are: Carlo M. Cipolla, *Guns and Sails in the Early Phase of European Expansion, 1400–1700* (New York: Random House, 1965); Geoffrey Parker, *The Military Revolution: Military Innovation and the Rise of the West, 1500–1800* (Cambridge/New York: Cambridge University Press, 1996), chapter 3; L.H.J. Sicking, "Naval Warfare in Europe, c.1330–c.1680," in *European Warfare, 1350–1750*, ed. Frank Tallett and D.J.B. Trim (Cambridge/New York: Cambridge University Press, 2010), 236–263; L.H.J. Sicking, *Neptune and the Netherlands: State, Economy, and War at Sea in the Renaissance* (Boston/Leiden: Brill, 2004).
5 Erik Odegard, "The Sixth Admiralty: The Dutch East India Company and the Military Revolution at Sea, c. 1639–1667," *International Journal of Maritime History* 26, no. 4 (2014): 669–684; Victor Enthoven, Henk den Heijer, Han Jordaan, ed., *Geweld in de West : een militaire geschiedenis van de Nederlandse Atlantische wereld, 1600–1800* (Boston/Leiden: Brill, 2013); Michiel de Jong, Gerrit Knaap and Henk den Heijer, *Oorlogen overzee: militair optreden door compagnie en staat buiten Europa 1595–1814* (Amsterdam: Uitgeverij Boom, 2015).
6 On these different forms of illegal activities in global history, see S. Amirel and L. Müller, ed., *Persistent Piracy: Maritime Violence and State-Formation in Global Historical Perspective* (New York: Palgrave Macmillan, 2014).
7 Adam Clulow, "European Maritime Violence and Territorial States in Early Modern Asia, 1600–1650," *Itinerario* 33, no. 3 (2009): 72–94, 79.
8 Clulow, "European Maritime Violence," 79.
9 Glete, *Warfare at Sea, 1500–1650*, 42.
10 Cipolla, *Guns and Sails*.
11 *Kancelliets brevbøger, 1627–1629*, 1.05.1628, Leyel appointed as captain in the Danish navy, 406–407.
12 See Chapter 4 for further discussion of this tension.
13 RAC, DK, B 246 A, Leyel to the directors, 22.11.1644.
14 RAC, DK, B 246 A, Instructions to the commander.

The sea was a violent place to work   167

15 Ibidem. On discipline onboard ships, see N.A.M. Rodger, *The Wooden World: An Anatomy of the Georgian Navy* (London: W. W. Norton & Company, 1996), 205–244.
16 Wellen, "The Danish East India," 439–461.
17 Clulow, "European Maritime Violence," 78.
18 Janice E. Thomson, *Mercenaries, Pirates, and Sovereigns: State-Building and Extraterritorial Violence in Early Modern Europe* (New Jersey: Princeton University Press, 1996); Kris Lane has extensively studied the different kinds of privateers, corsairs, sea rovers, and buccaneers. See Kris Lane, *Pillaging the Empire: Global Piracy on the High Seas, 1500–1750*, 1st edition (New York: Routledge, 2015).
19 Thomson, *Mercenaries, Pirates, and Sovereigns*, 22–23.
20 Terms like *corsair* and *buccaneer* also fell under the umbrella of the term *pirate*, but these are concepts directly related to the French and Spanish Caribbean, Lane, *Pillaging the Empire*, chapter 1.
21 Larsen, *Dansk-Ostindiske koloniers historie*, 435; Olsen, "Dansk Ostindien," 126; Wellen, "The Danish East India," 448.
22 RAC, DK, B247A, Manifest 24.08.1644; This manifest has been extensively studied by Wellen; her study will form the basis for this discussion. Wellen, "The Danish East India," 449–450.
23 Wellen, "The Danish East India," 449.
24 Wellen, "The Danish East India," 450.
25 RAC, DK, B 246 A, Leyel to the directors, 22.11.1644.
26 RAC, DK, B 246 A, Leyel to the directors, 22.11.1644.
27 Wellen, "The Danish East India," 451–452.
28 RAC, DK, B 246 A, Leyel to the directors, 12.12.1645.
29 The prince refers to the nawab/governor Shazada Muhammed Shah Shuja (1616–?). He was the son of the Mughal emperor Shah Jahan (1592–1666).
30 RAC, DK, B 246 A, Leyel to the directors, 12.12.1645.
31 RAC, DK, B 246 A, Leyel to the directors, 16.11.1646; RAC, DK, B 246 A, Leyel to P. Nielsen, 16.09.1646; RAC, DK, B 246 A, Leyel to J. Hansen and S. Janssen, 22.08.1644.
32 For example the letters: RAC, DK, B 246 A, Leyel to J. Hansen, 4.08.1647; RAC, DK, B 246 A, Leyel to J.Hansen, 9.08.1644; Wellen, "The Danish East India," 451.
33 RAC, DK, B247 B, Instruction S. Charstenson and W. Mouridsen 19.09.1645.
34 RAC, DK, B 246 A, Leyel to J. Hansen and S. Janssen, 22.08.1644.
35 Ibid.
36 RAC, DK, B247 B, Instruction S. Charstenson and W. Mouridsen, 19.09.1645.
37 RAC, DK, B 246 A, Leyel to J. Hansen and S. Janssen, 22.09.1644.
38 Wellen, "The Danish East India," 455.
39 Ibid., 457–459.
40 RAS, H&S, vol. 42, Henrich Carloff to Christer Bonde, 21.02.1657.
41 See Chapter 3 for further discussion on the topic. See also Nováky, *Handelskompanier*, 201.
42 Ibid.
43 RAS, H&S vol.42 Henrich Carloff to Christer Bonde, 21.02.1657; Nováky, *Handelskompanier*, 201.
44 RAC, TKIA, Diverse akter vedr. Det ostindiske kompagni og Guinea, Henrich Carloff to Fredrik III, 27.05.1657.
45 In 1654, at the meeting in Uppsala after de Geer's death, Carloff claimed that the de Geer family had too much power in the company. RAS, Kommerskollegium, Huvudarkivet (KKA), Protokoll, 1651–1654, A1 AA:1; see previous Chapters 3 and 4.
46 RAC, TKIA, Diverse akter vdr. Det ostindiske kompagni og Guinea, Henrich Carloff to Fredrik III, 27.05.1657.

168   *The sea was a violent place to work*

47 RAC, TKIA, Diverse akter vdr. Det ostindiske kompagni og Guinea, Contract: Henrich Carloff and Fredrik III, 1.08.1657; Justesen, *Danish Sources*, 1–3.
48 Nørregård, *Danish Settlements*, 16; Van Dantzig, *Forts and Castles*, 21.
49 Johan Müller was the priest of Glückstadt Company. He was originally from Hamburg and had entered service in the 1660s. Travel journal by Müller in Jones, *German Sources*; RAS, H&S 42, Krusenstiernas memorial, 25.06.1658.
50 Travel journal by Müller in, *German Sources*, 143.
51 Nováky, *Handelskompanier*, 202.
52 NL-HaNA, Staten-Generaal, 1.01.02, inv.nr. *12571.38.1*, Henrich Carloff to Jan Valckenburgh, 15.02.1658, FC, N8, 41–43; RAS, H&S vol. 42, Krusenstiernas memorial 25.06.1658; Nováky, *Handelskompanier*, 202.
53 Ibid., 203.
54 NL-HaNA, Staten-Generaal, 1.01.02, inv.nr. *12571.38.1*, Jan Claessen (Acrosan) to the directors of the SAC, 29.05.1659; FC, N8, 215.
55 For more about the two ships, see Nováky, *Handelskompanier*, 204.
56 See Chapter 4 on these relationships.
57 RAS, H&S 42, Krusenstiernas memorial 25.06.1658; NL-HaNA, Staten-Generaal, 1.01.02, inv.nr. *12571.38.1*, Henrich Carloff to Jan Valckenburgh 15.02.1658 and 16.02.1658; Nováky, *Handelskompanier*, 202–203.
58 Porter, *European Activity*, 380.
59 The events in the Caribbean during the 1670s have been studied by Cornelis de Jonge and Cornelis Goslinga. Goslinga, *The Dutch in the Caribbean*; De Jonge, *Geschiedenis van Het Nederlandsche Zeewezen*. Additonally, W. Menkman has studied the events in Tobago. See W.R. Menkman, "TOBAGO: een bijdrage tot de geschiedenis der Nederlandsche kolonisatie in tropisch Amerika IV," *De West-Indische Gids* 21 (1940): 33–46.
60 On the contract, see Chapter 5.
61 Goslinga, *The Dutch in the Caribbean*, 447.
62 Ibid., 449.
63 Pritchard, *In Search of Empire*, 269.
64 Ibid., 279.
65 Ibid., 450.
66 The Grand pensionary came from an influential political family. The position gave Fagel significant influence in the local politics and society; Cornelis De Jonge, *Geschiedenis van Het Nederlandsche Zeewezen*, pt. 2, Vol. 3, 295.
67 See the previous chapter for the slave trade voyages of Carloff.
68 Goslinga, *The Dutch in the Caribbean*, 450.
69 Pritchard, *In Search of Empire*, 280.
70 Ibid., 287.
71 "commissaris generaal en tweede persoon inde hooge kriegsraat ober deze expeditie, en bij nader acte tot een guverneur want Ejlandet Tabago," NL-HaNA, Raadpensionaris Fagel, 3.01.18, inv.nr. *191*, Jacob Binckes to Gaspar Fagel, 27.11.1676.
72 Goslinga, *The Dutch in the Caribbean*, 469–472; Pritchard, *In Search of Empire*, 277.
73 NL-HaNA, Raadpensionaris Fagel, 3.01.18, inv.nr. *191*, Henrich Carloff to Gaspar Fagel, 12.05.1676.
74 Pritchard, *In Search of Empire*, 288.
75 Ibid., 289.
76 Goslinga, *The Dutch in the Caribbean*, 478–479.
77 According to Goslinga, Bont set sail to Europe and sailed first to Cadiz, from where he continued to the Republic, where he was arrested and eventually beheaded. Why the naval officer decided leave the squadron is unclear. Ibid., 451.

The sea was a violent place to work 169

78 NL-HaNA, Raadpensionaris Fagel, 3.01.18, inv.nr. *191*, Henrich Carloff to Gaspar Fagel, 16.09.1676.
79 Goslinga, *The Dutch in the Caribbean*, 451.
80 Pritchard, *In Search of Empire*, 295–296.
81 Jan de Vries, *Verzwegen zeeheld; Jacob Benckes (1637–1677)* (Zutphen: Walburg Press 2018), 257–259.
82 NL-HaNA, Raadpensionaris Fagel, 3.01.18, inv.nr. *191*, Henrich Carloff to Gaspar Fagel, 12.05.1676.
83 Ibid.
84 NL-HaNA, Raadpensionaris Fagel, 3.01.18, inv.nr. *191*, Jacob Binckes to Gaspar Fagel 13.05.1676.
85 NL-HaNA, Raadpensionaris Fagel, 3.01.18, inv.nr. *191*, Instructions to Andreas Carloff, 14.05.1676.
86 NL-HaNA, Raadpensionaris Fagel, 3.01.18, inv.nr. *191*, Carloff to? (Recipient unclear but it was most likely Fagel), 8.10.1676.
87 NL-HaNA, Raadpensionaris Fagel, 3.01.18, inv.nr. *191*, Jacob Binckes to Gaspar Fagel, 27.11.1676.
88 NL-HaNA, Raadpensionaris Fagel, 3.01.18, inv.nr. *191*, Declaration by the council, 18.11.1676.
89 SAA NA: 4737, fol. 489, 17.10.1676.
90 De Vries, *Verzwegen*, 263–264, 271–273.

7   Conclusions

This book has analysed overseas business in northern Europe, especially in the Nordic kingdoms during the early stages of their expansion. In doing so, the book has discussed two interconnected topics in parallel, namely the early days of Nordic overseas business and the global business behaviour that characterised the early Nordic expansion. The book has revolved around questions such as: What were the backgrounds and the mechanisms of overseas entrepreneurship? How did these relate to the Nordic institutional context of the seventeenth century? In answering these questions, this book has examined the kind of entrepreneurship that these men represented, and has thereby shed new light on early modern business and entrepreneurship.

During the seventeenth century, two entrepreneurially driven men – Willem Leyel from Elsinore and Henrich Carloff from Rostock – were central to the establishment of Nordic overseas trade, in both the Indian and the Atlantic Oceans. Their international business behaviour provided the central focus of this book, which has demonstrated how the concept of overseas entrepreneurship can help us to better understand the ways in which the Nordic kingdoms (Sweden and Denmark) interjected themselves into the system of global commerce. Both men were trained in Dutch trading companies and were hired to use their skills to establish and maintain Nordic overseas business. They were experienced overseas veterans, who had up-to-date knowledge regarding local trading systems, and who were furthermore connected to local trading networks. In short, they were accustomed to non-European business patterns and rhythms. At the same time, Leyel and Carloff were sent to conduct business by either companies or monarchs and were willing to apply unconventional business strategies, such as violence and coercion, whenever necessary. Furthermore, they were able to manipulate flows of information in order to benefit their own careers. However, their entrepreneurship also had limitations. Without the company framework, they would have been unable to enjoy the protection that was essential for the type of international business they conducted.

Throughout their careers, they performed a complicated balancing act between social, political, and economic risks and uncertainties. The realities

Conclusions 171

of overseas business included multiple layers of risks and uncertainties, and these caused considerable problems for both men. The careers of Leyel and Carloff reveal hitherto unstudied modes of entrepreneurial behaviour. Taking into consideration the context of seventeenth-century European overseas trade, this book has thus brought about a better understanding of their entrepreneurship. Their behaviour offers new insights into how Nordic overseas business was developed alongside that of other European countries, and attests to just how globally connected this type of entrepreneurship was.

This book has argued that the type of entrepreneurship Leyel and Carloff represented was the product of a specific European and especially Nordic context. European overseas expansion had led to a European presence on all continents of the world. The expansion was encouraged by a dual interest – political prestige and economic gain. Several European powers were interested in being present in the overseas world and were even willing to fight to attain recognition. Equally, business prospects also attracted different European powers into overseas markets. During the period, several ambitious business enterprises were established in order to conduct business overseas on behalf of their patrons in Europe. This general tendency also included the Nordic kingdoms. In comparison to prominent European overseas actors such as the Portuguese and the Dutch, the Nordic projects were on a considerably smaller scale, being a curious mix of private business enterprises and royal-controlled companies. Nonetheless, their ambitions were the same as their rivals, namely to attain recognition within the European balance of power, both politically and economically. On top of this, Nordic participation was accelerated by the internal rivalry between the two Nordic powerhouses: Sweden and Denmark. Thus, the Nordic overseas expansion was as much about doing business overseas as it was about the rivalry for supremacy in the Baltic. As such, business, entrepreneurship, and Nordic ambitions have provided the driving forces of this book.

Despite the fact that this book has adopted an actor-centred approach, it has also discussed the careers of Leyel and Carloff within a larger interpretative framework. It thus stands in the tradition of microhistory, which takes in-depth studies of individuals (entrepreneurship) as an entry point into larger debates (overseas business). This approach allows for a study of the daily overseas business behaviour of individuals, and challenges the traditional narrative of European trading companies and empires as purely national entities. Particularly in Northern Europe, individuals frequently changed company affiliation, and this transformed the companies into multinational and cross-imperial enterprises.

In the Nordic kingdoms, the struggle for hegemony in the Baltic escalated into several wars, which sometimes drew in other European states. In the course of these political and economic conflicts, overseas possessions also played a role. The formative years of the companies were strongly influenced by a large number of international initiatives, as well as by experienced

172   *Conclusions*

international participants. Viewed through the activities of such individuals, Nordic overseas trade becomes an important part of the more general historiography of seventeenth-century European overseas business. In particular, this book has shown that Leyel and Carloff represented a business reality that was far more international than it was national.

Leyel and Carloff's careers demonstrate how individuals navigated overseas business: they participated actively and negotiated their role within trading institutions, and even established or maintained the companies for which they worked. Thus, they reveal the importance of individuals within the early modern trading companies. However, individuals operated within an even larger structure, including not only trading companies but also European governments, local traders, and local rulers. As such, individuals played an important role in several concurrent political processes, in both Europe and overseas.

It can plausibly be argued that at least in the Nordic context, individuals and their actions were the vehicles of such endeavours and aspirations. For the individual, the Nordic trading companies served as a mercantilist instrument through which to conduct overseas business. The newly founded Nordic companies (the DEIC, the SAC, and the Glückstadt Company) opened up significant room for manoeuvre for men like Leyel and Carloff. In terms of future research, it would be interesting to establish whether similar individual behaviour was in evidence during the formative years of the Dutch, English, German, and French trading companies, or even to investigate how overseas entrepreneurship changed during later periods.

Because of the many roles that such entrepreneurs performed, an entrepreneurial perspective serves to refine simplistic perceptions regarding the role of the individual, who is often seen as a mere employee of the companies. Depending on the perspective of the scholar concerned, individuals have variously been described as privateers, pirates, governors, commanders, merchants, soldiers, adventurers, and even traitors. However, in this book, Leyel and Carloff have been shown to transcend such simple categories. While they were colonial commanders and governors, they were also merchants. While serving as commanders, governors, and merchants, they were also engaged in what some would refer to as justified acts of violence, and others would condemn as piracy. Therefore, rather than restrictively confining individuals to a specific category, it is better to study them with reference to their all-encompassing entrepreneurial behaviour.

The structure of this book has followed five core mechanisms of overseas entrepreneurship: training, specialisation, balancing of connections, knowledge, and violence. Most of the time, these mechanisms overlapped, and they were also context-bound. Collectively, these mechanisms were the driving engine of overseas entrepreneurship. The first essential mechanism of overseas entrepreneurship was a cluster of factors, including background, education, and training. In this sense, Chapter 2 has demonstrated why the training that Leyel and Carloff had accumulated overseas represented an

Conclusions 173

entrepreneurial asset when negotiating with the Nordic kingdoms. Without doubt, when Leyel and Carloff were employed by the Nordic companies, their previous experience and training proved crucial. The Nordic kingdoms lacked knowledge and experience of overseas trade, and, in order to access the latter, they needed people who could provide these. Indeed, this was what brought several internationally experienced individuals to the North. Although a certain level of education and upbringing was important for starting an overseas career, family background was not the most important factor: to the contrary, joining a chartered company, such as the WIC or VOC, was a far better starting point. In effect, the Dutch trading companies served as training grounds for individuals who aspired to an overseas career.

During these formative years, Leyel and Carloff learnt about general practices of doing business: bookkeeping, languages, and sailing routes, to name but a few. Equally important were the lessons they learnt about how to act locally in a context that was very different from Europe. Experience gained through the Dutch companies gave individuals a competitive advantage when moving into the Nordic trading companies. Even starting out from a lowly position, it was possible to make a successful career. In exchange for employment, individuals offered their expertise in overseas business. This mutually beneficial arrangement developed into a symbiosis, which has been referred to in this book as institutional sheltering. In short, Chapter 2 has thus offered new insights into the political environment in which overseas entrepreneurship occurred.

As Chapter 3 has shown, overseas entrepreneurship was not necessarily about being self-employed but rather about behaving entrepreneurially within trading companies. Indeed, the individuals in question were hired as specialists in the establishment and maintenance of such trading companies. Their accumulated experience facilitated their ability to make decisions on behalf of the directors and investors in Europe. Chapter 3 has emphasised that although in theory the charter was the predominant form of organising overseas business, the practical operations of the company abroad were almost entirely dependent on the entrepreneurship of individuals. The reasons for this were the long distances involved, the different business milieus, and the other challenges with which the less experienced board members and investors were unfamiliar.

A unique feature of the Nordic context was that both Leyel and Carloff were engaged in the administration of the companies both in Europe and overseas. In the DEIC, Leyel was appointed director and bookkeeper, and was present at the boardroom meetings prior to his voyage in 1639, while in India, he was the overall commander of operations, having been personally appointed by the king. In the SAC, Carloff was the second largest investor, the co-director in Europe, and also the commander of the first SAC voyage in 1649. Both Leyel and Carloff were supposed to negotiate with local rulers; to maintain, coordinate, and develop business overseas; and to

174 *Conclusions*

be responsible to their patrons, whether these were directors or monarchs. They were supposed to know how to operate the business on the ground, including performing daily business transactions, communicating in several languages, maintaining contact with possible business partners, and providing knowledge of trade routes, products, and local business cultures. The chapter has thus shown that at least so far as the Nordic context was concerned, overseas entrepreneurship included business administration in direct connection with the trading companies. As such, it has offered an alternative way of studying early modern entrepreneurship inside the trading companies, rather than reducing entrepreneurship to mere self-employment.

In order to pursue an entrepreneurial career, individuals needed to be able to balance between several social networks, both in Europe and overseas. This provided the focus of Chapter 4. Indeed, the balancing of connections was essential to navigating various institutional and social environments. As Chapter 4 emphasised, for both Leyel and Carloff, being connected to both European and local merchants and rulers was absolutely essential to business.

The chapter argued that such social connections were not static, but rather loosely structured, being under constant pressure and tension. This altered the ways in which trade opportunities appeared or disappeared, for both individuals and trading institutions. Without well-maintained connections to local rulers and merchants, business could not develop. Indeed, this was why for both Leyel and Carloff, paying tributes and offering lavish gifts were essential to maintaining good business connections. However, both men failed to maintain good relationships with their colleagues and subordinates, having prioritised their own personal ambitions over the morale and motivation of the latter. In the end, Leyel was overthrown in a mutiny, while Carloff lost his position on the Gold Coast, due to the decision of his colleague, Samuel Smidt, to surrender the fort to the WIC. In this chapter, the question of trust was also addressed. Both Leyel and Carloff claimed that they had only a few colleagues whom they could trust. Significantly, even these "trustworthy" men eventually turned against Leyel and Carloff.

This chapter has also shown that trust was a rhetorical tool, which Leyel and Carloff employed in order to emphasise their own business partnerships and positions. However, since they were themselves engaged in smuggling and private trading, attempting to portray themselves as trustworthy was disingenuous. Nevertheless, they wanted to advertise the membership of their overseas networks, and to justify why they had chosen to work with these people. Both Leyel and Carloff were also prone to individualistic behaviour. Neither of them was able to sustain any kind of inner harmony within their companies, and their relationships with their colleagues and subordinates remained tense. On several occasions, their self-serving behaviour backfired on them, something which demonstrates the importance of social relationships within the companies.

Conclusions   175

As Chapter 5 has argued, another important mechanism was the accumulation of knowledge. In particular, day-to-day business experience and access to information formed the basis of overseas knowledge. Accumulated knowledge could be used to gain entrepreneurial advantage, and demonstrated how individuals could exploit a company's attempts to monitor and control overseas business. The companies requested that their employees write reports and keep the company books in good order. The need for control resulted from the problem of information asymmetry, which was caused by long distances and slow communication flows. Experienced individuals knew this, played along with the companies' requests, and manipulated reports and correspondence to demonstrate their own importance and indispensability.

Controlling the flow of information was one of Leyel's specialities. As the commander of the company, he alone was responsible for writing reports to the directors, and he used this correspondence to demonstrate his own importance to the company. Moreover, the reports could also function as a shield against possible accusations of wrong-doing. In many instances, Leyel wrote about who was a capable employee, or which problems had been caused by other employees. As he was the only person reporting from India, he held significant power over the distribution of information. Hence, control over knowledge and its distribution should be understood as a key entrepreneurial strategy overseas. Such documents were a way for individuals to advertise their knowledge of overseas trade, and to thereby make themselves indispensable to the organisations that employed them.

Finally, Chapter 6 focused on the role of violence and coercion in overseas entrepreneurial activity. This has traditionally been neglected in the historiography of entrepreneurship, since violence increases risks, thus creating uncertainty, something which entrepreneurs try to avoid. However, Chapter 6 has shown how politics and business became intertwined, and how individuals could use violence in order to further their goals, either out of a desire for profit or out of necessity. Individuals did not always plan acts of violence, but they were prepared to use them, since sometimes this was the only way to make a profit. Violence was considered a means to improve trade and to ensure quick revenue, as well as to advance one's overseas career.

Overseas entrepreneurship is thus best understood as a series of entrepreneurial mechanisms (activities, strategies, and behaviours), employed by individuals in a challenging overseas context. Overseas conditions were volatile and uncertain, and individuals were both shaped by and took advantage of them. Competition between Europeans, long distances, and the slow circulation of information made overseas business a lucrative opportunity for those who were willing to take risks. This book has thus defined overseas entrepreneurship as a mode of behaviour that was adopted by individuals in order to make a profit, and in order to improve their professional and social mobility in long-distance trade. In this sense, it departs from the

176   *Conclusions*

conventional belief that individuals involved in entrepreneurship were only interested in making a profit through trade. In the overseas context, balancing of social connections, violence, and exploitation of knowledge were also used as mechanisms of entrepreneurship.

By comparing the entrepreneurship of Leyel and Carloff, this book has shown just how fragile and vulnerable overseas business was. In fact, uncertain business prospects and risk were the basic conditions of trade. Overseas trade entailed even higher risks than European maritime trade, such as unknown diseases, shipwrecks, fraud, violent conflicts, and bankruptcy. Of course, all of these were possible in Europe, but the sheer scale was far larger overseas. As such, the aim of this book was not to focus solely on success but rather on the mechanisms of adaption that entrepreneurially minded individuals used in response to uncertain conditions. To be sure, this does not mean that every individual was successful. To the contrary, Leyel and Carloff eventually failed to achieve many of their long-term goals. Their individualistic approach to overseas business eventually cost them various career opportunities. Nevertheless, their careers manifested similar motives, mechanisms, and goals, in both the Indian and the Atlantic Oceans.

The international careers of Leyel and Carloff within the Nordic companies also reveal certain similarities in the Nordic overseas trade. First, both men exploited the immaturity of the Nordic trading companies. They had both been trained in the already established Dutch trading companies, and their experience was significant when they entered the Nordic companies. Second, both men were prepared to use violence to achieve their goals overseas. Third, both men obtained dual positions in the Nordic companies for which they worked. Indeed, the fact that they both held positions overseas and were involved in the administrations of the companies in Europe demonstrates that, at least in the case of the Nordic trading companies, the principal–agent theorem is problematic, since in cases such as these, the principal and the agent were the same person.

There were also differences in the Nordic careers of Leyel and Carloff. First of all, during the years covered in this study, Carloff was more mobile than Leyel. The latter worked in the Indian Ocean without a direct connection to Europe, whereas Carloff was able to sail back and forth across the Atlantic. This resulted in the second main difference: Carloff changed company affiliation more often than Leyel. The difference here was not necessarily a difference of setting but rather a difference of loyalty and character. Despite these differences, however, the similarities in their behaviour were striking. Changing company affiliation, participating in privateering, engaging in the slave trade, betraying patrons, and establishing cross-cultural trade connections were but a few examples.

In the Northern European context, companies remained the predominant form of conducting overseas business. Moreover, they remained especially attractive to individuals who were interested in a long-term career and upward social mobility. In order to achieve these aims, individuals needed the company framework. However, at the same time, the companies needed the individuals and their skills, in order to operate in highly competitive markets, far away from administrative centres. This interdependency was both the cause and the result of overseas entrepreneurship. In the overseas context, entrepreneurship was thus based on a constant interplay between individuals and the trading companies.

Overseas entrepreneurship should thus be seen as a response to the shortcomings of the early Nordic overseas ventures. During the seventeenth century, the Nordic kingdoms were ill-equipped, lacking the previous experience and capacity that were needed to kick-start and sustain overseas business. To these problems, entrepreneurially driven men such as Leyel and Carloff provided a solution. Through their entrepreneurship, Nordic overseas business was initiated, managed, and sustained.

Finally, this book has emphasised that through entrepreneurship, overseas trade became increasingly interconnected. Although the individuals concerned were not the same, their strategies were similar. Indeed, this was because overseas business tended to attract people like Leyel and Carloff, and because their entrepreneurial behaviour fulfilled the needs of overseas trade. For Leyel and Carloff, what mattered was overseas trade, rather than trade in the Indian or the Atlantic Ocean per se.

An actor-centred approach and a comparative perspective on entrepreneurial behaviour are valuable for business history, since they give an alternative outlook on European activities in early modern global history. Moreover, they also offer new insights into how seventeenth-century entrepreneurship was articulated. Because comparisons extend beyond one specific ocean, region, or company, they allow for a more connected overseas history. Using the concept of entrepreneurship has enabled this book to identify similarities and differences in the behaviour of business-minded individuals, moving beyond a restrictive focus on companies and empires. The comparison between Leyel and Carloff has yielded two important conclusions regarding business history in an overseas context. First, regardless of the geographical and cultural differences between the Indian and the Atlantic Oceans, similar entrepreneurial mechanisms were employed in both the East and the West. Second, the behaviour of men like Leyel and Carloff was quite typical of the early Nordic trading companies. Given the representative character of their behaviour, a study of their overseas entrepreneurship has allowed for new insights into the role of individuals in early modern overseas business, particularly from a global history perspective.

As a final conclusion, this book encourages other historians to carry out further in-depth studies of entrepreneurship in early modern overseas business, for five main reasons. First, the entrepreneurial careers of Leyel and Carloff shed light on those international business practices in which national and career-related affiliations were less pronounced. Second, research on entrepreneurship does not always have to be devoted to successful individuals. Indeed, less successful careers can provide essential information

178   *Conclusions*

about how business was developed. Third, the comparison of two different case studies in two different oceanic spaces suggests that the distinction between the Atlantic and the Indian Oceans is not necessarily that significant, especially if we apply a social perspective to the people conducting business there. Fourth, adopting the concept of overseas entrepreneurship permits a better understanding of how and why individuals used violence in their overseas business activities.

From this perspective, it also becomes clear just how important connections, experience, and knowledge were for the individual. All of these were mechanisms of overseas entrepreneurship, being characteristics that the companies desired, and for which they were willing to pay, in order to build up successful overseas business. As such, the concept of overseas entrepreneurship facilitates a better understanding of the social and institutional environment in which these individuals operated. Ultimately, this book has been a study of why and how individuals were willing to confront the manifold uncertainties and risks that were constantly and globally present in overseas business.

Sources and bibliography

Archival sources

The Netherlands

Nationaal Archief, den Haag (NL-HaNa)

Oude Westindische Compagnie (OWIC) – 1.05.01.01

- NL-HaNA, OWIC, 1.05.01.01, inv. nr.*11*: Overgkomen brieven en papieren uit Afrika.
- NL-HaNA, OWIC, 1.05.01.01, inv.nr. *13A*: Contracten en verdragen met ingezetenen van de Kust van Guinea en ander stukken betreffende de jurisdictie in het gebied.
- NL-HaNA, OWIC, 1.05.01.01, inv. nr. *25*: Resoluties of Notulen van de Kamer Zeeland.
- NL-HaNA, OWIC, 1.05.01.01, inv. nr. *47*: Journaal door Loys Dammaert van een reis met het schip Prins Willem naar Guinea.

Staten Generaal – 1.01.02

- NL-HaNA, Staten Generaal, 1.01.02, inv. nr. *5758*: Liassen Westindische Compagnie, 1645–1646.
- NL-HaNA, Staten Generaal, 1.01.02, inv. nr. *12571.36*: Stukken betreffende de bemoeiingen van de Staten-Generaal met de geschillen tussen de kamer van Amsterdam van de W.I.C. en Zweden over het aanhalen van het Zweedse schip 'Christina' door Gaspar van Heusden, directeur-generaal van het noorderdistrict van Afrika, 1660–1661.
- NL-HaNA, 1.01.02, inv. nr. *12571.38.1:* Stukken betreffende de bemoeiingen van de Staten-Generaal met de geschillen tussen de W.I.C. en de Zweedse Afrikaanse Compagnie over de kust van Guinea, 1662–1663.
- NL-HaNA, 1.01.02, inv. nr. *12572.41:* Stukken betreffende de bemoeiingen van de Staten-Generaal met de geschillen tussen de W.I.C. en de Deense Afrikaanse Compagnie over de kust van Guinea, 1662–1665.

180   *Sources and bibliography*

Raadpensionaris Fagel – 3.01.18

– NL-HaNA, 3.01.18, inv.nr. *191*: Missiven van Johan Apricius, [H.] Carloff en Johan Heinsius, allen gouverneurs van West-Indische koloniën, aan Gaspar Fagel; met bijlagen.

Verspreide West-Indische Stukken – 1.05.06

– NL-HaNa, 1.05.06, inv.nr. *1178*: Copie-request van Hendrick Carlof aan prins Willem III om met het vacante kommandeurschap van Suriname te worden begunstigd.

Amsterdam

Stadssarchief, (SAA)

Notarieel Archief (NA)

– SAA NA: 1289, fol. 28v–29v., 03.05.1644.
– SAA NA: 1133, fol. 107, 24.04.1660.
– SAA NA: 4737, fol. 489, 17.10.1676.
– SAA NA: 1117, fol. 191, 16.06.1656.
– SAA NA: 604, fol. 193, 12.12.1651.
– SAA NA: 2118, fol. -, 01.08.1657.
– SAA NA: 3188, fol. 386, 25.12.1665.
– SAA NA: 1761, fol. 834, 20.11.1660.
– SAA NA: 1134, fol. 143, 03.08.1660.
– SAA NA: 1128, fol. 272–273, 15.03.1659.
– SAA NA: 880, fol. 88, 30.07.1657.
– SAA NA: 878, fol. 170, 09.10.1653.
– SAA NA: 879, fol. 148, 29.08.1656.
– SAA NA: 875, fol. 170, 09.10.1653.
– SAA NA: 875, fol. 315, 12.10.1649.
– SAA NA: 870, fol.147, 29.08.1656.

Sweden

Stockholm

Riksarkivet, Stockholm (RAS)

Handel&Sjöfart (H&S)

– RAS, H&S, vol. 42.
– RAS, H&S, vol. 45.

Sources and bibliography 181

Leufsta Arkiv (LA),

- RAS, LA, vol. 82.
- RAS, LA, vol. 10.
- RAS, LA, vol. 111.

Kommerskollegium, Huvudarkivet (KKA)

- RAS, KKA, Protokoll, 1651–1654, A1 AA:1.

Riksregistraturen (RR)

- 1649

Vadstena

VLA (Vadstena Landsarkiv)

FBA (Finspångsbruk Arkiv)
- VLA, FBA, inv.nr.62A.

Uppsala

UUB (Uppsala Universitets Bibliotek),

- UUB, N430.

Denmark

Copenhagen

Rigsarkivet, Copenhagen (RAC)

Tyske Kancelli – Indenrigske Afdeling (TKIA)

- RAC, TKIA, B153-B154, 1627–1704, Memorialer vedr. Hertugdøm kgl. Undersåtters commercium.
- RAC, TKIA, A IX.171, Diverse akter vedr. det Ostindiske kompagni og Guinea 1618–1659.
- RAC, TKIA, A 10:1, 1626–1669: Patenten.
- RAC, TKIA, B.12. Inländische registratur: 1670–1770.

Tyske Kancelli – Udenrigske Afdeling (TKUA)

- RAC, TKUA, 70-14-70-15, Nederlanderne: akter vedr. Det poltiiska forhold, 1660–1665.

182　*Sources and bibliography*

Regeringskanclliet i Glückstadt

– RAC, Regeringskancelliet i Glückstadt, 146, Akter. Vedr. Glückstadt by og Fæstning 1630–1703.

Danske Kancelliet (DK)

– RAC, DK, (rentekammer afdelning 1588–1660), Wilum Leyel arkiv, B 246 A, B and C, Willum Leyel arkiv.
– RAC, DK, Tillæg till Willum Leyels arkiv, B247 B.
– RAC, DK, Diverse Breve Dokumenter og breve det ostindiska kompgani vedkommende 1616–1660.
– RAC, DK, Diverse kongelige ekspeditioner det Ostindiske Kompagni vedkommende, 1616–1639.

Håndskriftsamlingen

– RAC, VII E 1 a), De ostindiske Etablissementers Historie.

France

Aix-en-Provence

Archives nationales d'outre-mer and (FR ANOM).

Secrétariat d'État à la Marine – Correspondance à l'arrivée en provenance de la Guadeloupe (C7), accessible online: http://anom.archivesnationales.culture.gouv.fr/ark:/61561/be185yuxvuo (accessed 8 January 2020).

– FR ANOM C7A1 F° 253; 18.07.1670.
– FR ANOM C7A1 F° 275, 25.07.1670.
– FR ANOM C7A1 F° 279, 28.07.1670.
– FR ANOM C7A1 F° 46, 07.03.1672.
– FR ANOM C7A1 F° 371, 03.10.1670.

Paris

Archives nationales (AN)

Minutier central des notaires (MC)

– AN/MC/ET/VI/527.

Germany

Glückstadt

Sources and bibliography   183

Das Stadtarchiv

– Bürgerbuch.
– Urkunden.

Great Britain

London
National archives England, (NAE)

High Court of Admiralty (HCA)

– London, HCA (High Court of Admiralty), 24/111, no.182.

Printed sources

– Brieven, confessie; mitsgaders, advisen van verscheyden rechtsgeleerden in de saeck van Isaac Coymans gegeven; als mede de sententie daer op gevolgt (Rotterdam 1662).

Pamphlet collection Knuttel (Royal library, the Hague)

– Pamflet Knuttel 8905A, 'Remonstrantie aen de Ho: Mo: Heeren de Staten-Generael der Vereenighde Nederlanden: overgegeven den Junij 1664 Bij de Heeren de Bewint-hebberen van de Geoctroyeerde West-Indische Compagnie der Vereenighde Nederlanden. Opende jegens Verscheyde Memorien van den Heer Resident Charisius, wegens de (gepretendeerde) Deensche Africaensche Compagnie, aen haer Ho: Mo: overgegeven.' (Amsterdam 1664).

Published sources

Bergh, S., ed. *Svenska Riksrådets Protokoll* (RP), vol. XI: 1645–1646. Stockholm: Norstedt & Söner, 1906.
———, ed. *Svenska Riksrådets Protokoll*, 1649. Stockholm: Norstedt & Söner, 1912.
Bricka, C.F. and Fridericia, J.A., et al., eds. *Kong Christian den Fjerdes egenhændige breve 1626–1631*, vol. 2. Copenhagen: Selskabet for Udgivelse af Kilder til Dansk Historie, 1878–1947.
———, eds. *Kong Christian den Fjerdes egenhændige breve 1632–1635*, vol. 3. Copenhagen: Selskabet for Udgivelse af Kilder til Dansk Historie, 1878–1947.
———, eds. *Kong Christian Den Fjerdes egenhændige breve 1636–1640*, vol. 4. Copenhagen: Selskabet for Udgivelse af Kilder til Dansk Historie, 1969.
Colenbrander, H.T., ed. *Dagh-register gehouden int casteel Batavia vant passerende daer ter plaetse als over geheel Nederlandts-India: 1643–1644*. Gravenhage: Martinus Nijhoff, 1902.

184 *Sources and bibliography*

———, ed. *Dagh-register gehouden int casteel Batavia vant passerende daer ter plaetse als over geheel Nederlandts-India: 1636.* Gravenhage: Martinus Nijhoff, 1899.

Coolhas, W.P.H., ed. *Generale missiven van gouverneurs-generaal en raden aan heren XVII der Vereinigde Oostindische Compagnie*, deel 1, 1610–1638. Gravenhage: Martinus Nijhoff, 1960.

D'Elbée, F. *Journal du voyage du sieur Delbée, commissaire général de la marine, aux isles, dans la coste de Guynée, pour l'établissement du commerce en ces pays, en l'année 1669.* In vol. II, 347–494. Paris, 1671.

Feldbæk, O. *Danske Handelskompagnier 1616–1843: oktrojer og interne ledelsesregler.* Copenhagen: Selskabet for Udgivelse af Kilder til Dansk Historie, 1986.

Justeseen, O., ed. *Danish Sources for the History of Ghana 1657–1754, vol. 1: 1657–1753.* Copenhagen: The Royal Danish Academy of Science and Letters, 2005.

Laursen, L. *Danmark-Norges Traktater*, 1523–1750, vol. IV (1626–1649). Copenhagen: C.A. Reitzel Nielsen & Lydische, 1917.

———. *Kancelliets brevbøger, vedrørende Danmarks indre forhold*: 1624–1626. Copenhagen: C.A. Reitzel Nielsen & Lydische, 1925.

Marquard, E. *Kancelliets brevbøger, vedrørende Danmarks indre forhold*: 1627–1629. Copenhagen: C.A. Reitzel Nielsen & Lydische 1929.

———. *Kancelliets brevbøger, vedrørende Danmarks indre forhold*: 1633–1634. Copenhagen: C.A. Reitzel Nielsen & Lydische 1936.

———. *Kancelliets brevbøger vedrørende Danmarks indre forhold*: 1635–1636. Copenhagen: C.A. Reitzel Nielsen & Lydische, 1940.

———. *Kancelliets brevbøger vedrørende Danmarks indre forhold*: 1637–1639. Copenhagen: C.A. Reitzel Nielsen & Lydische 1944.

Mentz, Søren. *The English Gentleman Merchant at Work: Madras and the City of London 1660–1740.* Copenhagen: Museum Tusculanum Press, 2005.

Müller, J. Journal in the Fetu country, translated and printed in, Adam Jones, *German Sources for West African History, 1599–1669.* Wiesbaden: Franz Steiner Verlag, 1983.

Ratelband, K., ed. *Vijf Dagregisters van het kasteel São Jorge da Mina (Elmina) aan de Goudkust (1645–1647).* The Hague: Nijhoff, 1953.

Svensson, A. *Svensk agent ved Sundet: Toldkommissær og agent i Helsingør Anders Svenssons depecher til Gustav II Adolf og Axel Oxenstierna 1621–1626*, edited by Leo Tandrup. Aarhus: Universitetsforlaget i Aarhus, 1971.

Internet sources

Slave trade database. www.slavevoyages.org/voyage/search (accessed 8 January 2020).

State Papers, 1653: January. In *A Collection of the State Papers of John Thurloe*, vol. 1, 1638–1653, edited by Thomas Birch (London, 1742). www.british-history. ac.uk/thurloe-papers/vol1/ (accessed 21 November 2017).

Svenskt biografiskt lexikon. https://sok.riksarkivet.se/sbl/ (accessed 21 November 2017).

The Furley Collection (FC). The History of Gold Coast, the Netherlands collections (N4, N5, and N8), Balme Library, University of Ghana, http://ugspace.ug.edu.gh/ handle/123456789/3 (accessed 16 September 2015).

Sources and bibliography 185

Secondary literature

Abd-el Dayem, Torben. *Ove Geddes rejse til Ceylon og Indien 1618–1622*, No. 19. Esbjerg: Fiseri-og Søfartsmuseets, 2006.

Adams, Julia. *The Familial State: Ruling Families and Merchant Capitalism in Early Modern Europe* Ithaca: Cornell University Press, 2005.

Ames, Glenn. *Colbert Mercantilism & the French Quest for Asian Trade.* Dekalb: Northern Illinois University Press, 1996.

Amirel, S., and L. Müller, eds. *Persistent Piracy: Maritime Violence and State-Formation in Global Historical Perspective.* New York: Palgrave Macmillan, 2014.

Andaya, Leonard Y. "The 'Informal Portuguese Empire' and the Topasses in the Solor Archipelago and Timor in the Seventeenth and Eighteenth Centuries." *Journal of Southeast Asian Studies* 41, no. 3 (2010): 391–420.

Antunes, Cátia. "Amsterdam Cross-Cultural Partnerships in the Baltic-Atlantic Link, 1580–1674." In *The Rise of the Atlantic Economy and the North Sea/Baltic Trade, 1500–1800*, edited by Leos Müller, Philipp Robinson Rössner, and Toshiaki Tamaki, 103–119. Stuttgart: Franz Steiner Verlag, 2011.

Antunes, Cátia, and Amelia Polónia, eds. *Beyond Empires: Global, Self-Organizing, Cross-Imperial Networks, 1500–1800.* Boston/Leiden: Brill, 2016a.

———, eds. *Seaports in the First Global Age: Portuguese Agents, Networks and Interactions (1500–1800).* Porto: Uporto Edições, 2016b.

Antunes, Cátia, and Filipa Ribeiro da Silva. "Cross-Cultural Entrepreneurship in the Atlantic: Africans, Dutch and Sephardic Jews in Western Africa, 1580–1674." *Itinerario* 35, no. 1 (2011): 49–76.

———. "Amsterdam Merchants in the Slave Trade and African Commerce, 1580s–1670s." *Tijdschrift voor sociale en economische geschiedenis* 9, no. 4 (2012): 3–30.

Aslanian, Sebouh David. *From the Indian Ocean to the Mediterranean: The Global Trade Networks of Armenian Merchants from New Julfa.* Berkley/Los Angeles: University of California Press, 2011.

Bade, Klaus J., Pieter C. Emmer, Leo Lucassen, and Jochen Oltmer, eds. *The Encyclopedia of European Migration and Minorities: From the Seventeenth Century to the Present*, 1st edition. Cambridge/New York: Cambridge University Press, 2011.

Bailyn, Bernard. *Atlantic History: Concept and Contours.* Cambridge/London: Harvard University Press, 2005.

———. *The Barbarous Years: The Peopling of British North America: The Conflict of Civilizations, 1600–1675.* New York: Knopf Doubleday Publishing Group, 2012.

Baldaeus, Pilippus, *A True and Exact Description of the most Celebrated East-India Coasts of Malabar and Coromandel and also of the Isle of the Ceylon.* Amsterdam: 1672.

Barbour, Violet. *Capitalism in Amsterdam in the Seventeenth Century.* Ann Arbor: University of Michigan Press, 1950.

Birkenholz, Frans. "Merchant-Kings and Lords of the World: Diplomatic Gift-Exchange between the Dutch East India Company and the Safavid and Mughal Empires in the Seventeenth Century." In *Practices of Diplomacy in the Early Modern World c.1410–1800*, edited by Tracey Sowerby and Jan Hennings, 219–236. New York: Routledge, 2017.

Blussé, Leonard, and Femme Gaastra, eds. *Companies and Trade Essays on Overseas Trading Companies during the Ancien* Régime, Leiden: Leiden University Press, 1981.

186 Sources and bibliography

Bodian, Miriam. *Hebrews of the Portuguese Nation: Conversos and Community in Early Modern Amsterdam*. Bloomington/Indianapolis: Indiana University Press, 1999.

Boxer, C.R. *Salvador de Sá and the Struggle for Brazil and Angola, 1602–1686*. London: University of London, 1952.

———. *The Dutch in Brazil, 1624–1654*. Oxford: Clarendon Press, 1957.

———. *Francisco Vieira de Figueiredo: A Portuguese Merchant-Adventurer in South East Asia, 1624–1667*. Gravenhage: Martinus Nijhoff, 1967.

Brand, Hanno, ed. *Trade, Diplomacy and Cultural Exchange: Continuity and Change in the North Sea Area and the Baltic c. 1350–1750*. Hilversum: Uitgeverij Verloren, 2005.

Bredsdorff, Asta. *The Trials and Travels of Willem Leyel: An Account of the Danish East India Company in Tranquebar, 1639–1648*. Copenhagen: Museum Tusculanum Press, 2009.

Brennig, Joseph J. "Chief Merchants and the European Enclaves of Seventeenth-Century Coromandel." *Modern Asian Studies* 11, no. 3 (1977): 321–340.

Brøndsted, Johannes, ed. *Vore gamle tropenkolonier*. Vol I. Copenhagen: Westermann, 1952.

Bruijn, J.R., F.S. Gaastra, and I Schöffer, eds. *Dutch-Asiatic Shipping in the 17th and 18th Centuries*, vol. 1. Gravenhage: Martinus Nijhoff, 1979.

Caldeira, Arlindo. "Angola and 17th Century. South Atlantic Slave Trade." In *Networks and Trans-Cultural Exchange: Slave Trading in the South Atlantic, 1590–1867*, edited by Filipa Ribeiro da Silva and David Richardson, 101–142. Boston/Leiden: Brill, 2014.

Candido, Mariana. "The Formation of a Colonial Society in the African Coast: Benguela and the Atlantic World, 1600–1780." In *Seaports in the First Global Age Portuguese Agents, Networks and Interactions (1500–1800)*, edited by Cátia Antunes and Amelia Polónia, 197–219. Porto: Uporto Edições, 2016.

Carlos, Ann M., and Santhi Hejeebu. "Specific Information and the English Chartered Companies, 1650–1750." In *Information Flows: New Approaches in the Historical Study of Business Information*, edited by Leos Müller and Jari Ojala, 139–169. Helsinki: SKS, Finnish Literature Society, 2007.

Carlos, Ann M., and Stephen Nicholas. "Agency Problems in Early Chartered Companies: The Case of the Hudson's Bay Company." *The Journal of Economic History* 50, no. 4 (1990): 853–875.

———. "Theory and History: Seventeenth-Century Joint-Stock Chartered Trading Companies." *The Journal of Economic History* 56, no. 4 (1996): 916–924.

Casson, Mark. *The Entrepreneur: An Economic Theory*. 2 edition. Cheltenham; Northhampton: Edward Elgar, 2003.

———, ed. *Entrepreneurship: Theory, Networks, History*. Cheltenham; Northhampton: Edward Elgar, 2010.

Casson, Mark and Catherine Casson. *The Entrepreneur in History: From Medieval Merchant to Modern Business Leader*. Basingstoke: Palgrave MacMillan, 2013.

———. "The History of Entrepreneurship: Medieval Origins of a Modern Phenomenon." *Business History* 56, no. 8 (2014): 1223–1242.

Casson, Mark, and Marina Della Giusta. "Entrepreneurship and Social Capital: Analysing the Impact of Social Networks on Entrepreneurial Activity from a Rational Action Perspective." *International Small Business Journal* 25, no. 3 (2007): 220–244.

Sources and bibliography   187

Chaiklin, Martha. "Elephants and the Making of Early Modern India." In *The Indian Ocean in the Making of Early Modern India*, edited by Pius Malekandathil, 457–475. New York: Routledge, 2017.

Chaudhuri, K.N. *Trade and Civilisation in the Indian Ocean: An Economic History from the Rise of Islam to 1750*. Cambridge: Cambridge University Press, 1985.

Cipolla, Carlo M. *Guns and Sails in the Early Phase of European Expansion, 1400–1700*. New York: Random House, 1965.

Clulow, Adam. "European Maritime Violence and Territorial States in Early Modern Asia, 1600–1650." *Itinerario* 33, no. 3 (2009): 72–94.

Cruz, Maria Augusta Lima. "Exiles and Renegades in Early Sixteenth Century Portuguese India." *The Indian Economic & Social History Review* 23, no. 3 (1986): 249–262.

Daaku, Kwame Yeboa. *Trade and Politics on the Gold Coast, 1600–1720: A Study of the African Reaction to European Trade*. Oxford: Clarendon Press, 1970.

Dalgård, Sune. *Dansk-Norsk hvalfangst, 1615–1660 en studie over Danmarks-Norges stilling i Europæisk merkantil expansion*. Copenhagen: G.E.C. Gad, 1962.

Dahlgren, Erik Wilhelm. *Louis de Geer, 1587–1652, hans lif och verk*, vol. 1. Uppsala: Almqvist och Wicksell, 1923a.

———. *Louis de Geer, 1587–1652, hans lif och verk*, vol. 2. Uppsala: Almqvist och Wicksell, 1923b.

Dahlgren, Stellan and Norman, Hans. *The Rise and Fall of New Sweden: Gov. Johan Risingh's Journal*. Uppsala: Acta Universitatis Upsaliensis, 1988.

Dantzig, A. van. *Forts and Castles of Ghana*. Accra: Sedco Publishing, 1980.

———. *The Furley Collection: Its Value and Limitations for the Study of Ghana's History*, European Sources for Sub-Saharan Africa before 1900 : Use and Abuse, 423–432. Wiesbaden: Franz Steiner Verlag, 1987.

Dapper, Olfert. *Naukeurige beschrijvinge der Afrikaensche gewesten, van Egyten, Barbaryen, Libyen, Biledulgerid, Negroslant, Guinea, Ethiopiën, Abyssinië getrokken uit verscheyde hedendaegse lantbeschryvers en geschriften van bereisde onderzoekers dier landen*. Amsterdam 1668.

Davids, Karel, and Leo Noordegraaf, eds. *The Dutch Economy in the Golden Age*. Amsterdam: Nederlandsch Economisch-Historisch Archief, 1993.

De Geer, Louis de. *Louis de Geers brev och affärshandlingar 1614–1652*, edited by Erik Wilhelm Dahlgren. Stockholm: P.A. Norstedt & Söner, 1934.

Delafosse, Marcel. "La Rochelle et les Iles au XVlle siécle," *Revue d'histoire des colonies* 36, no. 127–128 (1949): 238–281.

De Jonge, Cornelis. *Geschiedenis van het Nederlandsche zeewezen*, pt. 2. vol. 3. Gravenhage: Gebroedersvan Cleef, 1837.

———. *De Oorsprong van Nederland's Bezittingen op de Kust van Guinea*. Gravenhage: Martinus Nijhoff, 1871.

De Roever, Nicholas. "Twee Concurrenten van de Eerste West-Indische Compagnie." *Oud-Holland. nieuw bijdragen voor de geschiedenis der Nederlandsche kunst, letterkunde, nijverheid, enz* 7 (1889): 195–220.

Den Blanken, W.B. "Imperium in Imperio Sovereign Powers of the First Dutch West India Company." M.A. dissertation, Leiden University, 2014.

Dekker, R.M. 'Van "grand tour" tot treur-en sukkelreis', Nederlandse reisverslagen van de 16e tot egin 19e eeuw', *Tijdschrift voor Historische en Kunstwetenschappen, in Opossum* 4 (1994), 8–25.

188 *Sources and bibliography*

Diller, Stephan. *Die Dänen in Indien, Südostasien und China (1620–1845)*. Wiesbaden: Otto Harrassowitz Verlag, 1999.

Disney, Anthony R. *The Portuguese in India and Other Studies, 1500–1700*. New York: Routledge, 2009.

Duindam, Jeroen, and Sabrine Dabringhaus, eds. *The Dynastic Centre and the Provinces: Agents and Interactions*. Boston/Leiden: Brill, 2014.

Ekama, Kate. "Courting Conflict: Managing Dutch East and West India Company disputes in the Dutch Republic." PhD dissertation, Leiden: Leiden University, 2018.

Elias, J.E. *De Vroedschap van Amsterdam 1578–1795*, vol. 1. Amsterdam: N. Israel, 1963.

Elliott, John. *Empires of the Atlantic World: Britain and Spain in America 1492–1830*. New Haven: Yale University Press, 2007.

Emmer, Piet. *The Dutch Slave Trade, 1500–1850*. Translated by Chris Emery. New York/Oxford: Berghahn Books, 2006.

Enthoven, Victor. "An assessment of Dutch Transatlantic commerce, 1585–1817." In *Riches of from Atlantic Commerce: Dutch Transatlantic trade and shipping, 1585–1817*, edited by Victor Enthoven and Johannes Postma, 385–445. Boston/ Leiden: Brill, 2003.

Enthoven, Victor, Henk den Heijer, and Jordaan, Han, eds. *Geweld in de West: een militaire Geschiedenis van de Nederlandse Atlantische wereld*, 1600–1800, Boston/ Leiden: Brill, 2013.

Enthoven, Victor, Steve Murdoch, Eila Williamson, and Ben Teensma, eds. *The Navigator: The Log of John Anderson, VOC Pilot-Major, 1640–1643*. Boston/ Leiden: Brill, 2010.

Feldbæk, Ole. "The Organization and Structure of the Danish East India, West India and Guinea Companies in the 17th and 18th Centuries." In *Companies and Trade*, edited by Leonard Blussé and Femme Gaastra, 131–158. Leiden: Leiden University Press, 1981.

———. "The Danish Trading Companies of the Seventeenth and Eighteenth Centuries." *Scandinavian Economic History Review* 34, no. 3 (1986): 204–218.

———. "No Ship for Tranquebar for Twenty-Nine Years. Or: The Art of Survival of a Mid-Seventeenth Century European Settlement in India." In *Emporia, Commodities and Entrepreneurs in Asian Maritime Trade, c. 1400–1750*, edited by Roderich Ptak and Dietmar Rothermund, 29–36. Stuttgart: Franz Steiner Verlag, 1991.

Feldbæk, Ole, and Justesen, Ole, eds. *Kolonierne i Asien og Afrika*. Copenhagen: Politiken, 1980.

Ferreira, Roquinaldo. "Transforming Atlantic Slaving: Trade, Warfare and Territorial Control in Angola, 1650–1800." PhD dissertation, Los Angeles: University of California, 2003.

Fihl, Esther. "Shipwrecked on the Coromandel: The First Indian-Danish Contact, 1620." In *Beyond Tranquebar Grappling across Cultural Borders in South India*, edited by Esther Fihl and A.R. Vēṅkaṭācalapati, 229–256. Delhi: Orient Blackswan, 2014.

Fihl, Esther, and Ā Irā Vēṅkaṭācalapati, eds. *Beyond Tranquebar: Grappling Across Cultural Borders in South India*. Delhi: Orient Blackswan, 2014.

Fortin, Jeffrey A., and Mark Meuwese, eds. *Atlantic Biographies: Individuals and Peoples in the Atlantic World*. Boston/Leiden: Brill, 2013.

Sources and bibliography 189

Fusaro, Maria. "A Reassessment of Mediterranean History between the Northern Invasion and the Caravane Maritime." In *Trade and Cultural Exchange in the Early Modern Mediterranean: Braudel's Maritime Legacy*, edited by Mohamed-Salah Omri, Colin Heywood, and Maria Fusaro, 1–22. London/New York: I.B. Tauris, 2010.

Fusaro, Maria, Colin Heywood, and Mohamed-Salah Omri, eds. *Trade and Cultural Exchange in the Early Modern Mediterranean: Braudel's Maritime Legacy*. London/New York: I.B. Tauris, 2010.

Fynn-Paul, Jeff, ed. *War, Entrepreneurs, and the State in Europe and the Mediterranean, 1300–1800*. Boston/Leiden: Brill, 2014.

Fynn-Paul, Jeff, Marjolein't Hart, and Griet Vermeesch. "Entrepreneurs, Military Supply, and State Formation in the Late Medieval and Early Modern Periods: New Directions." In *War, Entrepreneurs, and the State in Europe and the Mediterranean, 1300–1800*, edited by Jeff Fynn-Paul, 1–13. Boston/Leiden: Brill, 2014.

Games, Alison. *The Web of Empire: English Cosmopolitans in an Age of Expansion, 1560–1660*. New York: Oxford University Press, 2008.

García-Arenal, Mercedes, and Gerard Albert Wiegers. *A Man of Three Worlds: Samuel Pallache, a Moroccan Jew in Catholic and Protestant Europe*. Baltimore: John Hopkins University Press, 2003.

Gelder, Roelof van. *Het Oost-Indisch avontuur: Duitsers in dienst van de VOC (1600–1800)*. Nijmegen: SUN, 1997.

Gelderblom, Oscar. *Zuid-Nederlandse kooplieden en de opkomst van de Amsterdamse stapelmarkt (1578–1630)*. Hilversum: Uitgeverij Verloren, 2000.

Gerentz, Sven. *Kommerskollegium och näringslivet, 1651–1951*. Stockholm: Nordisk Rotogravyr, 1951.

Glamann, Kristoff. "The Danish East India Company." In *Societés et Compagnies de Commerce en Orient et dans I 'Océan Indien*, edited by Michiel Mollet, 471–481. Paris, 1970.

Glete, Jan. *Warfare at Sea, 1500–1650: Maritime Conflicts and the Transformation of Europe*. New York: Routledge, 2000.

Gøbel, Erik. "Danes in the Service of the Dutch East India Company in the Seventeenth Century." *International Journal of Maritime History* 16, no. 1 (2004): 77–94.

Goey, Ferry de, and Jan Willem Veluwenkamp, eds. *Entrepreneurs and Institutions in Europe and Asia, 1500–2000*. Amsterdam: Aksant, 2002.

Goslinga, Cornelis Christiaan. *The Dutch in the Caribbean and on the Wild Coast 1580–1680*. Assen: Van Gorcum, 1971.

Granlund, Victor. *En svensk koloni i Afrika: eller Svenska afrikanska kompaniets historia*. Stockholm: P.A. Norstedt, 1879.

Groesen, Michiel van. *Amsterdam's Atlantic: Print Culture and the Making of Dutch Brazil*. Philadelphia: University of Pennsylvania Press, 2016.

Gullov, H.C., et al., eds. *Danmark og kolonierna*, five volumes series. Copenhagen: Gads forlag, 2017.

Gunneriusson, Håkan. *Sociala nätverk och fält*. Uppsala: Historiska Inst., 2002.

Gupta, Ashin Das, and M.N. Pearson, eds. *India and the Indian Ocean 1500–1800*. Calcutta; New York: Oxford University Press, 1987.

Gustafsson, Harald. *Nordens historia: en europeisk region under 1200 år*. Lund: Studentlitteratur, 1997.

Harreld, Donald. "An Education in Commerce: Transmitting Business Information in Early Modern Europe." In *Information Flows: New Approaches in the*

190   *Sources and bibliography*

Historical Study of Business Information, edited by Leos Müller and Jari Ojala, 63–83. Helsinki: SKS, Finnish Literature Society, 2007.

Harris, Steven J. "Networks of Travel, Correspondance and Exchange." In *The Cambridge History of Science: Volume 3, Early Modern Science*, edited by Katharine Park and Lorraine Daston, 341–364. New York: Cambridge University Press, 2006.

Hasselberg, Ylva, Leos Müller, and Niklas Stenlås. "Åter till historians nätverk." In *Sociala nätverk och fält*, edited by Håkan Gunneriusson, 7–32. Uppsala: Historiska Inst., 2002.

Heijer, Henk den. "Een dienaar van hele Heren – De Atlantische carrier van Hendrick Caerloff." In *Het verre gezicht – politieke en culturele relaties tussen Nederland en Azie, Afrika en Amerika*, edited by Thomas Lindblad and Alicia Schrikker, 162–180. Franeker: Van Wijnen, 2011.

Heijmans, Elisabeth. "The Agency of Empire: Personal Connections and Individual Strategies of the French Early Modern Expansion (1686–1746)." PhD dissertation, Leiden: Leiden University, 2018.

Hill, Charles. *The Danish Sound Dues and the Command of the Baltic*. Durham: Duke University Press, 1926.

Holck, Harald. "Om slægten Leyel." *Personalhistorisk tidsskrift* 6, no. 13 (1958).

Hvidegaard, Torben. "Øresundstolden på Christian 4.'s tid – sundtoldens betydning 1613–1645 for forholdet mellem Danmark, Sverige og Nederlandene." *Fortid og nutid* 1 (2000): 199–219.

Israel, Jonathan. *Dutch Primacy in World Trade, 1585–1740*. Oxford: Clarendon Press, 1989.

———. *Empires and Entrepots: Dutch, the Spanish Monarchy and the Jews, 1585–1713*. London and Ronceverte: A&C Black, 1990.

———. *The Dutch Republic: Its Rise, Greatness and Fall, 1477–1806*. Oxford: Clarendon Press, 1998.

Jacobs, Jaap. *New Netherland: A Dutch Colony in Seventeenth-Century America*. Boston/Leiden: Brill, 2005.

———. *The Colony of New Netherland: A Dutch Settlement in Seventeenth-Century America*. Ithaca: Cornell University Press, 2009.

Jacobs, Joachim. "Der Jüdische Friedhof von Glückstadt." In *Erinnerungsorte – Im Auftrag des Heimatverbandes für den Kreis Steinburg*, edited by C Boldt, S Loebert, and K Puymnaa, 65–82. Itzehoe: Steinburger Jahrbuch, 2014.

Jespersen, Leon. *A Revolution from Above? The Power State of 16th and 17th Century Scandinavia*. Odense: University Press of Southern Denmark, 2000.

Jeyaraj, Daniel. *Bartholomäus Ziegenbalg, the Father of Modern Protestant Mission: An Indian Assessment*. New Delhi: ISPCK, 2006.

Johnson, Amandus. *The Swedish Settlements on the Delaware: Their History and Relation to the Indians, Dutch and English, 1638–1664: With an Account of the South, the New Sweden, and the American Companies, and the Efforts of Sweden to Regain the Colony*. Lancaster: The New Era Printing Company, 1911.

Jones, Adam. *German Sources for West African History, 1599–1669*. Wiesbaden: Franz Steiner Verlag, 1983.

Jones Geoffery and Daniel Wadhwani, "Entrepreneurship." In *The Oxford Handbook of Business History*, edited by Jones, Geoffery ja Zeitlin Jonathan, 501–528. Oxford: Oxford University Press, 2008.

Sources and bibliography 191

Jong Michiel de, Knaap, Gerrit and Heijer Henk den, *Oorlogen overzee: militair optreden door compagnie en staat buiten Europa 1595–1814*. Amsterdam: Uitgeverij Boom, 2015.

Jonsson, Mar. "Denmark-Norway as a Potential World Power in the Early Modern Seventeenth Century." *Itinerario* XXXIII, no. 2 (2007): 17–27.

Juynboll, W.M.C., *Zeventiende-eewsche Beoefenaars van het Arabisch in Nederland*. Utrecht: Kemink, 1931.

Karonen, Petri. *Pohjoinen suurvalta: Ruotsi ja Suomi 1521–1809*. Helsinki: WSOY, 1999.

Kellenbenz, Hermann. *Sephardim an der Unteren Elbe*. Wiesbaden: Franz Steiner Verlag, 1958.

———. *The Rise of the European Economy: An Economic History of Continental Europe from the Fifteenth to the Eighteenth Century*. New York: Holmes & Meier Publishers, 1976.

Kjeldstadli, Knut. "Denmark, Norway, Sweden, Finland." In *The Encyclopedia of European Migration and Minorities: From the Seventeenth Century to the Present*, edited by Klaus J. Bade, Pieter C. Emmer, Leo Lucassen, and Jochen Oltmer, 5–15. New York: Cambridge University Press, 2011.

Klein, Peter. *De Trippen in de 17e Eeuw: een studie over het ondernemersgedrag op de Hollandse stapelmarkt*. Rotterdam: Van Gorcum, 1965.

Klein, P.W., and Jan Willem Veluwenkamp. "The Role of the Entrepreneur in the Economic Expansion of the Dutch Republic." In *Dutch Republic in the Golden Age*, edited by Karel Davids and Leo Noordegraaf, 27–53. Amsterdam: Nederlandsch Economisch-Historisch Archief, 1993.

Klooster, Wim. "Curaçao as a Transit Center to the Spanish Main and the French West Indies." In *Dutch Atlantic Connections, 1680–1800: Linking Empires, Bridging Borders*, edited by Gert Oostindie and Jessica Vance Roitman, 25–51. Boston/Leiden: Brill, 2014.

———. *The Dutch Moment: War, Trade, and Settlement in the Seventeenth-Century Atlantic World*, 1st edition. Ithaca: Cornell University Press, 2016.

Köhn, Gerhard. *Die Bevölkerung der Residenz, Festung und Exulantenstadt Glückstadt von der Gründung 1616 bis zum Endausbau 1652: Methoden und Möglichkeiten einer historisch-demographischen Untersuchung mit Hilfe der elektronischen Datenverarbeitung*. Neumünster: Karl Wachholtz Verlag, 1974.

———. *Die Niederland und der Europäische Nordosten ein Jahrtausend weiträumiger Beziehungen*. Neumünster: Karl Wachholtz Verlag, 1992.

Kooijmans, L. "Risk and Reputation: On the Mentality of Merchants in the Early Modern Period." In *Entrepreneurs and Entrepreneurship in Early Modern Times: Merchants and Industrialists Within the Orbit of the Dutch Staple Market*, edited by Clé Lesger and Leo Noordegraaf, 25–35. Den Haag: Stiching Hollandse Historische Reeks, 1995.

———. *Vriendschap: en de kunst van het overleven in de zeventiende en achtiende eeuw*. Amsterdam: B. Bakker, 1997.

Koot, Christian J. "The Merchant, the Map, and Empire: Augustine Herrman's Chesapeake and Interimperial Trade, 1644–1673." *The William and Mary Quarterly* 67, no. 4 (2010): 603–644.

Krieger, Martin. *Kaufleute, Seeräuber und Diplomaten. Der Dänische Handel auf dem Indischen Ozean (1620–1868)*. Köln: Böhlau Verlag, 1998.

192   Sources and bibliography

———. "Der Dänische Sklavenhandel auf dem Indischen Ozean im 17. Und 18. Jahrhundert." In *Jahrbuch für Europäische Überseegeschichte*, vol. 12, 9–30. Wiesbaden: Harrassowitz Verlag, 2012.

Kuijpers, Erika. *Migrantenstad: immigratie en sociale verhoudingen in 17e-eeuws Amsterdam*. Hilversum: Uitgeverij Verloren, 2005.

Lane, Kris. *Pillaging the Empire: Global Piracy on the High Seas, 1500–1750*, 1st edition. New York: Routledge, 2015.

Lappalainen, Mirkka. *Suku, valta, suurvalta. Creutzit 1600-luvun Ruotsissa ja Suomessa*. Helsinki: WSOY, 2005.

———. *Maailman painavin raha*. Helsinki: WSOY, 2007.

Larsen, Kay. *Dansk-Ostindiske koloniers historie*. Copenhagen: Centralførlaget, 1907.

———. *Guvernører: residenter, kommandanter og chefer*. Copenhagen: Arthur Jensens Forlag, 1940.

Lauridsen, John. *Marselis konsortiet: en studie over forholdet mellem handelskapital og kongemagt i 1600-talets Danmark*. Copenhagen: Jysk Selskab for Historie, 1987.

Law, Robin. "Between the Sea and the Lagoons: The Interaction of Maritime and Inland Navigation on the Precolonial Slave Coast (Entre Mer et Lagune: Les Interactions de La Navigation Maritime et Continentale Sur La Côte Des Esclaves Avant La Colonisation)." *Cahiers d'Études Africaines* 29, no. 114 (1989): 209–237.

———. *The Slave Coast of West Africa 1550–1750: The Impact of the Atlantic Slave Trade on an African Society*. Oxford: Clarendon Press, 1991.

Leers, Arnout, *Pertinente Beschryvinge van Afrika* (Rotterdam, 1665).

Lesger, Clé. *The Rise of the Amsterdam Market and Information Exchange: Merchants, Commercial Expansion and Change in the Spatial Economy of the Low Countries, c.1550–1630*. Translated by J.C. Grayson. Aldershot; Burlington: Ashgate, 2006.

Lesger, Clé, and Leo Noordegraaf, eds. *Entrepreneurs and Entrepreneurship in Early Modern Times: Merchants and Industrialists within the Orbit of the Dutch Staple Market*. Den Haag: Stiching Hollandse Historische Reeks, 1995.

Lindblad, Thomas. *Sweden's Trade with the Dutch Republic 1738–1795: A Quantitative Analysis of the Relationship between Economic Growth and International Trade in the Eighteenth Century*. Assen: Van Gorcum, 1982.

———. "Louis de Geer (1587–1652); Dutch Entrepreneur and the Father of Swedish Industry." In *Entrepreneurs and Entrepreneurship in Early Modern Times; Merchants and Industrialists within the Orbit of the Dutch Staple Market*, edited by Clé Lesger and Leo Noordegraaf, 77–84. Den Haag: Hollandse Historische Reeks, 1995.

Lindblad, Thomas, and Alicia Schrikker. *Het verre gezicht – politieke en culturele relaties tussen Nederland en Azie, Afrika en Amerika*. Franeker: Van Wijnen, 2011.

Lindsay, Lisa A., and John Wood Sweet, eds. *Biography and the Black Atlantic*. Philadelphia: University of Pennsylvania Press, 2013.

Lockhart, Paul. "Denmark and the Empire A Reassessment of Danish Foreign Policy under King Christian IV." *Scandinavian Studies* 63, no. 3 (1992): 390–416.

Lottum, Jelle van. *Across the North Sea: The Impact of the Dutch Republic on International Labour Migration, c. 1550–1850*. Groeningen: Aksant Academic Publishers, 1632.

Lucassen, Jan, and Leo Lucassen. "The Netherlands." In *The Encyclopedia of European Migration and Minorities, from the Seventeenth Century to the Present*,

Sources and bibliography   193

edited by Klaus J. Bade, Pieter C. Emmer, Leo Lucassen, and Jochen Oltmer, 34–44. New York: Cambridge University Press, 2011.

Ly, A. *La Compagnie du Sénégal de 1675 à 1696*. Bordeaux: Universite Bordeaux, 1955.

Malekandathil, Pius, ed. *The Indian Ocean in the Making of Early Modern India*. New York: Routledge, 2017.

McCabe, Ina Baghdiantz, Gelina Harlaftis, and Ioanna Pepelasis Minoglou. *Diaspora Entrepreneurial Networks: Four Centuries of History*. Oxford/New York: Bloomsbury Academic, 2005.

Meersbergen van, Guido. "The Dutch Merchant-Diplomat in Comparative Perspective: Embassies to the Court Aurangzeb, 1660–1666." In *Practices of Diplomacy in the Early Modern World c.1410–1800*, edited by Tracey Sowerby and Jan Hennings, 147–165. New York: Routledge, 2017.

Menkman, W.R. "TOBAGO: een bijdrage tot de geschiedenis der Nederlandsche kolonisatie in tropisch Amerika IV." *De West-Indische Gids* 21 (1940): 33–46.

Meuwese, Mark."Indigenous Leaders and the Atlantic World: The Parallel Lives of Dom Antonio Filipe Camarao and Pieter Poty, 1600–1650." In *Atlantic Biographies: Individuals and Peoples in the Atlantic World*, edited by Jeffrey A. Fortin and Mark Meuwese, 213–233. Boston/Leiden: Brill, 2014.

Mims, Stuart. *Colbert's West India Policy*. New Heaven: Yale University Press, 1912.

Mo Svalastog, Julie. "The Transatlantic Slave Trade Database: Qualitative Possibilities and Quantitative Limitations." M.A. dissertation, King's College, 2012.

———. "Mastering the Worst of Trades: England's Early Africa Companies and Their Traders, 1618–1672." PhD dissertation, Leiden: Leiden University, 2018..

Mollet, Michiel, ed. *Societés et Compagnies de Commerce en Orient et dans I 'Océan Lndien*. Paris: S.E.V.P.E.N., 1970.

Mukherjee, Rila. "Portuguese Slave Ports in Bengal 1500–1700." In *Seaports in the First Global Age Portuguese Agents, Networks and Interactions (1500–1800)*, edited by Cátia Antunes and Amelia Polónia, 221–241. Porto: Uporto Edições, 2016.

Müller, Leos. "The Role of the Merchant Network – A Case History of Two Swedish Trading Houses 1650–1800." In *Entrepreneurship and Entrepreneurs in the Early Modern Times. Merchants and Industrialists within the Orbit of the Dutch Staple Market*, edited by Clé Lesger and Leo Noordegraaf, 147–163. Den Haag: Hollandse Historische Reeks, 1995.

———. *The Merchant Houses of Stockholm, C. 1640–1800: A Comparative Study of Early-Modern Entrepreneurial Behaviour*. Uppsala University Library, 1998.

———. "The Dutch Entrepreneurial Networks and Sweden in the Age of Greatness." In *Trade, Diplomacy and Cultural Exchange: Continuity and Change in the North Sea Area and the Baltic c.1350–1750*, edited by Hanno Brand, 58–74. Hilversum: Uitgeverij Verloren, 2005.

———. "Trading with Asia without a Colonial Empire in Asia: Swedish Merchant Networks and Chartered Company Trade, 1760–1790." In *Beyond Empires: Global, Self-Organizing, Cross-Imperial Networks*, edited by Cátia Antunes and Amelia Polónia, 236–2252. Boston/Leiden: Brill, 2016.

Müller, Leos, and Jari Ojala. "Information Flows and Economic Performance over the Long Term: An Introduction." In *Information Flows: New Approaches in the Historical Study of Business Information* edited by Leos Müller and Jari Ojala, 14–28. Helsinki: SKS, Finnish Literature Society, 2007.

194   Sources and bibliography

Müller, Leos, Philipp Robinson Rössner, and Toshiaki Tamaki, eds. *The Rise of the Atlantic Economy and the North Sea/Baltic Trades, 1500–1800: Proceedings of the XVth World Economic History Congress.* Stuttgart: Franz Steiner Verlag, 2011.

Munroe, John. *History of Delaware.* Newark: University of Delaware Press, 2006.

Murdoch, Steve. *Network North: Scottish Kin, Commercial and Covert Associations in Northern Europe 1603–1746.* Boston/Leiden: Brill, 2006.

Naum, Magdalena, and Jonas M. Nordin, eds. *Scandinavian Colonialism and the Rise of Modernity: Small Time Agents in a Global Arena.* New York: Springer, 2013.

Netten, Djoke, van, *Koopman in kennis, De uitgever Willem Jansz Blaeu n de geleerde wereld (1571–1638),* Zutphen: Walburg pers 2014.

Nergård, Maj Britt, *Mellan krona och markand: utlädnska och svenska entreprenörer inom svensk järnhantering från ca 1580 till 1700.* Uppsala: Acta Universitatis Upsaliensis, 2001.

Niebuhr, B.G. "Nogle efterretninger om Wilhelm Leyel og den Danske Ostindiske handel under hans bestyrelse." *Det Skandinaviske litteratuselskabs skriften* 1 (1805): 142–169.

Nørregård, Georg. *Danish Settlements in West Africa, 1658–1850.* Boston: Boston University Press, 1966.

Nováky, György. *Handelskompanier och kompanihandel – Svenska Afrikakompaniet 1649–1663 en studie i feodal handel.* Uppsala: Uppsala University Library, 1990.

———. "Small Company Trade and the Gold Coast: The Swedish Africa Company 1650–1663." *Itinerario,* 16, no. 01 (1992): 57–76.

Odegard, Erik. "The Sixth Admiralty: The Dutch East India Company and the Military Revolution at Sea, c. 1639–1667." *International Journal of Maritime History* 26, no. 4 (2014): 669–684.

———. "Colonial Careers: Johan Maurits van Nassau Siegen, Rijckloff Volckertsz. van Goens and Career-Making in the Early Modern Dutch Empire." PhD dissertation, Leiden: Leiden University, 2018.

Ogborn, Miles. *Indian Ink: Script and Print in the Making of the English East India Company.* Chicago: University of Chicago Press, 2008.

Olsen, Gunnar. *Dansk Ostindien.* In *Vore gamle tropenkolonier,* edited by Johannes Brøndsted. Copenhagen: Westermann, 1952.

Oostindie, Gert, and Jessica V. Roitman, eds. *Dutch Atlantic Connections, 1680–1800: Linking Empires, Bridging Borders.* Boston/Leiden: Brill, 2014.

Osterhammel, Jürgen. "The Imperial Viceroy: Reflections on an Historical Type." In *The Dynastic Centre and the Provinces: Agents and Interactions,* edited by Jeroen Duindam and Sabrine Dabringhaus, 13–29. Boston/Leiden: Brill, 2014.

Parker, Geoffrey. *The Military Revolution: Military Innovation and the Rise of the West, 1500–1800.* Cambridge/New York: Cambridge University Press, 1996.

Parrott, David. *The Business of War: Military Enterprise and Military Revolution in Early Modern Europe.* New York: Cambridge University Press, 2012.

Petto, Christine. *Mapping and Charting in Early Modern England and France: Power, Patronage, and Production.* Lanham/Boulder/New York/London: Lexington Books, 2015.

Porter, Robert. "European Activity on the Gold Coast, 1620–1667." PhD dissertation, Pretoria: University of South Africa, 1975.

Sources and bibliography   195

Postma, Johannes. *The Dutch in the Atlantic Slave Trade, 1600–1815*, 1st edition. Cambridge: Cambridge University Press, 2008.

Postma, Johannes, and Victor Enthoven. *Riches from Atlantic Commerce: Dutch Transatlantic Trade and Shipping, 1585–1817*. Boston/Leiden: Brill, 2003.

Powell, Walter. "Neither Market nor Hierarchy: Network Forms in Organization." In *Markets, Hierarchies and Networks: The Coordination of Social Life*, edited by Grahame Thompson, 265–276. London: SAGE, 1991.

Prak, Maarten. *Dutch Republic in the Seventeenth Century*. New York: Cambridge University Press, 2005.

Pritchard, James. *In Search of Empire: The French in the Americas, 1670–1730*. Cambridge/New York: Cambridge University Press, 2004.

Ptak, Roderich, and Dietmar Rothermund, eds. *Emporia, Commodities, and Entrepreneurs in Asian Maritime Trade, C. 1400–1750*. Stuttgart: Franz Steiner Verlag, 1991.

Ratelband, K. *Nederlanders in West-Afrika 1600–1650: Angola, Kongo en São Tomé*, 1st edition. Zutphen: Walburg Pers, 2000.

Raychaudhuri, Tapan. *Jan Company in Coromandel, 1605–1690: A Study in the Interrelations of European Commerce and Traditional Economies*. Gravenhage: Martinus Nijhoff, 1962.

Renders, Hans, Binne de Haan, and Jonne Harmsma, eds. *The Biographical Turn: Lives in History*. New York: Routledge, 2016.

Rian, Øystein. "Introduction: Government and Society in Early Modern Scandinavia 1560–1721." In *A Revolution from Above? The Power State of 16th and 17th Century Scandinavia*, edited by Leon Jespersen, 13–30. Odense: University Press of Southern Denmark, 2000.

Ribeiro da Silva, Filipa. "Crossing Empires: Portuguese, Sephardic, and Dutch Business Networks in the Atlantic Slave Trade, 1580–1674." *The Americas* 68, no. 1 (2011a): 7–32.

———. *Dutch and Portuguese in Western Africa: Empires, Merchants and the Atlantic System, 1580–1674*. Boston/Leiden: Brill, 2011b.

———. "Private Businessmen in the Angolan Trade, 1590s to 1780s: Insurance, Commerce and Agency." In *Networks and Trans-Cultural Exchange: Slave Trading in the South Atlantic, 1590–1867*, edited by David Richardson and Filipa Ribeiro da Silva, 71–100. Boston/Leiden: Brill, 2014.

Ribeiro da Silva, Filipa, and Stacey Sommerdyk. "Reexamining the Geography and Merchants of the West Central African Trade: Looking behind Numbers." *African Economic History* 28 (2010): 77–105.

Richardson, David, and Filipa Ribeiro da Silva, eds. *Networks and Trans-Cultural Exchange: Slave Trading in the South Atlantic, 1590–1867*. Boston/Leiden: Brill, 2014.

Riis, Thomas. *Should Auld Acquaintance Be Forgot...: Scottish–Danish Relations C. 1450–1707*. Odense: Odense University Press, 1988.

Rindom, Jan. "Ostindisk Kompagni 1616–1650 – et spørgsmål om organisatorisk udvikling og interne magtkampe." *Handels-og søfartsmuseets årbogsindeks* 6 (2000): 99–125.

Rogerius, Abraham, *De open-deure tot het verborgen heydendom: ofte waerachtigh vertoogh van het leven ende zeden; mitsgaders de religie, ende gods-dienst der Bramines, op de Cust Chormandel, ende de landen daar* ontrent, Leiden 1651.

196   Sources and bibliography

Roberts, Michael, *The Swedish Imperial Experience 1560–1718*. Cambridge: Cambridge University Press, 1979.

Rodger, N.A.M. *The Wooden World: An Anatomy of the Georgian Navy*. London: W. W. Norton & Company, 1996.

Roper, L.H. *Advancing Empire, English Interest and Overseas Expansion 1613–1688*. New York: Cambridge University Press, 2017.

Rossum, Matthias van, *Werkers van de Wereld: Globalisering, arbeid en interculturele ontmoetingen tussen Aziatische en Europese zeelieden in dienst van de VOC, 1600–1800*, Hilversum: Verloren, 2014.

Scammell, Geoffrey Vaughn. *The First Imperial Age: European Overseas Expansion C. 1400–1715*. New York: Routledge, 1989.

Schlegel Bernhard and Carl Arvid Klingspor, *Den med sköldebref förlänade men ej å riddarhuset introducerade Svenska adelns ättartaflor* (Stockholm, 1875).

Schmitt, Eberhard. "Die Französiche Westindienkompanie verhandlet mit dem König von Ardrah wegen einer Befestigten Handelsstation und Der Guinea-Küste 1670." In *Der Aufbau der Kolonialreiche*, 193–203. München: Otto Harrassowitz Verlag, 1987.

Schnurmann, Claudia. "Representative Atlantic Entrepreneur Jacob Leisler, 1640–1691." In *Riches from Atlantic Commerce: Dutch Transatlantic Trade and Shipping, 1585–1817*, edited by Victor Enthoven and Johannes Postma, 259–283. Boston/Leiden: Brill, 2003.

Seshan, Radhika. *Trade and Politics on the Coromandel Coast: Seventeenth and Early Eighteenth Centuries*. Delhi: Primus Books, 2012.

Sicking, L.H.J. *Neptune and the Netherlands: State, Economy, and War at Sea in the Renaissance*. Boston/Leiden: Brill, 2004.

———. "Naval Warfare in Europe, c.1330–c.1680." In *European Warfare, 1350–1750*, edited by Frank Tallett and D. J. B. Trim, 236–263. Cambridge/New York: Cambridge University Press, 2010.

Sieveking, Heinrich. "Die Glückstädter Guineafahrt im 17. Jahrhundert. Ein Stück deutscher Kolonialgeschichte." *Vierteljahrschrift für Sozial-und Wirtschaftsgeschichte* 30, no. 1 (1937): 19–71.

Smith, Stefan Halikowski. *Creolization and Diaspora in the Portuguese Indies: The Social World of Ayutthaya, 1640–1720*. Boston/Leiden: Brill, 2011.

Steensgaard, Niels. *The Asian Trade Revolution: The East India Companies and the Decline of the Caravan Trade*. Chicago: University of Chicago Press, 1973.

Subrahmanyam, Sanjay, ed. *Merchant Networks in the Early Modern World, 1450–1800*, vol. 8. London/New York: Routledge, 1976.

———. "The Coromandel Trade of the Danish East India Company, 1618–1649." *Scandinavian Economic History Review* 37, no. 1 (1989): 41–56.

———. *The Political Economy of Commerce: Southern India 1500–1650*. Cambridge: Cambridge University Press, 2002.

———. *The Portuguese Empire in Asia, 1500–1700: A Political and Economic History*. Chichester: John Wiley & Sons, 2012.

Sutton, Angela. "The Seventeenth-Century Slave Trade in the Documents of the English, Dutch, Swedish, Danish and Prussian Royal Slave Trading Companies." *Slavery & Abolition* 36, no. 3 (2015): 445–459.

Svensson, Anders, *Svensk agent ved Sundet: Toldkommissær og agent i Helsingør Anders Svenssons depecher til Gustav II Adolf og Axel Oxenstierna 1621–1626*, edited by Leo Tandrup. Aarhus: Universitetsforlaget i Aarhus, 1971.

Sources and bibliography   197

Tallett, Frank, and D.J.B. Trim, eds. *European Warfare, 1350–1750.* Cambridge/New York: Cambridge University Press, 2010.

Thomaz, Luis Felippe Ferreira Reis. "The Indian Merchant Communities in Malacca under the Portuguese Rule." In *Indo-Portuguese History: Old Issues, New Questions*, edited by Teotonio de Souza, 56–72. New Delhi: Concept Publishing Company, 1985.

Thompson, Grahame. *Markets, Hierarchies and Networks: The Coordination of Social Life.* London: Sage Publications, 1991.

Thomson, Janice E. *Mercenaries, Pirates, and Sovereigns: State-Building and Extraterritorial Violence in Early Modern Europe.* New Jersey: Princeton University Press, 1996.

Thornton, John. *Africa and Africans in the Making of the Atlantic World, 1400–1800.* Cambridge/New York: Cambridge University Press, 1998.

Tielhof, Milja van. *The "Mother of All Trades": The Baltic Grain Trade in Amsterdam from the Late 16th to the Early 19th Century.* Boston/Leiden: Brill, 2002.

Tracy, James D, ed. *The Rise of Merchant Empires: Long Distance Trade in the Early Modern World 1350–1750.* Cambridge: Cambridge University Press, 1993.

Trivellato, Francesca. "Is There a Future for Italian Microhistory in the Age of Global History?" *California Italian Studies* 2, no. 1 (2011).

———. *The Familiarity of Strangers: The Sephardic Diaspora, Livorno, and Cross-Cultural Trade in the Early Modern Period.* New Heaven: Yale University Press, 2014.

Trivellato, Francesca, Leor Halevi, and Cátia Antunes, eds. *Religion and Trade: Cross-Cultural Exchanges in World History, 1000–1900*, 1st edition. Oxford/New York: Oxford University Press, 2014.

Tønnesen, Allan. *'Al het Hollandse volk dat hier nu woont': Nederlanders in Helsingør, circa 1550–1600.* Hilversum: Verloren, 2003.

Tol van den, Joris. "Lobbying in Company Mechanisms of Political Decision-Making and Economic Interests in the History of Dutch Brazil, 1621–1656." PhD dissertation, Leiden: Leiden University, 2018.

Vries, Jan de, and Ad van der Woude. *The First Modern Economy: Success, Failure, and Perseverance of the Dutch Economy, 1500–1815.* Cambridge/New York: Cambridge University Press, 1997.

Vries, Jan de, *Verzwegen zeeheld; Jacob Benckes (1637–1677)*, Zutphen: Walburg Press 2018.

Wachelder, Tim. *Avonturen in Brazilië en op de Goudkust. Vier duitsers in dienst van de WIC (1623–1645).* Nijmegen: Radboud Universiteit Nijmegen, 2004.

Weibull, Jörgen. *Sveriges historia.* Stockholm: Förlags AB Wiken Svenska Institutet, 1993.

Weiss, Holger. ed. *Ports of Globalisation, Places of Creolisation: Nordic Possessions in the Atlantic World during the Era of the Slave Trade.* Boston/Leiden: Brill, 2015.

Wellen, Kathryn. "The Danish East India Company's War against the Mughal Empire, 1642–1698." *Journal of Early Modern History* 19, no. 5 (2015): 439–461.

Whitelocke, Bulstrode. *Journal of the Swedish Embassy in the Years 1653 and 1654.* Edited by Henry Reeve. London: Longman, Brown, Green and Longmans, 1855.

Willerslev, Richard. "Danmarks første aktieselskab." *Historisk Tidsskrift* 10, no. 6 (January 1, 1944): 609–636.

Winius, George. "The 'Shadow Empire' of Goa in the Bay of Bengal." *Itinerario* 7, no. 2 (July 1983): 83–101.

198 Sources and bibliography

Winius, George Davison. *The Fatal History of Portuguese Ceylon: Transition to Dutch Rule*. Cambridge: Harvard University Press, 1971.

Wirta, Kaarle. "Rediscovering Agency in the Atlantic: A Biographical Approach Linking Entrepreneurial Spirit and Overseas Companies." In *The Biographical Turn Lives in History*, edited by Hans Renders, Binne de Haan, and Jonne Harmsma, 118–129. New York: Routledge, 2016.

Wrangel, Ewert, *De Betrekkingen tusschen Zweden en de Nederlanden op het gebied van letteren en wetenschap*, Leiden: Brill, 1901.

Zickermann, Kathrin. *Across the German Sea: Early Modern Scottish Connections with the Wider Elbe-Weser Region*. Boston/Leiden: Brill, 2013.

Index

Accra 42–43, 77–78
Achin 34
Acrosan 75–76, 110–112, 155–156
actorcentered approach 4–5, 171, 177
Admiralty of Amsterdam 157–159, 163
alcohol 73, 125, 156
Amsterdam 10, 22, 24, 62, 65, 102–109, 121, 134–135, 138, 155, 163–164
Anglo-Dutch War 7, 106, 132, 157–158
Angola 24, 39, 131, 134
Anomabo 76, 78, 155
Antunes, Cátia 5–6
Antwerp 22
Arctic 12, 27
Ardres 137–138
Arminians 28–29
arrack 69, 73–74, 94, 96
Asiento 134
Axim 155

Baers, Marten 104
Balasore 34, 66, 72
Baldaeus, Philippus 121, 139
Baltic grain 8, 22
Bantam 34, 67–68, 71, 73, 93, 96, 129
Barbour, Violet 10, 30
Batavia 1, 26, 33, 35, 74, 101, 129
Batticaloa 95
Bay of Bengal 13, 69, 92, 148, 150–152, 165
Benada, Chedam 70
Benguela 131–132
van Beuningen, Coenrad 108
Binckes, Jacob 157, 159–164
Blommaert, Samuel 1, 23–24, 27, 46
Blaeu, Willem Jansz 121
Blussé, Leonard 3
Board of Commerce 63–66, 80
Bocca á Bocca 133–134

Bonde, Christer 63–65, 80, 153
Bont, Jan 157, 160–161
bookkeeper 37, 41, 65, 101, 173
de Boshouwer, Michielszoon 25–26
bottomry loans 103–104, 164
Braem, Johan 59, 129
Brazil 39, 45, 153–154
Bredsdorff, Asta 13, 37, 124–125
Bremer, Gerrit 103–104
broker 39, 42–43, 45, 70, 72–74, 81, 96–99, 101
Butri 76, 78

Cabiljau, Abraham 24
caboceer 75, 106, 110, 155–156
canoes 75, 99, 137–138
Canter, Johan 110–111, 156
Canton 71
Cape Apollonia 76
Cape Coast 74–75, 77–80, 103, 112, 155–156
Cape Comorin 97
Caribbean 7, 22, 24, 29, 132, 136, 138, 148, 157–165
Carical 91, 100
Carlos, Ann 123
Caron, François 1
carrier trade 8, 22, 29
cartazes 72–73
de Casseres, Henrique 29
de Casseres, Simon 29
Casson, Mark 5, 10–11, 57, 81, 124
Cayenne 134, 157, 159–162, 164–165
Central Western Africa 131–132
Ceylon 25–26, 66–70, 72, 74, 82, 94–96, 98, 121, 127, 129
Charabon 68, 71
Charstenson, Simon 72, 97, 152

200 *Index*

charter 24–25, 34, 37, 57–61, 63–65, 107, 127, 148, 173
Chetti, Chinanna 101
Chetti, Malaio Cinene 100–101
Christian IV 13, 25, 27, 29, 35, 37–38, 58, 60, 140, 149
cinnamon 69–70, 74, 96
Cipolla, Carlo 148
Claesz, Cornelis 121
cloves 69–71
Clulow, Adam 147
Cock, Arent 41, 77
Colbert, Jean-Baptiste 136, 158
commander 1, 34, 37, 38, 61, 63, 66, 75, 79, 90, 94, 98, 99, 101, 125, 149, 150, 163, 172–173, 175
Copenhagen 25, 30, 32, 33, 35–37, 59–60, 92, 98, 125–126, 128–129, 151
copper 8, 22, 24
Coromandel Coast 25, 26, 38, 66, 68–69, 71, 82, 97, 99, 100, 101, 127
Courland 24, 158
Coymans, Isaac 41–42, 105–106, 135
Cramer, Joost 79–80, 105–106, 112, 156
Crappe, Roeland 25–27, 35–36, 46–47, 59–61, 66, 96, 126, 129
Crispe Nicholas 75
Crispe, Thomas 74–77
cross-imperial 4, 23, 24, 31, 45, 74, 171
Curaçao 157, 161
Cutiara 70, 97, 129

D'Almeida, Simão 74, 91, 98, 149
Dale, Thomas 1
Dammert, Loys 79–80
Danish Chancellery 13
Danish East India Company (DEIC) 1, 13, 25–26, 33–36, 38, 46–47, 58–60, 66, 68–69, 71–74, 81, 90–97, 99–102, 113, 125–129, 139, 149–153, 165, 172–173
van Dantzig Albert 14, 38, 78
van Danzig, Michael 97
Dappert, Olfert 121, 138
Davids, Karel 10
De Boisseret, Jacques 137
Delaware 24
Delbée, François 133–134, 136–137
Den Blanken, W.B. 106
Den Heijer, Henk 13, 134, 147
Denmark 7–9, 25, 28–29, 32–33, 46, 59, 60, 68, 104–105, 108, 110, 129, 154–155, 170–171
Déstree, Jean 161
de Dieu, Ludovicus 124

Diller, Stephen 12
Director-General 26, 39–42, 44, 46, 75–78, 107
Doedens, Henrik 76–77
Du Lion, François 136–137
Dutch Brazil 39, 153
Dutch East India Company (VOC) 1, 3–4, 13, 16, 22–23, 25–27, 30–34, 38, 41, 58, 66, 69–72, 95–96, 98–102, 121, 124–125, 129, 147, 150–152, 173
Dutch Golden Age 10
Dutch Republic 4, 8, 22, 26–29, 33–34, 36, 101, 105–106, 108, 121, 129, 157–158
Dutch West India Company (WIC) 1, 3–4, 12, 22, 24, 27, 31, 38–41, 43–46, 60, 62–63, 75–80, 81–82, 104, 106, 108–113, 130, 132, 134–137, 153, 155–157, 159, 173–174
Dutch Whaling Company 26

Eighty Years War 29
Ekama, Kate 4
Ekman, Hans 72, 92
elephants 69–70, 72–74, 95–97, 151
Elias, Floris 102, 107
Elsinore 32, 46, 170
Emden 103
England 34, 45, 64, 129, 157–158
English East India Company (EIC) 59, 23
Enthoven, Victor 147
Estado da Índia 72, 74, 97, 99, 102
Evertsen, Cornelis 159
expedition 24–26, 39, 61, 68, 102, 107, 130, 136, 154, 155, 159–163

Fagel, Gasper 159, 162
Felbæk Ole 12, 25, 58
Fetu King 74–76, 130
Fidalgo 133
foreigners 22, 30–32, 60, 62, 64
Fort Carolusborg 102, 104, 105, 108, 109, 112, 114, 148, 155–156, 164–165
Fort Dansborg 34, 67, 68, 71, 74, 90–92, 98–100, 125–126, 128, 149
Fort Elmina 42–43, 75, 108, 155
Fort Nassau 41–42
Foullon, Jan 41, 135
France 131–132, 134, 157–159
Fredrik III (King of Denmark) 27, 102, 105, 110, 153–154
French West India Company (FWIC) 14, 130, 133, 136, 157, 159

Index

Fusaro, Maria 6
Fynn-Paul, Jeffrey 146

Gaastra, Femme 3
Gabbesen, Arent 42, 45–46, 135
de Geer family 14, 64, 154
de Geer, Laurens 41, 62
de Geer, Louis 61–63, 75, 130
van Gelder, Roelof 41
Gerloffsen, Dirck 135
ghost investing 65, 103–105, 113
Giedde, Ove 26
gift-giving 95, 126, 137
gifts 34, 43, 66, 70–73, 76–77, 81, 90, 95–96, 98, 100, 112–113, 134, 156, 174
Glamann Kristoff 22
Glete, Jan 146, 148–149
Glückstad Company 110, 112–113, 132, 134, 136, 172
Glückstadt 27–30, 45, 103–106, 112, 129, 154
Goa 73, 97, 99, 128–129
de Goey, Ferry 10
Gøbel, Erik 23
gold 64, 69, 70, 71, 74, 75, 80, 94, 98, 105, 106, 109–112, 125, 130, 136, 155, 157, 164–165
Gold Coast 14–15, 42, 45, 62, 75, 77, 80, 82, 103–108, 112, 130, 132, 134–139, 154–155, 157, 164, 174
Gomarians 28–29
Gomes, Antonio 70, 98
Goslinga, Cornelis 158
Gothenburg 24, 30
Grand pensionary 159, 162
Granlund, Victor 12
Groningen 38, 105, 121
de Groot, Arent 1, 130
Guadeloupe 134–136, 159–160, 162–163
Guinea 29, 108, 111, 132, 135, 155
Guinea Coast 45, 137
gunpowder 74, 98, 156
Gustav II Adolf 24
Guyana 135

Hamburg 29, 32, 45, 62, 105
Hansen Korsør, Poul 71, 74, 93–94
Hansen, Jørgen 72, 92, 129
Harreld, Donald 123
Harris, Steven 125, 129
Heeren XIX 40, 42–45
Heijmans, Elisabeth 4
Hendricksen, Cornelis 135
Hennequa 75–76
Hermann, Augustine 1

Heussen, Arnold 100
van Heussen, Casper 107, 109
Heyns, Cornelis Joosten 102, 107
Hogenhoeck, Joris 41

Iceland 29
immigrants 22
India 27, 35–37, 58, 68, 73–74, 90, 97, 99, 125–127, 129, 174–175
institutional environment 21, 27, 58, 60–61, 78, 81, 174, 178
institutional sheltering 14, 27, 29, 31, 47, 173
instructions 13, 70, 72–74, 92, 95–96, 137, 138, 140, 148, 149, 163
interloping 30, 40, 104, 164
investors 23, 25, 31, 35, 45, 59–65, 103–105, 107–109, 124, 133, 155, 173
iron 8, 22, 61, 137
Israel, Jonathan 22
ivory 75, 136–137

Jacobsen, Adrian 70
Janssen, Claes 136
Janssen, Simon 92
Japara 34, 66, 68, 71, 74, 96, 127
Java 27, 34, 69–71, 73, 92, 127
Jeunisch, Sigmund 80, 156
Jol, Cornelis 39
de Jong, Michiel 147
Jordaan, Han 147
Jumoree 76, 78, 155

Kamal-adin, Mir 58
van der Keer, Ambrosius 74
King Karl X Gustav 8, 64
King of Candy 25–26, 69, 70, 95–96, 98, 129
King of Oquy 43
Kingdom of Ardres 133–134
Kingdom of Golconda 68, 71, 90
Klein, Peter 10
Klingenberg, Poul 105, 109–110
Knaap, Gerrit 147
knowledge 29, 31, 35, 62, 93, 122, 136
Knutsen, Hans 91
Kooijmans, Luuc 10–11, 89
Krieger, Martin 12, 35, 58
Kroutsen, Michell 91

La Rochelle 132, 134, 136
Lagerfeldt, Israel 65
Lampsins family 158
Lappalainen, Mirkka 21
Larsen, Kay 12, 150

202 *Index*

Latif, Abdul 74, 96
Lauridsen, Jorgen 93
Law, Robin 134, 139
Le Havre 136
Leers, Arnout 121, 138
Leiden 121, 124
Leisler, Jacob 1
Lesger, Clé 10–11, 89
Lisbon 32
Loncq, Alexander 80
Loodewycksten, Carsten 92
Loten, Jeremia 41–42
Louis XIV 158
Luanda 39, 131, 134, 153
Luango Coast 131–132
Lumbroso, Samuel 135
van der Lyn, Cornelis 101

Macao 71, 99, 128
Makassar 34, 58, 66–71, 73–74, 82,
  92–93, 96, 98, 101, 126–127, 150
Malabar 121
Malay Peninsula 97
Man, Eduard 108–109
Manila 71, 74, 99, 128
manual 121, 137–140
Marie-Galante 137, 161, 163
Martinique 136, 159
Mascarenhas, Don Filipe 98–99
Masulipatnam 34, 58, 66, 69, 71, 74,
  90–92, 96–99, 150–151
Mathias, Henrique 135
van Meersbergen, Guido 95
Mendes, Francisco 74, 96
Mentz, Søren 33
merchant networks 4–5, 97
merchants 6–7, 10, 22–23, 25, 28–29, 30,
  33, 35, 40–41, 44, 46, 59, 65, 68–69,
  73, 78, 90–92, 94, 97–102, 104, 108,
  110, 113–114, 121–122, 125, 127–128,
  133–134, 136–137, 146, 150, 156,
  172, 174
Mickelsen, Jakob 59, 129
micro-analysis 6
Mims, Stewart 133
Minuit, Peter 1, 23–24, 27, 46
Mivilla, Isaac 79
mobility 40, 140
mobility, social 2, 46, 114, 175–176
van der Molen, Christoffer 27
de Moucheron, Hendrick 65
Mouridsen, Willem 72, 97, 152
Mughals 125, 150–151, 153

Müller, Johan 155
Müller, Leos 10–11, 89, 139
Murdoch, Steve 34
mutiny 1, 93–94, 114, 140, 174

van Nassau Siegen, Johan Maurits 39
Nayak of Tanjore 26, 68, 95–96, 100–101
Negapatnam 26, 74, 91, 98, 100, 149
The Netherlands 3, 14, 24, 158
New Netherland 24, 26
Nielsen, Anders 68, 70, 74, 92–98,
  126, 129
Nielsen, Poul 92, 101, 129
Nijmegen (peace treaty) 161
Nina, Ismael 72, 97
Nina, Seyed 72, 97
Noordegraaf, Leo 10
Nørregård, Georg 12
Nováky, György 12, 64, 79–80, 153, 156

Odegard, Erik 4, 33, 147
Oeges, Geert 108
Offra 133–134
Ojala, Jari 139
Olsen, Gunnar 150
Øresundtolden (Sound Toll) 8, 32–33,
  38, 46, 52
Orsu 76–77, 155
Oxenstierna, Axel 64–66
Oxenstierna, Erik 63–65

Pacheco 98
Pahsa, Razia 70, 98
Pallache family 29
Pancras, Nicholas 102, 106–107
Parrot, David 146
passports 13, 29, 72–74, 103, 165
patronage 43, 46, 108
Pedersen, Joachim 37
Persia 34, 124
Pessart, Barent 35, 37, 66, 68, 71, 90–96,
  125–126, 149–150
Pipley 34, 72, 100
piracy 147, 150, 153, 164, 172
plantation 133, 136, 137, 159, 162–164
Polónia, Amélia 5–6
Pondicherry 100
Porter, Robert 13, 77, 130, 157
Porto Novo 69, 71, 73, 98, 100
Portugal 24, 29, 106, 128, 129, 131
Postma, Johannes 38
Pötter, Joachim 65
principal-agent problem 123–124, 139, 176

Index

Pritchard, James 133, 158, 161
private trade 31, 35, 47, 59, 62, 72–73, 80–81, 90, 93, 95, 101, 153
privateering 94, 147–148, 150–154, 159, 164–166, 176
privileges 2, 7, 24, 28–31, 46, 60, 64, 103–105, 113
prosecutor 1, 40–44, 46, 62, 76–79, 103, 135
Pulicat 97, 99–101

Quedah 72, 97
Queen Christina 62–64, 66, 130

Raychaudri, Tapan 69, 98
rich trade 22
Rindom, Jan 59–60
risks 2, 10–12, 31, 47, 57, 104, 123, 128, 138–139, 146, 148, 170–171, 175–176, 178
Roem, Volkert Claas 134
Rogerius, Abraham 121
Rosa, Jan Daniel 79–80
Rosenkrantz, Herman 25
Roskilde (peace treaty) 8, 104, 110
van Rossum, Matthias 41
Rostock 38, 170
rumours 43, 45, 111, 123, 128–129
Ruychaver, Jan 39, 40–41, 44, 46, 77–79
Rytter, Claus 34, 93

Sael, Andries 103
Saint-Domingue Company (French) 133
Samson, Nikolai 94
São Tomé 39, 42, 75, 105, 130, 132, 138, 153
São Tomé of Meliapor 91, 97–98
Scammel, George 3
Schleswig-Holstein 28
Schmitt, Eberhart 134
Schröder, Jürgen (Schroeder, Jorrien) 105
Scotland 32, 34, 46, 129
self-organised networks 6
Senegal Company (French) 133
Sephardic Jews 28–29
Seshan, Radika 101
shareholder 30, 35–36, 38, 58–60, 64
ships: *Christianshavn* 38, 67, 71, 92, 101, 128, 149, 151; *Christina* 45, 62; *Coninck Salomon* 111; *De Eendracht* 41, 135; *De Liefde* 62; *Den Forgylte Sol* 38; *Diamant* 102; *Die Liebe* 104–105; *Ellefant* 96; *Eyckenboom* 111; *Fortuna* 93; *Fredricus* 104; *Glückstadt*

102, 104, 108; *Graaf Enno* 104; *La Justice* 133, 135; *Poppiesbergh* 163; *Postellion von Venedig* 104; *Prince of Denmark* 44; *St Anna* 36–37; *St Jacob* 42; *St Joris* 134–135; *St Marten* 104–105; *St Michael* 67, 72, 94, 97, 152; *St Peter* 93; *St Poul* 93; *Stockholms Slott* 104–105, 155; *Tijdsverdrijf* 135–136; *Trangabara* 97; *Wahlby* 67, 91, 151
Sierra Leone 103–104
Sieveking, Heinrich 12
silk 69, 71
silver 71, 99, 128
simulation 62
Skeel, Albert 36
skipper 22, 25, 28–30, 41, 44–45, 72–73, 80, 91, 97, 103–105, 135, 152, 165
Slave Coast 130, 134, 136–140
slave trade 26, 71–72, 74–75, 132, 134–140, 162–164
Smidt, Samuel 108–111, 114, 156, 174
Smith, John 1
Smith, Stefan Halikowski 74
Sommerdyk, Stacey 135
Sound Toll (Øresundtolden) 8, 32–33, 38, 46, 52
South Company (Söderkompaniet) 24
spices 69–71
Spranger, Quirijn 135
Stael, Josias 70, 94
States General 14, 28–29, 108, 158
Steensgaard, Niels 3
Stephen, Nicholas 123
Stockholm 24, 45, 64
Stolwijk, Pieter 163
Strait of Malacca 68, 128
Sturm, Christer 93
Subrahmanyam, Sanjay 58, 97–98, 146
sugar 29, 39, 69, 75, 130, 132, 158, 162, 164
Surat 34
Suriname 108, 157, 161
de Swaen, Jan 105–107, 110
Sweden 7–8, 22–24, 30, 45, 61, 63–66, 79, 105, 110, 129–130, 132, 154–155, 170–171
Swedish Africa Company (SAC) 1, 12, 47, 59, 61–66, 74, 76–81, 102–103, 105, 107–109, 112, 130, 132, 134, 136, 153, 155–156, 164, 172–174
Swedish Shipping Company 24, 63
Synod of Dordrecht 29
Spain 24, 29, 161

204 Index

Takorari 76, 78–79, 137, 155
Tamil 13, 68, 97
Tayapa, Canacpel 73, 98
van Tets, Gerard 105
Texel 79, 134, 136
textiles 69, 70–71, 96, 156
Thirty Years War 7–8, 28, 35, 60, 149
Tiagapule 68–69, 94, 100
tobacco 94, 98, 158, 162
Tobago 157, 158, 159–165
Tracy, James 3
Tranquebar 1, 13, 26–27, 34, 38, 60, 66,
    68–69, 91–93, 95–96, 98, 100–102
Transatlantic Slave Trade Database 134
translator 68, 73, 96
Treaty of Westphalia 7
Trincomalee 26
Trivellato, Francesca 6
trust 92, 94–95, 107, 110–111, 114, 126,
    129, 174
Twelve Years' Truce 28–29

Udbyneder, Niels 93, 149
Ulfeldt, Corfiz 129
uncertainty 11, 31, 47, 89, 92, 94, 123,
    146, 175
Uppsala 64
Usselincx, Willem 24, 27, 30, 46

Vainqueur, Jean 102, 107
Valckenburg, Jan 75, 77, 107–109, 155

Van der Wel, Jan 39–45
Veluwenkamp, Jan Willem 10
Verbeeck, Abel 103
Vermeesch, Griet 146
Viceroy 73, 98, 99
Vieira, Francisco 1, 58
Vijayanagara 68
Vinckel, Jasper 102, 104, 107–108
Vingboons, Johannes 121
Vlasblom, Jan 102, 107
Von Krusenstierna, Johann Philip 79–80,
    155–156
Von Stakenborrig, Jakob 91, 149
de Vries, Jan 21, 161

Wellen, Kathryn 13, 150–152
Westminster (peace treaty) 158
Whitelocke, Bulstrode 64
Whydah 136
de Wildt, Hiob 159
Wilkens, Thielman 44–46, 103, 136
de Willem, Jan 24
Willerslev, Richard 25, 59–60
Winius, Georg 98
Woltzogen, Jan (Jean-Andre) 63, 130
Woltzogen, Lodewijk 63
Woltzogen, Sophia Felicitas 63
van der Woude, Ad 21
Wouters, Jan 62

Zeeland 136, 158